KB084795

적중100

영어 기출 문제집

중2

지학 | 민찬규

Best Collection

구성과 특징

교과서의 주요 학습 내용을 중심으로 학습 영역별 특성에 맞춰 단계별로 다양한 학습 기회를 제 공하여 단원별 학습능력 평가는 물론 중간 및 기말고사 시험 등에 완벽하게 대비할 수 있도록 내용을 구성

Words & Expressions

Step1 Key Words 단원별 핵심 단어 설명 및 풀이
Key Expression 단원별 핵심 숙어 및 관용어 설명
Word Power 반대 또는 비슷한 뜻 단어 배우기
English Dictionary 영어로 배우는 영어 단어

Step2 실력평가 단원별 수시평가 대비 주관식, 객관식 문제풀이

Step3 서술형 대비 학업성취도 및 수행능력평가 대비 서술형 문제풀이

Conversation

Step1 핵심 의사소통 의사소통에 필요한 주요 표현 방법 요약
핵심 Check 기본적인 표현 방법 및 활용능력 확인

Step2 대화문 익히기 상황에 따른 대화문 활용 및 연습

Step3 기본평가 시험대비 기초 학습 능력 평가

Step4 실력평가 단원별 수시평가 대비 주관식, 객관식 문제풀이

Step5 서술형 대비 학업성취도 및 수행능력평가 대비 서술형 문제풀이

Grammar

Step1 주요 문법 단원별 주요 문법 사항과 예문을 알기 쉽게 설명
핵심 Check 기본 문법사항에 대한 이해 여부 확인

Step2 기본평가 시험대비 기초 학습 능력 평가

Step3 실력평가 단원별 수시평가 대비 주관식, 객관식 문제풀이

Step4 서술형 대비 학업성취도 및 수행능력평가 대비 서술형 문제풀이

Reading

Step1 구문 분석 단원별로 제시된 문장에 대한 구문별 분석과 내용 설명
확인문제 문장에 대한 기본적인 이해와 인지능력 확인

Step2 확인학습A 빈칸 채우기를 통한 문장 완성 능력 확인

Step3 확인학습B 제시된 우리말을 영어로 완성하여 작문 능력 키우기

Step4 실력평가 단원별 수시평가 대비 주관식, 객관식 문제풀이

Step5 서술형 대비 학업성취도 및 수행능력평가 대비 서술형 문제풀이
교과서 구석구석 교과서에 나오는 기타 문장까지 완벽 학습

Composition

|영역별 핵심문제|

단어 및 어휘, 대화문, 문법, 독해 등 각 영역별 기출문제의 출제 유형을 분석하여 실전에 대비하고 연습할 수 있도록 문제를 배열

|서술형 실전 및 창의사고력 문제|

학교 시험에서 점차 늘어나는 서술형 시험에 집중 대비하고 고득점을 취득하는데 만전을 기하기 위한 학습 코너

|단원별 예상문제|

기출문제를 분석한 후 새로운 시험 출제 경향을 더하여 새롭게 출제될 수 있는 문제를 포함하여 시험에 완벽하게 대비할 수 있도록 준비

|단원별 모의고사|

영역별, 단계별 학습을 모두 마친 후 실전 연습을 위한 모의고사

on the textbook

교과서 파헤치기

- **단어Test1~2** 영어 단어 우리말 쓰기와 우리말을 영어 단어로 쓰기
- **대화문Test1~2** 대화문 빈칸 완성 및 전체 대화문 쓰기
- **본문Test1~5** 빈칸 완성, 우리말 쓰기, 문장 배열연습, 영어 작문하기 복습 등 단계별 반복 학습을 통해 교과서 지문에 대한 완벽한 습득
- **구석구석지문Test1~2** 지문 빈칸 완성 및 전문 영어로 쓰기

Contents

Lesson 1

New Beginnings

 의사소통 기능

- 주의 끌기
  You know what?

- 의도 표현하기
  I'm thinking of learning *taekwondo*.

언어 형식

- One ... The other ~
  I have two pets. **One** is a dog. **The other** is a cat.

- If 조건절
  If you exercise every day, you will become healthier.

Words & Expressions

Key Words

- **art** [ɑːrt] 명 미술, 예술
- **beef** [biːf] 명 소고기
- **bite** [bait] 동 물다 명 물린 자국
- **break** [breik] 동 깨뜨리다, 부수다
- **care** [kɛər] 명 주의, 조심
- **clean** [kliːn] 동 청소하다, 깨끗하게 하다
- **cupcake** [kʌ́pkèik] 명 컵케이크
- **dear** [diər] 형 친애하는
- **decide** [disáid] 동 결정하다
- **during** [djúəriŋ] 전 ~ 동안
- **email** [íːmèil] 동 이메일을 보내다
- **fall** [fɔːl] 명 가을
- **false** [fɔːls] 형 틀린, 거짓의
- **funny** [fʌ́ni] 형 재미있는, 익살맞은
- **habit** [hǽbit] 명 습관
- **handle** [hǽndl] 명 손잡이
- **healthy** [hélθi] 형 건강한, 튼튼한
- **hobby** [hábi] 명 취미
- **hold** [hould] 동 잡다, 쥐다
- **homeroom teacher** 담임 선생님
- **jogging** [dʒágiŋ] 명 달리기
- **kind** [kaind] 명 종류
- **lie** [lai] 동 거짓말을 하다
- **nail** [neil] 명 손톱
- **past** [pæst] 명 과거
- **personal** [pɔ́rsənl] 형 개인적인
- **planet** [plǽnit] 명 행성
- **print** [print] 동 인쇄하다
- **soon** [suːn] 부 곧
- **spring** [spriŋ] 명 봄
- **smart** [smɑːrt] 형 똑똑한, 명석한
- **space** [speis] 명 우주
- **sure** [ʃuər] 형 확실한, 확신하고 있는
- **ticket** [tíkit] 명 표, 입장권
- **tip** [tip] 명 조언, 정보
- **toy** [tɔi] 명 장난감
- **traffic** [trǽfik] 명 교통
- **truth** [truːθ] 명 사실, 진실
- **try** [trai] 동 시도하다
- **upset** [ʌ́pset] 형 화난, 속상한
- **vacation** [veikéiʃən] 명 방학
- **vegetable** [védʒətbl] 명 야채
- **wish** [wiʃ] 명 소망
- **yoga** [jóuɡə] 명 요가

Key Expressions

- **be interested in** ~에 흥미가 있다
- **be into** ~에 열중하다
- **break a bad habit** 나쁜 습관을 버리다
- **by the way** 그건 그렇고, 그런데
- **change into** ~로 변하다
- **come true** 실현되다
- **do one's best** 최선을 다하다
- **each other** 서로
- **hear from** ~로부터 소식을 듣다
- **It's time to** ~할 때다
- **make changes** 변화를 이루다
- **not ~ anymore** 더 이상 ~하지 않다
- **on one's way home** 집에 오는 길에
- **take a class** 수업을 듣다
- **take care** 몸 건강해, 잘 있어
- **these days** 요즘에
- **those days** 그 당시에
- **think of** ~할 생각이다

Words Power

※ 서로 반대되는 뜻을 가진 어휘

□ **healthy** 건강한 ↔ **unhealthy** 건강하지 못한

□ **funny** 재미있는 ↔ **boring** 지겨운, 지루한

□ **private** 사적인, 사사로운 ↔ **public** 공공의

□ **clean** 깨끗한 ↔ **dirty** 더러운

□ **lie** 거짓말 ↔ **truth** 진실, 사실

□ **true** 사실인, 참인 ↔ **false** 거짓의

□ **buy** 사다 ↔ **sell** 팔다

□ **honest** 정직한 ↔ **dishonest** 정직하지 못한

□ **smart** 영리한, 똑똑한 ↔ **foolish** 어리석은

□ **thin** 얇은 ↔ **thick** 두꺼운

□ **save** 저축하다 ↔ **waste** 낭비하다

□ **wet** 젖은 ↔ **dry** 마른

English Dictionary

□ **art** 미술
→ the methods and skills used for painting, sculpting, drawing, etc.
회화, 조각, 그리기 등에 사용되는 기법이나 기술

□ **beef** 소고기
→ meat from a cow
소에서 나는 고기

□ **bite** 물다
→ to press down on or cut into someone or something with the teeth
치아로 누군가나 무엇인가를 누르거나 베다

□ **decide** 결정하다
→ to make a choice about something
무언가에 대해 선택을 하다

□ **handle** 손잡이
→ a part that is designed especially to be grasped by the hand
특히 손에 의해 쥐어질 수 있도록 고안된 부분

□ **homeroom teacher** 담임 선생님
→ a teacher in charge of a class
학급을 담당하는 교사

□ **nail** 손톱
→ the hard covering at the end of a finger or toe
손가락이나 발가락의 끝을 덮고 있는 딱딱한 부분

□ **personal** 개인적인
→ belonging or relating to a particular person
특정한 개인에게 속하거나 관련된

□ **planet** 행성
→ a large, round object in space that travels around a star
별 주위를 도는 우주의 크고 둥근 물체

□ **traffic** 교통
→ the movement of vehicles or pedestrians through an area or along a route
한 지역을 통과하거나 길을 따라 가는 자동차나 보행자들의 움직임

□ **try** 시도하다
→ to do or use something in order to find out if you like it
당신이 좋아하는지를 알아내기 위해 무언가를 사용하거나 하다

□ **wish** 소망
→ a feeling of wanting to do or have something
무언가를 하고 싶거나 갖고 싶은 감정

서답형

01 다음 짝지어진 단어의 관계가 같도록 빈칸에 알맞은 말을 쓰시오.

> funny : boring = _____ : public

중요

02 다음 중 밑줄 친 부분의 뜻풀이가 바르지 <u>않은</u> 것은?

① She used to bite <u>nails</u>. 손톱
② Jupiter is the biggest <u>planet</u> in the solar system. 우주
③ I <u>decided</u> to become an English teacher. 결심했다
④ Minju is working for a <u>toy</u> store. 장난감
⑤ I missed the train because of a <u>traffic</u> jam. 교통

03 다음 주어진 문장의 밑줄 친 handle(s)의 의미와 같은 의미로 쓰인 것은?

> My special cup has two <u>handles</u>.

① I can't <u>handle</u> this matter anymore.
② I'm not sure if I can <u>handle</u> this car.
③ I don't expect you can <u>handle</u> this problem.
④ My department <u>handles</u> the information you need.
⑤ She grasped the <u>handle</u> of the knife.

04 다음 문장에 공통으로 들어갈 말을 고르시오.

> • Would you do me a favor? I need to hammer the _____ on the wall.
> • I have cut my _____ too close.
> • My sweater was caught on the _____.

① net   ② needle   ③ pin
④ nail   ⑤ toe

서답형

05 다음 문장의 빈칸에 들어갈 말을 보기에서 골라 알맞은 형태로 쓰시오.

> ┤ 보기 ├
> make changes / hear from /
> be into / be interested in

(1) I _____ _____ _____ playing soccer these days.
(2) My brother _____ _____ playing computer games.
(3) Have you _____ _____ Sumi recently?
(4) She made lots of efforts to _____ _____.

중요

06 다음 문장에 공통으로 들어갈 말을 고르시오.

> • I know the answer. It's on the _____ of my tongue.
> • How much should I give as a _____?
> • Could you give me a useful _____ on how to spend time wisely?

① advice   ② information
③ edge   ④ tip
⑤ fee

01 다음 짝지어진 단어의 관계가 같도록 빈칸에 알맞은 말을 쓰시오.

clean : dirty = true : _____

[02~03] 다음 영영풀이에 해당하는 말을 쓰시오.

02
a teacher in charge of a class
➡ _____

03
a large, round object in space that travels around a star
➡ _____

04 다음 우리말과 일치하도록 주어진 단어를 알맞게 배열하여 완성하시오.

(1) 집에 오는 길에 우유 좀 사다 주겠니?
(way / home / milk / for / you / me / your / on / would / buy)
➡ _____

(2) 변화를 이루기 위해 새로운 프로그램을 사용할 때이다.
(make / time / it's / a / program / to / use / to / changes / new)
➡ _____

(3) 그는 더 이상 컴퓨터 수업을 듣지 않는다.
(class / anymore / he / the / doesn't / computer / take)
➡ _____

05 다음 우리말에 맞게 빈칸에 알맞은 말을 쓰시오.

(1) 나는 나쁜 습관을 그만 두기 위해 노력하고 있다.
➡ I'm trying to _____ _____ _____ _____.

(2) 그건 그렇고, 내가 너를 위해 이 책을 샀어.
➡ _____ _____ _____, I bought this book for you.

(3) 나는 너의 소망이 이루어지길 바라.
➡ I hope your wish _____ _____.

(4) 주제에 대해 토론해 볼 시간이다.
➡ _____ _____ _____ discuss the topic.

06 다음 문장의 빈칸에 들어갈 말을 〈보기〉에서 골라 쓰시오.

┌─ 보기 ─┐
handles   kind   bite   wish
└─────┘

(1) I often _____ my nails when I feel nervous.
(2) What _____ of music do you like most?
(3) I _____ I can make lots of friends.
(4) A pot usually has two _____.

07 다음 문장의 빈칸에 들어갈 말을 순서대로 쓰시오.

• I hope to hear (A)_____ my daughter soon.
• (B)_____ the way, why do we get together?
• It can change (C)_____ a different style of clothes.

➡ (A) _____, (B) _____, (C) _____

Conversation

1 주의 끌기

> **You know what?** (너 그거 아니?)

■ 대화에서 상대방이 자기의 말에 귀를 기울이도록 주의를 끌기 위한 표현으로 새로운 사실이나 놀라운 일을 소개하거나 또는 새로운 주제로 이야기를 시작할 때 'You know what?'을 이용하여 상대방의 주의를 끌 수 있다.

주의 끌기의 여러 가지 표현

- You know what? (너 그거 아니?)
- Guess what? (있잖아.)
- Look! (여기 봐!)
- Listen. (들어 봐.)

핵심 Check

1. 다음 우리말과 일치하도록 빈칸에 알맞은 말을 쓰시오.

   A: _____ _____ _____? I'm thinking of taking a Chinese class. (그거 아니? 나 중국어 수업을 들을까 생각 중이야.)

   B: That's great.

2. 다음 우리말과 일치하도록 빈칸에 알맞은 말을 쓰시오.

   A: _____ _____? I decided to learn swimming. (있잖아. 나 수영을 배우기로 결심했어.)

   B: Sounds great.

3. 다음 우리말과 일치하도록 빈칸에 알맞은 말을 쓰시오.

   A: _____ You should clean your room before going out. (여기 봐! 너는 외출 전에 네 방을 치워야 해.)

   B: I see. I _____ to clean everything now. (알겠어요. 제가 지금 모두 치울 것을 약속해요.)

② 의도 표현하기

> **I'm thinking of learning _taekwondo_.** (나는 태권도를 배울 생각이야.)

■ 'I'm thinking of ~'는 '나는 ~할 생각이다'라는 뜻으로 '의도'를 나타낼 때 쓰는 표현이다. 이 표현은 'I'm planning to ~'로 바꿔 쓸 수 있다. of 뒤에는 명사(구)나 동명사가 오지만 'I'm planning to ~'를 쓸 때는 뒤에 동사원형을 사용한다는 점에 유의한다.

의도 표현하기

- I'm thinking of saving money. (나는 돈을 저금할 생각이야.)
- I'm planning to learn yoga. (나는 요가를 배울 계획이다.)
- I'm going to take a badminton class. (나는 배드민턴 수업을 들을 거야.)
- I will keep a diary in English. (나는 영어로 일기를 쓸 거야.)
- I made a plan to go jogging in the morning. (나는 아침에 조깅을 갈 계획을 세웠다.)

핵심 Check

4. 다음 우리말과 일치하도록 빈칸에 알맞은 말을 쓰시오.

    A: What are you going to do this weekend? (이번 주말에 무엇을 할 예정이니?)

    B: _____ _____ _____ visit my grandfather. (나는 할아버지 댁을 방문할 계획이야.)

5. 다음 우리말과 일치하도록 빈칸에 알맞은 말을 쓰시오.

    A: _____ _____ _____ keep a diary in English. (나는 영어로 일기를 쓸 거야.)

    B: Why did you _____ to do that? (왜 너는 그렇게 하기로 결심했니?)

6. 다음 우리말과 일치하도록 빈칸에 알맞은 말을 쓰시오.

    A: _____ _____ _____ _____ _bulgogi_ for dinner. (나는 저녁으로 불고기를 요리할 생각이야.)

    B: Oh, can you make it by yourself? (오, 너 혼자서 그것을 만들 수 있니?)

A. Listen and Speak 2-A

Jane: Minsu, Sujin and I ❶are thinking of starting a club.

Minsu: Really? What kind of club?

Jane: We want to learn about stars and ❷planets. So, we're thinking of starting a space science club.

Minsu: ❸Sounds good. How often are you going to meet?

Jane: Maybe once a week.

Minsu: I see. Where will you meet?

Jane: In Room 101. Minsu, do you want to join our club?

Minsu: Yes, ❹I'm interested in space, too.

Jane: 민수야, 수진이와 나는 동아리를 만들 생각이야.

Minsu: 정말? 어떤 종류의 동아리야?

Jane: 우리는 별과 행성에 대해 알고 싶어. 그래서 우주 과학 동아리를 만들 생각이야.

Minsu: 그거 멋지다. 얼마나 자주 모일 예정이니?

Jane: 아마도 일주일에 한 번쯤.

Minsu: 그렇구나. 어디에서 모일 거니?

Jane: 101호에서. 민수야, 우리 동아리에 가입할래?

Minsu: 응, 나도 우주에 관심 있어.

❶ 'be thinking of ∼'는 '∼할 생각이야'라는 의미로 '의도'를 나타낸다.
❷ planet: 행성
❸ (That) Sounds good. = That's wonderful. = What a great idea!
❹ be interested in ∼: ∼에 관심이 있다

Check(√) True or False

(1) Sujin and Jane want to learn about stars and planets.   T ☐ F ☐

(2) Minsu is thinking of starting a new club.   T ☐ F ☐

B. Real Life Communication

Emily: ❶You know what, Junsu? I'm thinking of taking a painting class.

Junsu: Really? Why did you ❷decide to ❸take a painting class, Emily?

Emily: Because I want to go to an art high school.

Junsu: Are you thinking of becoming an artist in the future?

Emily: I hope so. I'm interested in painting pictures.

Junsu: That's great. I hope your wish ❹comes true.

Emily: Thanks. ❺I'll do my best.

Emily: 준수야, 그거 아니? 나는 미술 수업을 들을 생각이야.

Junsu: 정말? 왜 미술 수업을 들으려고 결심했니, Emily?

Emily: 예술 고등학교에 가고 싶어서야.

Junsu: 장래에 미술가가 될 생각이니?

Emily: 그러고 싶어. 나는 그림 그리는 것에 흥미가 있어.

Junsu: 그거 잘 됐다. 네 꿈이 이뤄지길 바라.

Emily: 고마워. 최선을 다할 거야.

❶ 상대방의 주의를 끌기 위해 사용하는 표현이다.
❷ decide to: ∼하기로 결심하다
❸ take a class: 수업을 듣다
❹ come true: 실현되다
❺ do one's best: 최선을 다하다

Check(√) True or False

(3) Emily is interested in painting pictures.   T ☐ F ☐

(4) Junsu wants to be an artist in the future.   T ☐ F ☐

Listen and Speak 1 A

Brian: Julia, how was your winter vacation?

Julia: It was great. ❶You know what? I ❷took *muay thai* lessons ❸during the vacation.

Brian: That's amazing. I didn't know that you ❹ were interested in *muay thai*.

Julia: Yes. ❺It was really fun.

Brian: Really? I want ❻to try ❼it.

❶ You know what?: '너 그거 아니?'라는 뜻으로 상대방의 주의를 끌고자 할 때 사용한다. 이 다음에는 말하고자 하는 새로운 사실이 나온다.

❷ take a lesson: 수업을 듣다

❸ during은 '~ 동안에'라는 의미로 뒤에 기간을 나타내는 명사가 이어진다.

❹ be interested in: ~에 관심이 있다

❺ it은 *muay thai*를 가리킨다.

❻ want의 목적어로 to부정사가 쓰이고 있다. try는 '한 번 해보다'의 의미이다.

❼ it은 *muay thai*를 가리킨다.

Listen and Speak 1 B

Jimin: You know what, Tim? Mr. Smith is my ❶ homeroom teacher ❷this year.

Tim: That's great, Jimin. His science class last year was ❸a lot of fun.

Jimin: Who's your homeroom teacher this year?

Tim: It's Ms. Kim. She's a new teacher.

Jimin: What does she teach?

Tim: She teaches ❹art.

❶ homeroom teacher: 담임 선생님

❷ this year: 올해

❸ a lot of는 수(= many)와 양(= much) 두 가지의 경우 모두 쓰인다.

❹ 과목 명 앞에서 관사는 생략한다.

Listen and Speak 2 B

Alex: Mom, I made *bulgogi* at school today. ❶I'm thinking of cooking *bulgogi* for dinner.

Mom: That ❷sounds great, Alex.

Alex: Do we have ❸any vegetables at home, Mom? ❹ What about beef?

Mom: We have ❺some vegetables, but we don't have beef. I'll buy ❻some for you ❼on my way home.

Alex: Great.

❶ I'm thinking of ~: '나는 ~할 생각이야'라는 뜻으로, '의도'를 나타내는 표현이다. 'I'm planning to ~'로 바꾸어 쓸 수 있다. of 뒤에는 (동)명사(구)가 오지만, to 다음에는 동사원형이 온다.

❷ 감각동사(sound) 다음에 형용사(great)가 보어로 나왔다.

❸ 의문문이므로 any가 쓰였다.

❹ What about ~?: '~는 어때요?'라는 뜻으로 여기서는 '소고기는 있어요?'라는 뜻이다.

❺ 긍정문이므로 some이 쓰였다.

❻ 여기서 some은 대명사로 '약간의 소고기'를 의미한다.

❼ on one's way home: 집에 오는 길에

Real Life Communication

Sue: You know what? Jenny's family is going to move to Japan.

Jack: Is that right? Jenny didn't tell me about ❶it.

Sue: She learned about ❶it just last week and she's very ❷upset now.

Jack: I can understand her feelings. I am going to ❸miss her so much.

Sue: ❹Me, too. She said she would ❺keep in touch with us.

❶ it은 일본으로 이사 가는 것을 가리킨다.

❷ upset : 속상한

❸ miss는 '그리워하다'라는 의미로 쓰였다.

❹ Me, too. = So am I.: 나도 그래.

❺ keep in touch: 연락하다

● 다음 우리말과 일치하도록 빈칸에 알맞은 말을 쓰시오.

Listen & Speak 1 A

Brian: Julia, how was your winter vacation?

Julia: It was great. _____ _____ _____? I took *muay thai* lessons during the vacation.

Brian: That's amazing. I didn't know that _____ _____ _____ _____ *muay thai*.

Julia: Yes. It was really fun.

Brian: Really? I want to try it.

Listen & Speak 1 B

Jimin: You know what, Tim? Mr. Smith is my _____ _____ this year.

Tim: That's great, Jimin. His science class last year was a lot of _____.

Jimin: Who's your homeroom teacher this year?

Tim: It's Ms. Kim. She's a new teacher.

Jimin: _____ _____ _____ _____?

Tim: She teaches _____.

Listen & Speak 2 A

Jane: Minsu, Sujin and I _____ _____ _____ _____ a club.

Minsu: Really? _____ _____ _____ _____?

Jane: We want to learn about _____ and _____. So, we're thinking of starting a space science club.

Minsu: Sounds good. How often are you going to meet?

Jane: Maybe _____ _____ _____.

Minsu: I see. Where will you meet?

Jane: In Room 101. Minsu, do you want to join our club?

Minsu: Yes, _____ _____ _____ space, too.

해석

Brian: Julia, 네 겨울 방학은 어땠니?
Julia: 좋았어. 그거 아니? 나는 방학 동안 무에타이 수업을 받았어.
Brian: 그거 멋지다. 나는 네가 무에타이에 관심이 있는지 몰랐어.
Julia: 응. 아주 재미있었어.
Brian: 그래? 나도 해 보고 싶다.

Jimin: 그거 아니, Tim? Smith 선생님이 올해 우리 반 담임 선생님이야.
Tim: 그거 잘됐다, 지민아. 작년 Smith선생님의 과학 수업은 아주 재미있었어.
Jimin: 올해 너희 반 담임 선생님은 누구니?
Tim: 김 선생님이야. 그녀는 새로 오신 선생님이야.
Jimin: 그분은 어떤 과목을 가르치시니?
Tim: 미술을 가르치셔.

Jane: 민수야, 수진이와 나는 동아리를 만들 생각이야.
Minsu: 정말? 어떤 종류의 동아리야?
Jane: 우리는 별과 행성에 대해 배우고 싶어. 그래서 우주 과학 동아리를 만들 생각이야.
Minsu: 그거 멋지다. 얼마나 자주 모일 예정이니?
Jane: 아마도 일주일에 한 번쯤.
Minsu: 그렇구나. 어디에서 모일 거니?
Jane: 101호에서. 민수야, 우리 동아리에 가입할래?
Minsu: 응, 나도 우주에 관심 있어.

Listen & Speak 2 B

Alex: Mom, I made *bulgogi* at school today._____ _____ _____
_____ *bulgogi* for dinner.

Mom: That sounds great, Alex.

Alex: Do we have any vegetables at home, Mom? _____ _____
_____?

Mom: We have some vegetables, but we don't have beef. _____
_____ _____ _____ _____ _____ _____ _____
_____ _____.

Alex: Great.

Alex: 엄마, 오늘 학교에서 불고기를 만들었어요. 오늘 저녁으로 불고기를 요리할 생각이에요.
Mom: 그거 멋지구나, Alex.
Alex: 집에 채소 있어요, 엄마? 소고기는요?
Mom: 채소는 좀 있는데 소고기는 없어. 집에 오는 길에 좀 사올게.
Alex: 좋아요.

Real Life Communication A

Emily: You know what, Junsu? _____ _____ _____ _____
a _____ _____.

Junsu: Really? Why did you _____ to take a painting class, Emily?

Emily: Because _____ _____ _____ _____ _____
_____ _____ _____ _____.

Junsu: Are you thinking of becoming an _____ in the future?

Emily: I hope so. I'm interested in painting pictures.

Junsu: That's great. I hope your wish _____ _____.

Emily: Thanks. I'll _____ _____ _____.

Emily: 준수야, 그거 아니? 나는 미술 수업을 들을 생각이야.
Junsu: 정말? 왜 미술 수업을 들으려고 결심했니, Emily?
Emily: 예술 고등학교에 가고 싶어서야.
Junsu: 장래에 미술가가 될 생각이니?
Emily: 그러고 싶어. 나는 그림 그리는 것에 흥미가 있어.
Junsu: 그거 잘 됐다. 네 꿈이 이뤄지길 바라.
Emily: 고마워. 최선을 다할 거야.

Real Life Communication B

Sue: You know what? Jenny's family is going to _____ to Japan.

Jack: Is that right? Jenny didn't tell me about it.

Sue: She learned about it just last week and she's very _____ now.

Jack: _____ _____ _____ _____ _____ _____ _____. I am going to
miss her so much.

Sue: Me, too. She said she would _____ _____ _____
_____ us.

Sue: 있잖아, Jenny 가족이 일본으로 이민을 간대.
Jack: 정말이야? Jenny가 그것에 관해 얘기하지 않았는데.
Sue: Jenny도 지난주에야 알았어. 그래서 지금 매우 기분이 안 좋아.
Jack: 나는 Jenny의 기분을 이해할 수 있어. Jenny가 정말 그리울 거야.
Sue: 나도 그래. Jenny는 우리와 계속 연락할 거라고 했어.

01 다음 대화의 우리말을 주어진 단어를 사용하여 영작하시오.

> A: 너 그거 아니? I'm thinking of buying a bike. (what)
> B: Why did you decide to do that?

➡ _____?

02 다음 대화가 자연스럽게 이어지도록 순서대로 배열하시오.

You know what? Jenny's family is going to move to Japan.

> (A) Me, too. She said she would keep in touch with us.
> (B) Is that right? Jenny didn't tell me about it.
> (C) She learned about it just last week and she's very upset now.
> (D) I can understand her feelings. I am going to miss her so much.

➡ _____

[03~04] 다음 대화를 읽고 물음에 답하시오.

Jimin: You know what, Tim? Mr. Smith is my homeroom teacher this year.
Tim: That's great, Jimin. His science class last year was a lot of fun.
Jimin: (A)올해 너의 반 담임 선생님은 누구니?
Tim: It's Ms. Kim. She's a new teacher.
Jimin: What does she teach?
Tim: She teaches art.

03 위 대화에서 (A)의 우리말을 영어로 쓰시오.

➡ _____

04 위 대화의 내용과 일치하지 않는 것은?

① Jimin의 올해 담임 선생님은 Mr. Smith이다.
② Mr. Smith는 과학 선생님이다.
③ Tim은 작년에 Mr. Smith에게 과학을 배웠다.
④ Ms. Kim은 미술 선생님으로 새로 왔다.
⑤ Jimin과 Tim은 서로 같은 반이 되었다.

[01~02] 다음 대화를 읽고 물음에 답하시오.

Brian: Julia, (A)[what / how] was your winter vacation?

Julia: It was great. You know what? I took *muay thai* lessons during the vacation.

Brian: That's (B)[amazing / amazed]. I didn't know that you were (C)[interesting / interested] in *muay thai*.

Julia: Yes. It was really fun.

Brian: Really? I want to try it.

01 위 대화의 괄호 (A)~(C)에 알맞은 말로 바르게 짝지어진 것은?

	(A)	(B)	(C)
①	what	amazing	interesting
②	what	amazed	interested
③	how	amazed	interesting
④	how	amazing	interested
⑤	how	amazing	interesting

02 위 대화의 내용과 일치하지 <u>않는</u> 것은?

① Julia는 겨울 방학을 잘 보냈다.
② Julia는 겨울 방학에 무에타이 수업을 들었다.
③ Brian은 Julia가 무에타이에 관심이 있다는 것을 알고 있었다.
④ Julia는 무에타이 수업이 재미있었다.
⑤ Brain은 무에타이를 한 번 해보고 싶어 한다.

03 다음 대화가 자연스럽게 이어지도록 순서대로 배열하시오.

Emily: You know what, Junsu? I'm thinking of taking a painting class.

(A) Are you thinking of becoming an artist in the future?

(B) Because I want to go to an art high school.

(C) That's great. I hope your wish comes true.

(D) I hope so. I'm interested in painting pictures.

(E) Really? Why did you decide to take a painting class, Emily?

Emily: Thanks. I'll do my best.

➡ _____

[04~05] 다음 대화를 읽고 물음에 답하시오.

Jimin: (A) Mr. Smith is my homeroom teacher this year.

Tim: (B) That's great, Jimin. His science class last year was a lot of fun.

Jimin: (C) Who's your homeroom teacher this year?

Tim: (D) It's Ms. Kim. She's a new teacher.

Jimin: (E) What does she teach?

Tim: She teaches art.

04 위 대화의 (A)~(E) 중 주어진 문장이 들어가기에 적절한 곳은?

You know what?

① (A) ② (B) ③ (C) ④ (D) ⑤ (E)

05 위 대화를 읽고 대답할 수 <u>없는</u> 것은?

① Who is Jimin's homeroom teacher?
② What did Tim learn from Mr. Smith?
③ What is Ms. Kim going to teach?
④ How was Ms. Kim's class last year?
⑤ Who is the new teacher?

[06~07] 다음 대화를 읽고 물음에 답하시오.

> Sue: You know what? Jenny's family is going to move to Japan.
>
> Jack: Is that right? Jenny didn't tell me about it.
>
> Sue: She learned about it just last week and she's very upset now.
>
> Jack: I can understand her feelings. I am going to miss her so much.
>
> Sue: Me, too. She said she would (A)_____ us.

서답형

06 위 대화의 빈칸 (A)에 '~와 연락하다'를 의미하는 숙어를 4단어로 완성하시오.

➡ _____

07 위 대화를 통해 알 수 있는 Jenny의 심경으로 적절한 것은?

① pleased   ② nervous

③ frustrated   ④ lonely

⑤ excited

[08~09] 다음 대화를 읽고 물음에 답하시오.

> Alex: Mom, I made *bulgogi* at school today. I'm thinking ⓐ<u>of</u> cooking *bulgogi* for dinner.
>
> Mom: ⓑ<u>That</u> sounds great, Alex.
>
> Alex: Do we have any vegetables ⓒ<u>at</u> home, Mom? What ⓓ<u>about</u> beef?
>
> Mom: We have some vegetables, but we don't have beef. I'll buy some for you ⓔ<u>in</u> my way home.
>
> Alex: Great.

서답형

08 위 대화의 밑줄 친 ⓐ~ⓔ 중 어법상 틀린 것을 찾아 바르게 고쳐 쓰시오.

➡ _____

09 위 대화를 읽고 대답할 수 <u>없는</u> 것은?

① What did Alex make at school?

② What is Alex planning to make for dinner?

③ What does Alex need to cook *bulgogi*?

④ To cook *bulgogi*, what doesn't Alex have?

⑤ Where is Alex's mom now?

[10~12] 다음 대화를 읽고 물음에 답하시오.

> Jane: Minsu, Sujin and I are thinking of starting a club.
>
> Minsu: Really? What kind of club?
>
> Jane: We want to learn about stars and planets. So, we're thinking of starting a space science club.
>
> Minsu: Sounds good. (A)_____
>
> Jane: Maybe once a week.
>
> Minsu: I see. Where will you meet?
>
> Jane: In Room 101. Minsu, do you want to join our club?
>
> Minsu: Yes, I'm interested in space, too.

서답형

10 위 대화의 빈칸 (A)에 들어갈 말을 주어진 단어를 모두 사용하여 완성하시오.

┌─── 보기 ───
│ to are meet how going often you
└

➡ _____

서답형

11 About what do Sujin and Jane want to learn in a space science club?

➡ _____

서답형

12 What is Minsu interested in?

➡ _____

[01~03] 다음 대화를 읽고 물음에 답하시오.

Brian: Julia, how was your winter vacation?
Julia: It was great. You know what? I took *muay thai* lessons during the vacation.
Brian: That's amazing. I didn't know that you were interested in *muay thai*.
Julia: Yes. It was really fun.
Brian: Really? I want to try (A)it.

01 위 대화의 밑줄 친 (A)it이 가리키는 것을 영어로 쓰시오.

➡ _____

02 What did Julia do during the winter vacation?

➡ _____

03 What was Julia interested in?

➡ _____

04 다음 주어진 문장에 이어질 대화가 자연스럽게 이어지도록 순서대로 배열하시오.

You know what? Mr. Smith is my homeroom teacher this year.

(A) She teaches art.
(B) What does she teach?
(C) It's Ms. Kim. She's a new teacher.
(D) Who's your homeroom teacher this year?
(E) That's great. His science class last year was a lot of fun.

➡ _____

05 다음 대화의 우리말을 주어진 단어를 이용하여 영작하시오.

A: You know what? 나는 요가를 배울 생각이야. (am, think, learn)
B: I think it's good for your health.

➡ _____

06 다음 대화의 내용과 일치하도록 민수의 일기를 완성하시오.

Jane: Minsu, Sujin and I are thinking of starting a club.
Minsu: Really? What kind of club?
Jane: We want to learn about stars and planets. So, we're thinking of starting a space science club.
Minsu: Sounds good. How often are you going to meet?
Jane: Maybe once a week.
Minsu: I see. Where will you meet?
Jane: In Room 101. Minsu, do you want to join our club?
Minsu: Yes, I'm interested in space, too.

⬇

Wed, March 27th, 2019
Today, Jane told me about starting a space science club. Sujin and she were interested in (A)_____, so they wanted to make a space science club. They were planning to meet (B)_____ in (C)_____. It sounded good. So, I decided to join the club. I'm really looking forward to learning about space.

➡ (A) _____ (B) _____
(C) _____

Grammar

1 One ... The other ~

> • I have two pencils. **One** is short and **the other** is long. 내게는 연필 두 자루가 있다. 하나는 짧고 다른 하나는 길다.
>
> • There are three umbrellas. **One** is yellow, **another** is blue, and **the other** is black. 우산이 세 개 있다. 하나는 노란색이고, 또 다른 하나는 파란색이고, 남은 하나는 검정색이다.

■ 둘 중에 하나를 가리킬 때에 'one'을 쓰고 남은 하나를 가리킬 때 'the other'를 쓴다. '하나는 …', '나머지 다른 하나는 ~'이라는 뜻으로 사용된다.
  • There are two balls. **One** is baseball. **The other** is basketball. 공이 두 개 있다. 하나는 야구공이다. 나머지 다른 하나는 농구공이다.

■ 셋을 지칭할 때에는 제일 처음 가리키는 것을 'one', 그 다음으로 가리키는 것을 'another', 마지막으로 남은 하나를 가리킬 때에는 'the other'를 쓴다. 'the other+복수명사'가 올 경우 'the others'로 대명사화 할 수 있다.
  • I'm fixing three cars. **One** is a truck. **Another** is a minivan. **The other** is a sports car.
  나는 차 세 대를 고치는 중이야. 한 대는 트럭이야. 다른 한 대는 미니밴이야. 나머지 한 대는 스포츠카야.

■ 지칭하는 것이 복수일 때에는 'some'을 쓰고, 이미 언급한 것과는 다른 것을 묶어서 이야기할 때에는 'other+복수명사'를 쓴다.
  • **Some** students want to be teachers. **Other** students(= Others) want to be politicians.
  몇몇 학생들은 선생님이 되기를 원한다. 다른 학생들은 정치인이 되기를 원한다.
  • The persons in the lounge have different jobs. **One** is a dentist. **Some** people are tennis players. **Others** are chefs.
  라운지에 있는 사람들은 여러 가지 직업을 가지고 있다. 한 사람은 치과의사이다. 몇몇 사람들은 테니스 선수들이다. 다른 사람들은 요리사이다.

핵심 Check

1. 다음 우리말과 같도록 빈칸에 알맞은 말을 쓰시오.
  (1) 그녀에게는 책 두 권이 있다. 한 권은 소설이고, 나머지 한 권은 잡지이다.
  ➡ She has two books. _____ is a novel and _____ is a magazine.
  (2) 사과 다섯 개가 있다. 하나는 엄마 것이다. 다른 하나는 내 것이다. 나머지 모두는 아빠 것이다.
  ➡ There are five apples. _____ is Mom's. _____ is mine. _____ are Dad's.
  (3) 몇몇 책은 과학에 관한 것이고, 다른 책들은 영화에 관한 것이다.
  ➡ _____ are about science, and _____ are about movies.

② If가 이끄는 조건절

> • **If** you meet him, you will like him. 네가 그를 만난다면, 너는 그를 좋아할 거야.
>
> • **If** you have some time tomorrow, what will you do? 내일 시간이 좀 있으면, 넌 뭘 할 거야?

■ 조건의 부사절에서는 현재시제를 사용하여 미래를 나타내며 '만약 ~라면'이라고 해석한다.

- **If** he goes by taxi, he will get there soon. 그가 택시를 타고 간다면, 그곳에 곧 도착할 거야.

- **If** you are hungry, she will make you a pizza. 네가 배고프다면, 그녀가 너에게 피자를 만들어 줄 거야.

■ 때를 나타내는 부사절에서도 현재시제를 사용하여 미래를 나타낸다.

- We will go out **after** we finish watching this movie. 이 영화를 보는 걸 끝낸 후에 우리는 나갈 것이다.

■ If절이 명사 역할을 하는 경우도 있다. 명사절을 이끄는 접속사 if와 부사절을 이끄는 접속사 if의 쓰임을 구별하자. 명사절을 이끄는 접속사 if의 경우 '~인지 아닌지'로 해석하며 미래를 나타낼 때에는 미래시제를 써야 한다.

- I wonder **if** you **will accept** the offer. 나는 네가 그 제안을 받아들일지 궁금해.

- No one can tell **if** he **will** really **sign** the contract or not.
  그가 정말 그 계약서에 서명할지 서명하지 않을지는 아무도 알 수 없다.

- I can't decide **if** I **will take** a vacation with her or not.
  나는 그녀와 휴가를 갈지 안 갈지 결정할 수 없어.

■ If ~ not은 '만약 ~하지 않으면'의 의미인 Unless로 쓸 수 있다. Unless 역시 조건절이므로 현재시제로 미래를 나타낸다.

- **If** you **don't hurry**, you will miss the train. 서두르지 않으면 그 기차를 놓칠 거야.
  = **Unless** you **hurry**, you will miss the train.

핵심 Check

2. 다음 우리말과 같도록 빈칸에 알맞은 말을 쓰시오.

(1) 그들이 일찍 도착한다면, 우리는 일찍 떠날 거야.

➡ If they _____ early, _____ _____ leave early.

(2) 네가 그의 파티에 오지 않는다면, 그는 아주 슬플 거야.

➡ _____ you come to his party, he _____ _____ very sad.

(3) 나는 네가 여행에서 돌아왔는지 알고 싶어.

➡ I want to know _____ you came back from the trip.

01 다음 문장에서 어법상 <u>어색한</u> 부분을 바르게 고쳐 쓰시오.

(1) If you will tell me the truth, I won't tell it to anyone.

_____ ➡ _____

(2) Some people like oranges. Another people like apples.

_____ ➡ _____

(3) I don't know if she practices hard tomorrow.

_____ ➡ _____

(4) There are two seats. One is mine and other is yours.

_____ ➡ _____

02 다음 빈칸에 알맞은 말을 쓰시오.

(1) If it _____ tomorrow, I will lend you my umbrella.

(2) She is holding two cameras. _____ is mine, and _____

_____ is hers.

(3) _____ you wake up early, you will be late for the meeting.

(4) I bought five skirts. One is red, _____ is pink, and _____

_____ are white.

03 다음 우리말에 맞게 주어진 어구를 바르게 배열하시오. (필요하다면 단어를 추가할 것)

(1) 어떤 꽃들은 흰색이고, 또 다른 꽃들은 노란색이다.

(flowers / are / yellow / white / some / are / and / others)

➡ _____

(2) 만약 네가 이 잡지를 원한다면, 내가 그것을 네게 빌려줄게.

(want / lend / you / to / if / this magazine / I / it / you)

➡ _____

(3) 너는 두 개의 시계를 가지고 있잖아. 하나는 여기에 있어. 다른 하나는 어디
에 있니?

(two watches / have / one / you / here / the other / is / where / is)

➡ _____

(4) 네가 이기면, 우리는 행복할 거야. (if / be / you / we / win / happy)

➡ _____

01 다음 빈칸에 들어갈 말로 어법상 적절한 것을 모두 고르시오.

> _____ I can see you arrive here safely, I won't leave.

① Unless ② Because ③ Although
④ Until ⑤ Since

02 다음 빈칸에 들어갈 말로 가장 적절한 것은? 중요

> A: What is the difference between these two bikes?
> B: Well, this one is more comfortable than _____ .

① some ② another ③ other
④ one ⑤ the other

03 다음 빈칸에 들어갈 말이 바르게 짝지어진 것은?

> If you _____ a problem, we _____ it later.

① will have – will discuss
② had – can solve
③ have had – discuss
④ have – will discuss
⑤ have – discuss

04 서답형 다음 빈칸에 알맞은 말을 쓰시오.

> Mr. Robinson has three daughters. _____ is a teacher, _____ is a pianist, and _____ is a writer.

➡ _____

05 다음 우리말을 영어로 바르게 옮긴 것은?

> 네가 하나를 선택하면, 내가 남은 하나를 선택할게.

① If you choose it, I will choose another.
② If you choose one, I will choose other.
③ If you will choose one, I will choose the other.
④ If you will choose it, I will choose another.
⑤ If you choose one, I will choose the other.

06 다음 중 어법상 바르지 않은 것은?

> There ①are many people ②downstairs. ③Some want to have peach juice, ④other want to have lemonade. If you want me ⑤to ask what the others want to have, I will.

07 다음 중 밑줄 친 if의 쓰임이 나머지와 다른 하나는? 중요

① If anyone finds it, I will call you.
② You will regret if you don't listen to me.
③ It is hard to tell if he liked it or not.
④ She will stay longer if you ask her to.
⑤ If the tree is cut, we will plant another one.

08 서답형 주어진 어구를 이용하여 다음 우리말을 영어로 쓰시오.

> 네게 시간이 있다면, 내 부탁 하나 들어주겠니?
> (have time / do / a favor)

➡ _____

09 다음 중 어법상 옳은 것은?

① Please move your car because you are blocking another cars.

② Unless you are not an expert, it is difficult to do the job.

③ If I make some mistakes, can you help me?

④ Angela has three necklaces. One is short and the other are long.

⑤ I wonder if you buy a lap top computer this weekend.

서답형

10 주어진 단어를 활용하여 밑줄 친 우리말을 8 단어로 이루어진 문장으로 쓰시오.

This copy machine is broken. 다른 복사기가 있는지 혹시 아니? (know / if / there / one)

➡ _____

11 다음 빈칸에 공통으로 들어갈 말은? **중요**

• I will go skiing _____ it snows this weekend.

• Can you tell me _____ James will join the party tonight?

① because   ② while   ③ if
④ unless   ⑤ although

12 다음 중 빈칸에 들어갈 말이 바르게 짝지어진 것은? **중요**

There are two cats under the tree. _____ is sleeping, and _____ is playing with a ball.

① It – another   ② The one – other
③ One – two   ④ One – the other
⑤ One - another

서답형

13 다음 빈칸에 알맞은 말을 쓰시오.

I got three letters. _____ was from my grandfather. _____ was from my brother. _____ was from my girlfriend.

➡ _____

14 다음 중 밑줄 친 부분과 바꾸어 쓸 수 있는 것은?

I bought a blue hat but I want to buy a different one.

① one   ② it   ③ the other
④ other   ⑤ another

15 다음 중 밑줄 친 부분이 문맥이나 어법상 옳은 것은? **중요**

① If they will throw a party, will they invite Tom?

② Some people like bowling and another like badminton.

③ Let me know if you will be there.

④ If you say sorry, Mom will be upset.

⑤ This shirt is too bright. Can you show me the other one in this size?

서답형

16 다음 빈칸 ⓐ~ⓔ에 알맞은 말을 쓰시오.

Look at your hand. You have five fingers. ⓐ_____ is your thumb. ⓑ_____ is your index finger. ⓒ_____ is your middle finger. ⓓ_____ is your ring finger. And ⓔ_____ finger is your little finger.

➡ ⓐ: _____   ⓑ: _____   ⓒ: _____
　 ⓓ: _____   ⓔ: _____

서답형

17 주어진 단어를 이용하여 다음 우리말을 영어로 쓰시오.

> 만약 그녀가 널 초대하면, 너는 그 파티에 갈거니? (invite / go) (if로 시작할 것)

➡ _____

18 다음 빈칸에 들어갈 말로 가장 적절한 것은?

> A: What are you doing?
> B: I'm watching Timmy. He is writing something with one hand, and holding a hamburger with _____.

① the others　　② another
③ the other　　④ one hand
⑤ other

서답형

19 두 문장의 의미가 같도록 빈칸에 알맞은 말을 쓰시오.

> If you don't read the book carefully, you will not pass the test.
> = _____ you read the book carefully, you will not pass the test.

➡ _____

중요

20 다음 중 빈칸에 들어갈 말이 바르게 짝지어진 것은?

> If you look at _____ side of the coin, you _____ a small castle on it.

① other – will discover
② another – discover
③ the other – discovered
④ another – discovered
⑤ the other – will discover

21 다음 빈칸에 들어갈 말로 가장 적절한 것은?

> Jenny has two sisters. _____

① One is taller than another.
② She is taller than others.
③ One is taller than the other.
④ She is taller than other.
⑤ One is taller than others.

중요

22 다음 빈칸에 들어갈 말이 바르게 짝지어진 것은?

> Many students have their favorite K-pop idols. These students often show their love in various ways. _____ scream wildly at concerts. _____ wait hours just to see their stars.

① One – The other　　② Some – Others
③ Few – Others　　④ Some – Another
⑤ One – Others

23 다음 빈칸에 가장 적절한 것은?

> I have been to two cities. One is Busan and _____ is Seoul.

① it　　② others　　③ other
④ another　　⑤ the other

서답형

24 적절한 부정대명사를 이용하여 다음 우리말을 영어로 쓰시오. (8 letters)

> 어떤 사람들은 파란색을 좋아하고, 어떤 사람들은 초록색을 좋아한다.

➡ _____

01 괄호 안에 주어진 동사를 이용하여 다음 우리말을 영어로 쓰시오.

> A: I think I left my lip balm at your house. Have you seen it?
> B: No, but 내가 그것을 찾으면, 네게 말해 줄게. (find, tell)

➡ _____

02 다음 빈칸에 알맞은 말을 쓰시오.

> Ms. Jefferson has five children. One of them has red hair. _____ children have brown hair.

➡ _____

03 다음 주어진 문장과 같은 의미의 문장을 쓰시오.

> If it doesn't rain tomorrow, I will play tennis with my friends.
> = _____ _____ _____ tomorrow, I will play tennis with my friends.

➡ _____

04 주어진 어구를 활용하여 다음 우리말을 두 개의 문장으로 쓰시오.

> 내일 몸이 좋지 않으면, 집에 머물 거야.
> (feel well / stay / at)

➡ _____

➡ _____

05 주어진 단어를 활용하여 다음 우리말을 영어로 쓰시오.

> 나는 두 개의 언어를 말할 수 있다. 하나는 한국어이고, 다른 하나는 영어이다.
> (speak / language)

➡ _____

06 괄호 안에 주어진 동사를 어법에 맞게 쓰시오.

> A: What are you going to do this weekend?
> B: My sister is going to come home this weekend. So if she (come) home early, I (go) shopping with her.

➡ _____

07 주어진 동사를 이용하여 다음 우리말을 영어로 쓰시오.

> 만약 네가 Jerry를 본다면, 너는 그를 좋아할 거야. (see / like)

➡ _____

08 빈칸에 알맞은 말을 쓰시오.

> I have been in only three cities since I came to the United States. _____ is Chicago, and _____ is San Francisco, and _____ is Miami.

➡ _____

09 주어진 어구를 어법에 맞게 빈칸에 각각 쓰시오.

another	the other	the others
one	some	other	others

(1) _____ people prefer classic music, but _____ prefer pop music.

(2) Molly has two goals in her life. _____ is to become a famous singer. _____ is to read many books.

(3) Jason got _____ birthday presents from his family. _____ is a computer. _____ is a bike. _____ is a long padding coat.

(4) There are ten bananas on the table. _____ is mine. _____ are yours.

(5) Some students like to study English, but _____ students like to study math.

(6) I lost my pencil, so I have to buy _____ one.

(7) In summer, _____ friends want to go to the beach, _____ want to go to the mountains.

10 두 개의 문장을 연결하여 자연스러운 하나의 문장으로 만드시오.

- You cheat on the test.
- You have a car.
- You don't wear a helmet.

- You will be hurt.
- You will get caught.
- Will you take me to the airport?

➡ _____

➡ _____

➡ _____

11 다음 빈칸에 적절한 것을 쓰시오.

There were ten chairs in the room, but I can count only five now. Where are _____?

➡ _____

12 괄호 안에 주어진 단어를 활용하여 빈칸 ⓐ와 ⓑ에 알맞은 말을 쓰고, 빈칸 ⓒ에는 적절한 부정대명사를 쓰시오.

A: What will do you if it rains after school?
B: If ⓐ _____ (rain) after school, I ⓑ _____ (use) one of my umbrellas. Actually, I have two umbrellas.
A: Then, can you borrow me ⓒ _____ one?
B: Sure.

➡ ⓐ _____ ⓑ _____ ⓒ _____

13 다음 글을 읽고 물음에 완전한 문장의 영어로 답하시오.

Helen took a cookie from the cookie jar and ate it. Then she took the other one and ate it, too. There were no more cookies in the cookie jar.

Q: How many cookies were there in the cookie jar?

➡ _____

14 다음 빈칸에 알맞은 말을 쓰시오.

There are two boys. _____ is wearing glasses and _____ is tall.

➡ _____

My New Changes

My friend Eric and I made some interesting changes during the
vacation. We emailed each other and talked about our changes.

My friend와 Eric은 동격으로 동일 인물을 나타냄 　 ~ 동안(숫자를 포함하지 않은 특정 기간)

Dear Eric,

It's a beautiful spring in Seoul. The last winter vacation was a great
time for me. I made two personal changes during the vacation. One is
my new hobby. It's making cupcakes. Making my own cupcakes is a
lot of fun. The other change is breaking one of my bad habits. In the
past, I often bit my nails. Now I don't anymore. I feel great about the
changes I made. If you try to make some changes, I'm sure you'll feel
great like me. I hope to hear from you soon.

날씨, 날짜, 거리, 명암 등을 나타내는 비인칭 주어 it
나에게
two changes 중 하나를 가리키며 '하나'라는 뜻을 나타냄
=My new hobby　동명사(보어)　동명사(주어)　동명사 주어는 단수 취급
two changes 중 나머지를 가리키며 '나머지 다른'이란 뜻을 나타냄
빈도부사로 일반동사 bite 앞에 위치. bite-bit-bitten　'not ~ anymore'는 '더 이상 ~ 않다'는 뜻이며, Now I don't bite my nails anymore.에서 bite my nails를 생략한 문장이다
앞에 관계대명사 목적격 that[which] 생략　=I'm sure (that)~: ~을 확신한다
~처럼　hope의 목적어

Your friend, Junho.

친한 친구 사이의 편지글의 마무리 말

---

make changes: 변화를 이루다
email: 이메일을 보내다
each other: 서로
personal: 개인적인
break a bad habit: 나쁜 습관을 그
만두다
bite: 깨물다
nail: 손톱
not ~ anymore: 더 이상 ~하지 않다
hear from: ~로부터 연락을 받다

✎ 확인문제

● 다음 문장이 본문의 내용과 일치하면 T, 일치하지 않으면 F를 쓰시오.

1 Junho isn't good at making cupcakes. ☐

2 Junho used to bite his nails. ☐

3 Junho feels great about not biting his nails. ☐

4 Junho doesn't like making his own cupcakes so much. ☐

Dear Junho,

In Sydney, it's fall in March. You talked about your changes in your
_{비인칭 주어}

email. Now, it's time to talk about my new changes.
_{'it's time to ~'는 '~할 시간이다'라는 뜻이고, 뒤에 동사원형이 옴}

These days, I'm into 3D printing. I printed two things with a 3D
_{~에 빠져 있다} _{~으로 (도구)}

printer. One is a model of my dream car. If the traffic is heavy, it will
_{(둘 중에서) 하나} _{if는 '조건'을 나타냄. 조건절의 동사는 미래시제 대신
현재시제를 사용하며, 주절은 그대로 미래시제를 쓴다.}

change into a flying car. The other is a special cup for my grandfather.
_{The other는 '(둘 중) 나머지 다른 하나'라는 뜻으로 'One ~'을 언급한 후 나머지 다른 하나를 설명할 때 쓰는 표현이다.}

He can't hold his cup well because he's sick. My special cup has three
_{'이유'를 나타내는 접속사}

handles, so it is easy to hold. My grandfather is very happy. By the
_{'결과'를 나타내는 접속사} _{형용사를 수식하는 부사적 용법}

way, I want to try your cupcakes some day, Junho.
_{먹어 보다} _{언젠가}

Take care.

Best wishes,
_{행운을 빌어}

Eric.

It's time to ~: ~할 때다
these days: 요즈음에는
be into: ~에 빠져 있다
traffic: 교통
change into: ~로 변하다
handle: 손잡이
by the way: 그건 그렇고
take care: 잘 있어

📎 **확인문제**

● 다음 문장이 본문의 내용과 일치하면 T, 일치하지 않으면 F를 쓰시오.

1 Eric wrote the email in March. ☐

2 Eric wants to talk about his new changes. ☐

3 Eric printed three things with a 3D printer. ☐

4 A flying car is Eric's dream car. ☐

5 Eric made the special cup for his grandmother. ☐

6 Eric's grandfather is healthy. ☐

● 우리말을 참고하여 빈칸에 알맞은 말을 쓰시오.

1 My friend Eric and I _____ _____ _____ _____ _____ the vacation.

2 We _____ _____ _____ and _____ _____ our changes.

3 _____ Eric,

4 _____'s a beautiful _____ _____ Seoul.

5 _____ _____ _____ was a great _____ for me.

6 I _____ two _____ _____ _____ the vacation.

7 _____ is my new hobby.

8 It's _____ cupcakes.

9 _____ my _____ cupcakes _____ a lot of fun.

10 _____ _____ _____ is _____ one of my bad habits.

11 In the past, I _____ _____ my nails.

12 Now I _____ _____.

13 I _____ _____ _____ the changes I _____.

14 _____ you _____ _____ _____ some changes, I'm sure you _____ _____ great _____ me.

15 I hope to _____ _____ you soon.

16 Your _____, Junho.

1	내 친구 Eric과 나는 방학 동안 흥미로운 변화가 있었다.
2	우리는 서로에게 이메일을 보냈고 우리의 변화에 관해 이야기했다.
3	안녕 Eric,
4	서울은 아름다운 봄이야.
5	지난 겨울 방학은 나에게 멋진 시간이었어.
6	나는 방학 동안 두 가지 개인적인 변화가 있었어.
7	하나는 나의 새로운 취미야.
8	그것은 컵케이크를 만드는 거야.
9	나만의 컵케이크를 만드는 것은 정말 재미있어.
10	나머지 다른 변화는 나의 나쁜 습관 중 하나를 없애는 거야.
11	예전에 나는 종종 손톱을 물어뜯곤 했어.
12	이제 나는 더 이상 그러지 않아.
13	나는 내가 만든 변화가 정말 기분 좋아.
14	만약 네가 변화하려고 노력한다면, 너도 나처럼 기분이 좋을 거라고 확신해.
15	곧 소식 전해 줘.
16	너의 친구 준호가

17 _____ Junho,

18 _____ Sydney, _____'s fall _____ March.

19 You talked _____ your _____ in your email.

20 Now, it's _____ _____ _____ _____ my new changes.

21 _____ _____, I'm _____ 3D printing.

22 I printed _____ _____ _____ a 3D printer.

23 _____ is a model of my _____ _____.

24 _____ the traffic _____ _____, it _____ _____ _____ a flying car.

25 _____ _____ is a special cup _____ my grandfather.

26 He can't _____ his cup _____ because he's _____.

27 My special cup has _____ _____, so it is easy _____ _____.

28 My grandfather is very _____.

29 _____ _____ _____, I want _____ _____ your cupcakes some day, Junho.

30 _____ _____.

31 Best _____, Eric.

---

17 안녕 준호,

18 시드니에서는 3월이 가을이야.

19 너는 이메일에서 너에게 일어난 변화들을 말해 주었지.

20 이제 나의 새로운 변화를 말해 줄 차례야.

21 요즈음, 나는 3D 프린팅에 빠져 있어.

22 나는 3D 프린터로 2가지를 인쇄했어.

23 하나는 나의 꿈의 자동차의 모형이야.

24 교통이 혼잡할 때, 그것은 날 수 있는 차로 바뀌어.

25 나머지 다른 하나는 우리 할아버지를 위한 특수 컵이야.

26 할아버지는 편찮으셔서 컵을 잘 들지 못하셔.

27 나의 특수 컵은 손잡이가 3개 있어서 들기 쉬워.

28 할아버지는 아주 행복해 하셔.

29 그건 그렇고, 너의 컵케이크를 언젠가 먹어 보고 싶다, 준호야.

30 잘 지내.

31 행운을 빌어, Eric

● 우리말을 참고하여 본문을 영작하시오.

1 내 친구 Eric과 나는 방학 동안 흥미로운 변화가 있었다.

➡ _____

2 우리는 서로에게 이메일을 보냈고 우리의 변화에 관해 이야기했다.

➡ _____

3 안녕 Eric,

➡ _____

4 서울은 아름다운 봄이야.

➡ _____

5 지난 겨울 방학은 나에게 멋진 시간이었어.

➡ _____

6 나는 방학 동안 두 가지 개인적인 변화가 있었어.

➡ _____

7 하나는 나의 새로운 취미야.

➡ _____

8 그것은 컵케이크를 만드는 거야.

➡ _____

9 나만의 컵케이크를 만드는 것은 정말 재미있어.

➡ _____

10 나머지 다른 변화는 나의 나쁜 습관 중 하나를 없애는 거야.

➡ _____

11 예전에 나는 종종 손톱을 물어뜯곤 했어.

➡ _____

12 이제 나는 더 이상 그러지 않아.

➡ _____

13 나는 내가 만든 변화가 정말 기분 좋아.

➡ _____

14 만약 네가 변화하려고 노력한다면, 너도 나처럼 기분이 좋을 거라고 확신해.

➡ _____

15 곧 소식 전해 줘.

➡ _____

16 너의 친구 준호가

➡ _____

17 안녕 준호,

➡ _____

18 시드니에서는 3월이 가을이야.

➡ _____

19 너는 이메일에서 너에게 일어난 변화들을 말해 주었지.

➡ _____

20 이제 나의 새로운 변화를 말해 줄 차례야.

➡ _____

21 요즈음, 나는 3D 프린팅에 빠져 있어.

➡ _____

22 나는 3D 프린터로 2가지를 인쇄했어.

➡ _____

23 하나는 나의 꿈의 자동차의 모형이야.

➡ _____

24 교통이 혼잡할 때, 그것은 날 수 있는 차로 바뀌어.

➡ _____

25 나머지 다른 하나는 우리 할아버지를 위한 특수 컵이야.

➡ _____

26 할아버지는 편찮으셔서 컵을 잘 들지 못해서.

➡ _____

27 나의 특수 컵은 손잡이가 3개 있어서 들기 쉬워.

➡ _____

28 할아버지는 아주 행복해 하셔.

➡ _____

29 그건 그렇고, 너의 컵케이크를 언젠가 먹어 보고 싶다, 준호야.

➡ _____

30 잘 지내.

➡ _____

31 행운을 빌어, Eric.

➡ _____

[01~06] 다음 글을 읽고 물음에 답하시오.

My friend Eric and I made some interesting changes during the vacation. We emailed each other and talked about our changes.

　Dear Eric,
　(A)It's a beautiful spring in Seoul. The last winter vacation was a great time for me. I made two personal changes during the vacation. (B)[It / One] is my new hobby. It's making cupcakes. Making my own cupcakes (C)[is / are] a lot of fun. ⓐ_____ change is breaking one of my bad (D)[habit / habits]. In the past, I often bit my nails. Now I don't anymore. I feel great about (a)내가 만든 변화. If you try to make some changes, I'm sure you'll feel great like me. I hope to hear ⓑ_____ you soon.
　Your friend, Junho.

서답형

01 빈칸 ⓐ에 알맞은 말을 쓰시오.

➡ _____

02 다음 중 빈칸 ⓑ에 들어갈 말과 같은 것은?

① She is thinking _____ taking a trip to Europe.
② Jerry called his father _____ his way home.
③ Are you interested _____ breaking your bad habit?
④ Listen _____ what others say carefully.
⑤ Where did you come _____?

서답형

03 밑줄 친 우리말 (a)를 영어로 쓰시오.

➡ _____

04 다음 중 밑줄 친 (A)와 쓰임이 같은 것끼리 바르게 묶은 것은?

Ⓐ It is getting dark outside. Let's go home.
Ⓑ It is four kilometers from the school to my house.
Ⓒ It is climbing up the tree.
Ⓓ It is important to always tell the truth to your friend.
Ⓔ It is eight o'clock already.

① Ⓐ, Ⓑ, Ⓒ　　　② Ⓒ, Ⓓ, Ⓔ
③ Ⓑ, Ⓓ, Ⓔ　　　④ Ⓐ, Ⓑ, Ⓔ
⑤ Ⓐ, Ⓒ, Ⓓ

05 **중요** (B)~(D)에서 어법상 옳은 것끼리 바르게 짝지은 것은?

① It – is – habit
② It – are – habit
③ One – is – habit
④ One – is – habits
⑤ One – are – habits

06 위 글의 내용과 일치하지 <u>않는</u> 것은?

① The writer is Junho.
② The writer made two changes.
③ Changes were made during the vacation.
④ The writer and Eric didn't contact each other.
⑤ The writer wrote the email in spring.

[07~14] 다음 글을 읽고 물음에 답하시오.

Dear Junho,

In Sydney, it's fall in March. You talked about your changes in your email. Now, it's time to talk about my new changes. These days, I'm ⓐ_____ 3D printing. I printed two things with a 3D printer. One is a model of my dream car. If the traffic is heavy, it will change ⓑ_____ a (A)_____ car. The other is a special cup for my grandfather. He can't hold his cup well ⓒ_____ he's sick. My special cup has three handles, so ⓓit is easy to hold. My grandfather is very happy. ⓔ By the way, I want (B)_____ your cupcakes some day, Junho.

Take care.

Best wishes,

Eric.

07 다음 중 빈칸 ⓐ와 ⓑ에 공통으로 들어갈 말은?

① on　　　② about　　　③ into
④ by　　　⑤ from

08 다음 중 빈칸 ⓒ에 들어갈 말로 가장 적절한 것은?

① if　　　② so　　　③ because
④ when　　⑤ although

서답형

09 주어진 단어를 어법에 맞게 빈칸 (A)와 (B)에 각각 쓰시오.

(fly / try)

➡ (A)_____ (B)_____

서답형

10 밑줄 친 ⓓ가 가리키는 것은?

➡ _____

11 다음 중 밑줄 친 ⓔ의 의미로 가장 적절한 것은?

① 집에 가는 길에　　② 그 길목에서
③ 그건 그렇고　　　④ 길옆에서
⑤ 혹시

12 위 글의 내용과 일치하지 <u>않는</u> 것은?

① 준호의 편지에 대한 Eric의 답장이다.
② Eric은 3D 프린터로 꿈의 자동차 모형을 인쇄하였다.
③ Eric이 만든 컵은 손잡이가 3개 있다.
④ Eric이 만든 컵은 들기 쉽다.
⑤ Eric은 준호에게 컵케이크를 보내달라고 요청하고 있다.

13 다음 빈칸에 들어갈 말로 가장 적절한 것은?

According to the letter, it is thought that Junho's email was about _____.

① how he spent his time with his family
② some changes he made
③ how to make cupcakes
④ why he wanted to buy a 3D printer
⑤ changes in our environment

서답형

14 다음은 Eric이 자신의 컵을 소개하는 글이다. 위 글의 내용에 맞게 빈칸에 알맞은 말을 쓰시오.

This cup is very special. I made it for _____ _____. It has _____ _____. So it is easy to hold this _____.

➡ _____

[15~21] 다음 글을 읽고 물음에 답하시오.

My friend Eric and I made some ⓐ_____ changes during the vacation. We emailed each other and talked ⓑ_____ our changes.

Dear Eric,
It's a beautiful spring in Seoul. The last winter vacation was a great time for me. ① I made two personal changes during the vacation. ② One is my new hobby. ③ Making my own cupcakes is a lot of fun. ④ The other change is (A)_____. ⑤ In the past, I often bit my nails. Now I don't anymore. I feel great about the changes I made. If you try to make some changes, I'm sure you'll feel great like me. I hope (B) to hear from you soon.
Your friend, Junho.

15 ①~⑤ 중 주어진 문장이 들어가기에 가장 적절한 곳은?

It's making cupcakes.

①   ②   ③   ④   ⑤

16 빈칸 ⓐ와 ⓑ에 들어갈 말이 바르게 짝지어진 것은?

① interesting – in
② interested – with
③ interesting – about
④ interest – to
⑤ interested – into

17 다음 단어를 바르게 배열하여 빈칸 (A)를 채우시오. (하나의 단어를 어법에 맞게 변형하시오.)

habits / break / one / my / of / bad

➡ _____

18 다음 중 위 글을 읽고 답할 수 없는 것은?

① Who is Eric?
② To whom did Junho write the email?
③ How does Junho feel about making his own cupcakes?
④ Why did Junho bite his nails so much?
⑤ What is Junho's new hobby?

19 다음과 같이 풀이되는 단어를 위 글에서 찾아 쓰시오.

(1)
the hard covering at the end of a finger

➡ _____

(2)
the time before the present, and the things that have happened

➡ _____

20 위 글의 내용에 맞게 대화의 빈칸을 채우시오.

Amelia: Junho, how do you feel about the changes you made?
Junho: _____ _____ _____

➡ _____

21 다음 중 밑줄 친 (B)와 그 쓰임이 같은 것은?

① We will be glad to see you again.
② I decided to become a lawyer.
③ She felt sorry not to be honest with her friend.
④ Do you have a friend to trust?
⑤ Is there anyone to help you?

[22~26] 다음 글을 읽고 물음에 답하시오.

Dear, Junho,

In Sydney, it's fall in March. You talked about your changes in your email. Now, it's time (A)[talking / to talk] about my new changes. These days, ⓐI'm into 3D printing. I printed two things with a 3D printer. One is a model of my dream car. If the traffic is heavy, it will (B)[change / change into] a flying car. The other is a special cup for my grandfather. He can't hold his cup well because he's sick. My special cup has three handles, so it is easy (C)[holding / to hold]. My grandfather is very happy. By the way, I want to try your cupcakes some day, Junho.

Take care.

Best wishes,

Eric.

 22 (A)~(C) 중 어법상 옳은 것끼리 바르게 짝지은 것은?

① talking – change – holding

② to talk – change into – holding

③ talking – change into – to hold

④ to talk – change into – to hold

⑤ talking – change – to hold

23 How many handles does Eric's cup have? Answer in English with a full sentence.

➡ _____

24 밑줄 친 ⓐ의 의미로 가장 적절한 것은?

① I look into a 3D printer.

② I would like to have a 3D printer.

③ I am interested in making a 3D printer.

④ I imagine 3D printing.

⑤ I am crazy about 3D printing.

25 주어진 어구를 사용하여 다음 물음에 12 단어로 이루어진 하나의 문장으로 답하시오.

Q: Why did Eric make a special cup for his grandfather? (wanted to help / because / hold)

➡ _____

_____

 26 위 글의 내용과 일치하지 <u>않는</u> 것은?

① It is a letter written by Eric.

② Eric is writing about his new changes.

③ Eric printed two things with his 3D printer.

④ Eric's grandfather is sick.

⑤ Eric's grandfather doesn't like the special cup that much.

27 주어진 문장과 자연스럽게 이어지도록 (A)~(C)를 바르게 나열한 것은?

It's a beautiful spring in Seoul. The last winter vacation was a great time for me.

(A) If you try to make some changes, I'm sure you'll feel great like me. I really think so.

(B) The other change is breaking one of my bad habits. In the past, I often bit my nails. Now I don't anymore. I feel great about the changes I made.

(C) I made two personal changes during the vacation. One is my new hobby. It's making cupcakes. Making my own cupcakes is a lot of fun.

① (A)-(C)-(B)　　② (B)-(A)-(C)

③ (B)-(C)-(A)　　④ (C)-(A)-(B)

⑤ (C)-(B)-(A)

[01~08] 다음 글을 읽고 물음에 답하시오.

My friend Eric and I made some interesting changes during the vacation. (A)우리는 서로에게 이메일을 보냈다 and talked about our changes.

Dear Eric,
It's a beautiful spring in Seoul. The last winter vacation was a great time for me. I made two personal changes during the vacation. ⓐ_____ is my new hobby. It's making cupcakes. Making my own cupcakes is a lot of fun. ⓑ_____ change is breaking one of my bad habits. In the past, I often bit my nails. ⓒNow I don't anymore. I feel great about the changes I made. If you try to make some changes, I'm sure you'll feel great like me. I hope to hear from you soon.
Your friend, Junho.

01 밑줄 친 우리말 (A)를 영어로 쓰시오.

➡ _____

02 빈칸 ⓐ와 ⓑ에 알맞은 어구를 쓰시오.

➡ ⓐ_____ ⓑ_____

03 밑줄 친 ⓒ를 완전한 문장으로 쓰시오.

➡ _____

04 According to the passage, where does Junho live? Answer in English with a full sentence.

➡ _____

05 위 글의 내용에 맞게 대화의 빈칸을 채우시오.

Jenny: Junho, do you have a _____ _____ that you want to _____?
Junho: I had it before. But I broke it.

➡ _____

06 위 글의 내용에 맞게 대화의 빈칸에 알맞은 말을 쓰시오.

Julia: Junho, what are you doing?
Junho: I am ____ ____ ____ ____. It is my new hobby.
Julia: Is there _____ hobby?
Junho: Yes, there is.

➡ _____

07 위 글의 표현을 참고하여 다음 우리말을 영어로 쓰시오.

너의 나쁜 습관 중 하나를 없앤다면, 너는 기분이 좋을 거야.

➡ _____

08 괄호 안에 주어진 단어를 사용하여 다음 물음에 완전한 문장의 영어로 답하시오.

Q: Why does Junho say that the last winter vacation was a great time for him?
A: _____
_____ (because, vacation)

[09~17] 다음 글을 읽고 물음에 답하시오.

Dear Junho,

In Sydney, it's fall in March. You talked about your changes in your email. Now, it's time to talk about my new changes. These days, I'm into 3D printing. I printed two things with a 3D printer. One is a model of my dream car. ⓐIf the traffic will be heavy, it will change into a flying car. ⓑ나머지 다른 하나는 우리 할아버지를 위한 특수 컵이야. He can't hold his cup well because he's sick. ⓒ My special cup has three handles, so it is easy to hold. My grandfather is very happy. By the way, I want to try your cupcakes some day, Junho.

Take care.

Best wishes,

Eric.

09 다음은 Eric이 친구들에게 할 수 있는 말이다. 밑줄 친 우리말을 영어로 쓰시오.

> Eric: I made a special cup for my grandfather. 네가 이 컵을 들면, 너는 이 컵이 들기 쉽다는 것을 알게 될 거야.

➡ _____

10 Where and when did Eric write the letter? Answer in English with a full sentence.

➡ _____

11 밑줄 친 ⓐ에서 어법상 틀린 것을 바르게 고치고, 그렇게 고친 이유를 서술하시오.

➡ _____ ➡ _____

➡ 이유: _____

12 다음은 Eric이 만든 컵을 본 할아버지의 반응이다. 괄호 안에 주어진 단어를 어법에 맞게 고쳐 쓰고, 빈칸에 들어갈 말은 위 글에서 찾아 쓰시오.

> Grandfather: Eric, I (satisfy) this cup. I feel _____.

➡ _____

13 주어진 단어를 바르게 배열하여 밑줄 친 우리말 ⓑ를 영어로 쓰시오. 필요하다면 단어를 추가하시오..

> (my / other / cup / grandfather / a / is / special / for)

➡ _____

14 What is Eric into these days? Answer in English with a full sentence.

➡ _____

15 주어진 단어를 사용하여 밑줄 친 ⓒ와 같은 의미의 문장을 쓰시오.

> (because)

➡ _____
_____

16 What do they talk about through email? Answer in English with a full sentence.

➡ _____

17 According to the passage, what can Junho make? Answer in English with a full sentence.

➡ _____

Real Life Communication - Step 2

A: You know what? I'm thinking of keeping a diary in English.
그거 아니?   동명사(전치사의 목적어)

B: Why did you decide to do that?
결심하다   = keep a diary in English

A: It's because I want to be good at English writing.
because+주어+동사   ~를 잘하다

B: That's great.

구문해설 · think of: ~에 대해 생각하다 · keep a diary: 일기를 쓰다 · decide: 결심하다

A: 그거 아니? 나는 영어로 일기를 쓸 생각이야.
B: 왜 그런 결심을 했어?
A: 왜냐하면 영어 쓰기를 잘하고 싶기 때문이야.
B: 멋지다.

My Writing Portfolio

Dear me,

You are very smart and funny. However, you still want to make two changes,
그러나   want의 목적어

don't you? One is to have more good friends. The other is to become healthier.
부가의문문 (둘 중에서) 하나는   나머지 다른 하나

Here are my tips for your wishes. If you are nicer to others and eat more
my tips에 수의 일치   조건의 부사절에서 현재시제로 미래를 나타냄 =other people

vegetables, you'll make these changes.

Love, Me

구문해설 · still: 아직, 여전히 · change: 변화 · healthier: 더 건강한 · tip: 조언 · wish: 소망

나에게

너는 매우 영리하고 재미있어. 하지만 너는 아직 두 가지 변화를 이루고 싶어 해. 그렇지 않니? 하나는 더 많은 좋은 친구를 사귀는 거야. 다른 하나는 더 건강해지는 거야. 여기 너의 소망을 위한 조언이 있어. 다른 사람들에게 더 친절하고 더 많은 채소를 먹는다면, 너는 이러한 변화들을 이룰 수 있을 거야.

사랑하는,

내가

Words in Action B

Bobo is my pet dog. She has two brothers. One is black. The other is white.
둘 중 첫 번째로 언급하는 것을 one   나머지 하나를 언급하는 것은 the other이다.

She has two toys. One is a ball. The other is a plastic duck. She has two habits.

One is watching TV. The other is sleeping on my chair.
동명사(is의 보어)   동명사

구문해설 · pet: 애완동물 · plastic: 플라스틱 · habit: 습관

보보는 내 애완견이다. 그녀는 남동생이 둘 있다. 하나는 검정색이다. 다른 하나는 하얀색이다. 그녀는 장난감이 두 개 있다. 하나는 공이다. 다른 하나는 플라스틱 오리이다. 그녀는 두 가지 습관이 있다. 하나는 TV를 보는 것이다. 다른 하나는 내 의자 위에서 자는 것이다.

Words & Expressions

01 다음 우리말에 맞게 빈칸에 알맞은 말을 쓰시오.

(1) 그는 재즈 음악에 열중해 있다.
➡ He _____ _____ jazz music.

(2) 내가 집에 가는 길에 빵을 살게.
➡ I'll buy some bread _____ _____ _____ _____.

(3) 그녀는 아들한테 소식을 듣기를 기다리고 있어.
➡ She is waiting to _____ _____ her son.

02 다음 중 밑줄 친 부분의 뜻풀이가 바르지 <u>않은</u> 것은?

① The rumor is proved to be <u>false</u>. 사실의
② She made me laugh with a <u>funny</u> story. 재미있는
③ How was your summer <u>vacation</u>? 휴가
④ I'm not sure if I can make it, but I'll <u>try</u>. 시도하다
⑤ <u>Hold</u> the baby in your arms. 안다

03 다음 우리말을 주어진 단어를 이용하여 영작하시오.

(1) 나는 나의 나쁜 습관을 그만두기로 결심했다. (decide, break)
➡ _____

(2) 나는 시험에 통과하기 위해 최선을 다할 것이다. (do, pass, test)
➡ _____

(3) 그는 골프에 열중하고 있다. (playing, into)
➡ _____

04 다음 문장에 공통으로 들어갈 말을 고르시오.

• Did your dog _____ you?
• I'm hungry. Let's grab a _____.
• Tom has an itchy hand because of a mosquito _____.

① eat　② beat　③ bite　④ catch　⑤ bend

05 다음 주어진 문장의 밑줄 친 kind와 같은 의미로 쓰인 것은?

What <u>kind</u> of music do you like?

① They didn't sell that <u>kind</u> of cake.
② My grandmother has a <u>kind</u> heart.
③ Somi is a very <u>kind</u> and helpful person.
④ Thank you for your <u>kind</u> comments.
⑤ Let's make a <u>kind</u> and safe society.

Conversation

06 다음 대화의 빈칸에 들어갈 말로 어색한 것은?

A: What is your plan for this weekend, Sejun?
B: _____

① I'm thinking of visiting my grandparents.
② I'm planning to play soccer with my friends.
③ I'm going to have dinner with my uncles.
④ I have a plan to do my homework.
⑤ I planted trees in the garden.

[07~09] 다음 대화를 읽고 물음에 답하시오.

Brian: Julia, ⓐhow was your winter vacation?
Julia: It was great. (A)그거 아니? I took *muay thai* lessons ⓑfor the vacation.
Brian: That's ⓒamazing. I didn't know that you were ⓓinterested in *muay thai*.
Julia: Yes. It was really fun.
Brian: Really? I want ⓔto try it.

07 위 대화의 밑줄 친 (A)의 우리말을 3단어를 사용하여 영어로 쓰시오.

➡ _____

08 위 대화의 밑줄 친 ⓐ~ⓔ 중 어법상 어색한 것을 찾아 바르게 고치시오.

➡ _____

09 위 대화를 읽고 대답할 수 없는 것은?

① What did Julia learn during the winter vacation?
② How were *muay thai* lessons?
③ What was Julia interested in?
④ What does Brian want to try?
⑤ What class did Brian take during the winter vacation?

10 다음 대화가 자연스럽게 이어지도록 순서대로 배열하시오.

(A) That sounds great.
(B) We have some vegetables, but we don't have beef. I'll buy some for you on my way home.
(C) Do we have any vegetables at home? What about beef?
(D) I made *bulgogi* at school today. I'm thinking of cooking *bulgogi* for dinner.

➡ _____

[11~13] 다음 대화를 읽고 물음에 답하시오.

Jane: Minsu, (A)Sujin and I are thinking of starting a club.
Minsu: Really? What kind of club?
Jane: We want to learn about stars and planets. So, we're thinking of starting a space science club.
Minsu: Sounds good. How often are you going to meet?
Jane: Maybe once a week.
Minsu: I see. Where will you meet?
Jane: In Room 101. Minsu, do you want to join our club?
Minsu: Yes, I'm interested in space, too.

11 위 대화에서 다음의 영영풀이가 가리키는 말을 찾아 쓰시오.

> a large, round object in space that travels around a star

➡ _____

12 밑줄 친 (A)와 바꾸어 쓸 수 없는 것은?

① Sujin and I are planning to start a club.
② Sujin and I are going to start a club.
③ Sujin and I are into starting a club.
④ Sujin and I are considering starting a club.
⑤ Sujin and I will start a club.

13 위 대화의 내용과 일치하지 않는 것은?

① Sujin and Jane are thinking of starting a club.
② Jane and Sujin are interested in learning about stars and planets.
③ Jane and Sujin are planning to meet once a month.
④ The members of the space science club will meet in Room 101.
⑤ Minsu wants to join the space science club.

[14~15] 다음 대화를 읽고 물음에 답하시오.

> Jimin: You know what, Tim? Mr. Smith is my homeroom teacher this year.
> Tim: That's great, Jimin. His science class last year was a lot of fun.
> Jimin: Who's your homeroom teacher this year?
> Tim: It's Ms. Kim. She's a new teacher.
> Jimin: What does she teach?
> Tim: She teaches art.

14 According to Tim, how was Mr. Smith's class last year?

➡ _____

15 What are Tim and Jimin going to learn from the new teacher?

➡ _____

Grammar

16 다음 빈칸에 가장 적절한 것은?

> Hawaii is a popular tourist destination. Italy is _____ popular tourist destination.

① other　　　　　② the other
③ another　　　　④ others
⑤ one

17 다음 중 어법상 바르지 <u>않은</u> 것은?

> ①Will you ②give this message ③to her ④if Susan ⑤will come back?

①　　　②　　　③　　　④　　　⑤

18 다음 중 밑줄 친 부분을 대신하여 쓸 수 있는 것은?

> Some of the birds are flying. <u>Other birds</u> are sitting on a fence.

① Another　　　② The other
③ The others　　④ Others
⑤ Other

19 주어진 단어를 이용하여 다음 우리말을 영어로 쓰시오.

> 내게는 세 명의 외국인 친구가 있다. 한 명은 일본에서 왔고, 다른 두 명은 프랑스에서 왔다. (have / foreign / from)

➡ _____

　_____

20 다음 중 if의 쓰임이 같은 것끼리 바르게 묶인 것은?

> ⓐ Robert will be here on time <u>if</u> he doesn't miss the bus.
> ⓑ <u>If</u> you don't mind, I will pay for it.
> ⓒ I wonder <u>if</u> there is some food in the refrigerator.
> ⓓ <u>If</u> you need lots of paper, I will give you some.
> ⓔ How can I know <u>if</u> someone is my true friend or not?

① ⓐⓑⓒ, ⓓⓔ　　　② ⓐⓑⓓ, ⓒⓔ
③ ⓐⓒⓓ, ⓑⓔ　　　④ ⓐⓓⓔ, ⓑⓒ
⑤ ⓐⓑⓒⓓⓔ

21 다음 중 어법상 바르지 <u>않은</u> 것은?

> ①Some of ②his books ③are novels and 　④others ⑤are all comics.

22 주어진 단어를 바르게 배열하여 다음 우리말을 영어로 쓰시오.

> 최선을 다하지 않는다면, 너는 아무것도 성취할 수 없을 거야. (unless로 시작할 것)
> (anything / unless / not / achieve / you / will / you / your / do / best)

➡ _____

　_____

23 다음 대화의 빈칸에 들어갈 말로 가장 적절한 것은?

> **A:** What are your two daughters doing now?
> **B:** _____

① One is sleeping, and another is listening to music.
② A daughter is cleaning her room, and the others is hanging out with her friend.
③ One is answering a phone, and other is doing her homework.
④ One is baking bread, and one is playing a computer game.
⑤ One is watching TV, and the other is reading a book.

24 주어진 어구를 이용하여 다음 우리말을 두 개의 영어 문장으로 쓰시오. (부사절을 주절의 앞에 쓸 것)

> 따뜻한 옷을 입지 않으면, 너는 감기에 걸릴 거야. (wear / clothes / catch a cold)

➡ _____

➡ _____

25 다음 빈칸에 들어갈 말을 바르게 짝지은 것은?

> There are three balls in the box. _____ is blue. _____ is red. _____ is gray.

① It – The other – Other
② It – The other – The other
③ One – Another - Another
④ One – Another – The other
⑤ One – Other – The other

26 주어진 단어를 어법에 맞게 활용하여 다음 우리말을 영어로 쓰시오. (if로 시작할 것)

> 네가 매일 조깅하러 가면, 너는 더 건강해 질 거야. (go / jog / get / healthy)

➡ _____

Reading

[27~30] 다음 글을 읽고 물음에 답하시오.

> My friend Eric and I made some interesting changes ⓐ_____ the vacation. We emailed ① each other and talked about our changes.
>
> Dear Eric,
> It's a beautiful spring ②in Seoul. The last winter vacation was a great time for me. I made ⓑ_____ personal changes during the vacation. One is my new hobby. It's making cupcakes. Making my own cupcakes is a lot of fun. ③The other is breaking one of my bad habits. In the past, I often ④bite my nails. Now I don't ⑤anymore. I feel great about the changes I made. ⓒ만약 네가 변화하려고 노력한다면, I'm sure you'll feel great like me. I hope to hear from you soon.
> Your friend, Junho.

27 다음 중 빈칸 ⓐ에 들어갈 말과 같은 것은?

① I'm going away _____ a few days.
② We only saw her once _____ our stay in Korea.
③ I've studied English _____ three hours.
④ They went down to the sea _____ a day.
⑤ Helen stayed there _____ a couple of weeks.

28 빈칸 ⓑ에 들어갈 말로 가장 적절한 것은?

① a great deal of   ② a number of
③ a couple of   ④ a lot of
⑤ so much

29 주어진 단어를 바르게 배열하여 밑줄 친 ⓒ를 영어로 옮기시오.

(changes / if / make / you / some / try / to)

➡ _____

30 밑줄 친 ①~⑤ 중 어법상 바르지 않은 것은?

①   ②   ③   ④   ⑤

[31~34] 다음 글을 읽고, 물음에 답하시오.

Dear Junho,
In Sydney, it's fall in March. You talked about your changes in your email. Now, it's time to talk about my new changes. These days, I'm into 3D printing. I printed two things with a 3D printer. One is a model of my dream car. If the traffic is heavy, it will change into a flying car. The other is a special cup for my grandfather. He can't hold his cup well because he's sick. My special cup has three handles, so it is easy to hold. My grandfather is very happy. By the way, I want to try your cupcakes some day, Junho.
Take care.
Best wishes,
Eric.

31 다음 중 위 글을 읽고 답할 수 없는 것은?

① What did Junho talk about in his email?
② What season is it in Sydney in March?
③ What does Eric want to talk about in his email?
④ When does Eric's dream car change into a flying car?
⑤ Why is Eric's grandfather sick?

32 다음 빈칸에 해당하는 단어를 위 글에서 찾아 쓰시오.

A _____ is the part that is designed especially to be grasped by the hand.

➡ _____

33 위 글의 내용에 맞게 빈칸에 알맞은 말을 쓰시오.

Eric lives in _____. He is interested _____ _____ _____.

➡ _____

34 Write the reason why Eric's special cup is easy to hold. Use the word 'because.'

➡ _____

[01~02] 다음 대화를 읽고 물음에 답하시오.

> **Alex:** Mom, I made *bulgogi* at school today. I'm thinking of cooking *bulgogi* for dinner.
> **Mom:** That sounds great, Alex.
> **Alex:** Do we have any vegetables at home, Mom? What about beef?
> **Mom:** We have some vegetables, but we don't have beef. I'll buy some for you on my way home.
> **Alex:** Great.

✏️ 출제율 90%

01 위 대화의 표현을 사용하여 다음 주어진 문장을 영작하시오.

> 나는 도서관에 가는 길에 Mike를 만났다.

➡ _____

✏️ 출제율 95%

02 위 대화의 내용과 일치하지 <u>않는</u> 것은?

① Alex is planning to make *bulgogi* for dinner.
② Alex needs some vegetables and beef to make *bulgogi*.
③ Alex has some vegetables at home.
④ Alex's mom is thinking of buying some beef for Alex.
⑤ Alex and his mom are talking in the kitchen together.

[03~05] 다음 대화를 읽고 물음에 답하시오.

> **Emily:** You know what, Junsu? I'm thinking of taking a painting class.
> **Junsu:** Really? Why did you decide to take a painting class, Emily?
> **Emily:** Because I want to go to an art high school.
> **Junsu:** Are you thinking of becoming an artist in the future?

> **Emily:** I hope so. I'm interested in painting pictures.
> **Junsu:** That's great. (A)_____
> **Emily:** Thanks. I'll do my best.

✏️ 출제율 100%

03 위 대화의 빈칸 (A)에 들어갈 말을 〈보기〉에 주어진 단어를 배열하여 완성하시오.

> ┤ 보기 ├
> true / hope / your / I / wish / comes

➡ _____

✏️ 출제율 80%

04 What does Emily want to be in the future?

➡ _____

✏️ 출제율 90%

05 What is Emily planning to do to go to an art high school?

➡ _____

[06~07] 다음 대화를 읽고 물음에 답하시오.

> **A:** You know what? (A)나는 영어로 일기를 쓸 생각이야. (think, keep)
> **B:** Why did you (B)decide to do that?
> **A:** It's because I want to be good at English writing.
> **B:** That's great.

✏️ 출제율 90%

06 위 대화의 (A)를 주어진 단어를 이용하여 영작하시오.

➡ _____

✏️ 출제율 95%

07 위 대화의 밑줄 친 (B)와 바꾸어 쓸 수 있는 것은?

① determine   ② refuse
③ postpone   ④ delay
⑤ bite

Sue: You know what? Jenny's family is going to move to Japan.

Jack Is that right? Jenny didn't tell me about it.

Sue: She learned about it just last week and she's very upset now.

Jack: I can understand her feelings. I am going to miss her so much.

Sue: (A)Me, too. She said she would keep in touch with us.

08 위 대화의 밑줄 친 (A)와 바꾸어 쓸 수 있는 것은?

① So do I.
② So am I.
③ Nether do I.
④ Neither am I.
⑤ Nether did I.

09 위 대화의 내용과 일치하지 않는 것은?

① Jenny의 가족이 일본으로 이민을 갈 예정이다.
② Jenny는 Jack에게 이민 가는 것에 대해 이야기 하지 않았다.
③ Jenny는 지금 Jack에게 매우 화가 나 있다.
④ Jenny는 일본에서도 Sue와 Jack에게 연락할 것이다.
⑤ Jack은 Jenny의 심정을 이해한다.

10 다음 대화가 자연스럽게 이어지도록 순서대로 배열하시오.

(A) Really? I want to try it.
(B) Yes. It was really fun.
(C) That's amazing. I didn't know that you were interested in *muay thai*.
(D) How was your winter vacation?
(E) It was great. You know what? I took *muay thai* lessons during the vacation.

➡ _____

11 다음 빈칸에 가장 적절한 것은?

This hat is not good for me. Show me _____.

① other one
② the others
③ another
④ others
⑤ one

12 다음 문장의 빈칸에 들어갈 말로 가장 적절한 것은?

_____ into reading, there will be many interesting books you can borrow anytime.

① When you will be
② If you are
③ Though you are
④ Because you were
⑤ If you will be

13 빈칸에 들어갈 말이 바르게 짝지어진 것은?

• Cindy invited five friends to her party. But only two of them came. _____ didn't came.
• There are many students in the classroom. Some study Korean, _____ study English.

① The other – other
② Others – others
③ The others – the others
④ The other – others
⑤ The others – others

✏️ 출제율 90%

14 주어진 단어를 이용하여 다음 빈칸에 알맞은 말을 쓰시오.

lend / pay

A: I have to buy some chocolate for Valentine's Day. But I am short of money.
B: How much?
A: About ten dollars. If you ＿＿＿＿ ＿＿＿＿ ten dollars, I ＿＿＿＿ ＿＿＿＿ you back tomorrow.

➡ ＿＿＿＿＿＿＿＿＿＿＿＿＿＿＿

✏️ 출제율 85%

15 주어진 단어를 이용하여 각 빈칸에 적절한 문장을 쓰시오.

- There are three colors that I really like.
- ＿＿＿＿＿＿＿＿＿＿＿＿(blue).
- ＿＿＿＿＿＿＿＿＿＿＿＿(hot pink).
- ＿＿＿＿＿＿＿＿＿＿＿＿(yellow).

➡ ＿＿＿＿＿＿＿ ➡ ＿＿＿＿＿＿＿
➡ ＿＿＿＿＿＿＿

✏️ 출제율 90%

16 다음 우리말을 영어로 바르게 옮긴 것은?

내가 그것들 중 하나를 사용하면, 네가 나머지 하나를 쓸 거니?

① If I use one of them, do you use the other?
② If I use one, will you use the others?
③ If I use one of them, will you use the other?
④ If I use one of them, do you use others?
⑤ If I use one, will you use another?

[17~20] 다음 글을 읽고 물음에 답하시오.

My friend Eric and I made some ①interesting changes during the vacation. We emailed each ⓐ＿＿＿ and talked about our changes.

Dear Eric,
It's a beautiful spring in Seoul. The last winter vacation was ②a great time for me. I made two personal changes during the vacation. One is my new hobby. It's ⓑ＿＿＿ cupcakes. ⓒ＿＿＿ my own cupcakes is ③a lot of fun. The other change is ⓓ＿＿＿ one of my bad habits. In the past, I often bit my nails. Now I ④am not anymore. I feel great about the changes I made. If you try to make some changes, I'm sure you ⑤will feel great like me. I hope to hear from you soon.
Your friend, Junho.

✏️ 출제율 95%

17 다음 중 빈칸 ⓐ에 들어갈 말과 같은 것은?

① Can you show me ＿＿＿＿ color of this scarf?
② There are two people. One is sitting, and ＿＿＿＿ is cleaning.
③ Some friends want to eat pizza, and ＿＿＿＿ friends want to eat noodle.
④ One of my three dolls is new, and ＿＿＿＿ are a little old.
⑤ Some people have brown hair, but ＿＿＿＿ have black hair.

✏️ 출제율 90%

18 주어진 동사를 빈칸 ⓑ~ⓓ에 문맥과 어법에 맞게 쓰시오.

(make / break)

➡ ⓑ ＿＿＿＿＿＿＿ ⓒ ＿＿＿＿＿＿＿
ⓓ ＿＿＿＿＿＿＿

19 ①~⑤ 중 어법상 어색한 것을 골라 바르게 고치시오. *출제율 100%*

_____ ➡ _____

20 위 글의 내용과 일치하지 않는 것은? *출제율 90%*

① Junho made personal changes during the winter vacation.

② Eric is Junho's friend.

③ Junho wrote a letter to Eric in winter.

④ Junho can make his own cupcakes.

⑤ Junho used to bite his nails.

[21~25] 다음 글을 읽고, 물음에 답하시오.

Dear Junho,

In Sydney, it's fall in March. You talked about your changes in your email. Now, it's time ①to talk about my new changes. These days, I'm into 3D printing. I printed two things ②with a 3D printer. One is a model of my dream car. If the traffic is (A)[light / heavy], it will change into a flying car. ③The others is a (B)[common / special] cup for my grandfather. He can't hold his cup well (C) [because / unless] he's sick. My special cup has three handles, so it is easy ④to hold. My grandfather is very happy. ⑤By the way, I want to try your cupcakes some day, Junho.

Take care.

Best wishes,

Eric.

21 ①~⑤ 중 어법상 바르지 않은 것은? *출제율 90%*

①   ②   ③   ④   ⑤

22 (A)~(C)에서 글의 흐름상 적절한 것끼리 바르게 묶인 것은? *출제율 90%*

① light – common – because

② heavy – common – unless

③ light – special – because

④ heavy – special – because

⑤ light – special – unless

23 What did Eric print with a 3D printer? Answer in English with a full sentence. *출제율 95%*

➡ _____

_____

24 According to the passage, what does Eric want to try some day? Answer in English with a full sentence. *출제율 95%*

➡ _____

25 위 글의 내용으로 보아 대답할 수 없는 질문은? *출제율 85%*

① What did Junho talk about in his email?

② What is Eric talking about?

③ What is Eric interested in now?

④ What is Eric print with a 3D printer?

⑤ When will Eric eat Junho's cupcakes?

[01~03] 다음 대화를 읽고 물음에 답하시오.

> **Alex:** Mom, I made *bulgogi* at school today. (A)<u>오늘 저녁으로 불고기를 요리할 생각이에요.</u> (think, *bulgogi*, cook)
>
> **Mom:** That sounds great, Alex.
>
> **Alex:** Do we have any vegetables at home, Mom? What about beef?
>
> **Mom:** We have some vegetables, but we don't have beef. I'll buy some for you on my way home.
>
> **Alex:** Great.

01 위 대화의 (A)의 우리말을 주어진 표현을 이용하여 영작하시오.

➡ _____

02 What does Alex need to cook *bulgogi*?

➡ _____

03 What is Alex's mom going to do for Alex?

➡ _____

04 괄호 안에 주어진 어구를 이용하여 다음 대화를 완성하시오.

> **A:** Do you see the two people in the kitchen? What are they doing?
>
> **B:** (making food / washing the dishes)

➡ _____

05 두 개의 문장을 연결하여 자연스러운 하나의 문장으로 만드시오.

> • You need it.
> • You want her to help you.
> • Your alarm clock is out of order.

> • She will help you.
> • You can have it.
> • I will buy you a new one.

➡ _____
➡ _____
➡ _____

06 주어진 문장과 같은 의미의 문장을 두 개 쓰시오.

> Listen carefully, or you won't know what to do.

➡ _____
➡ _____

07 다음 빈칸에 알맞은 말을 쓰시오.

> I have three cats. _____ has blue eyes. _____ have yellow eyes.

➡ _____

08 괄호 안에 주어진 단어를 어법에 맞게 쓰시오.

> **A:** If you (finish) your homework early, what (do, you)?
> **B:** I (clean) my room if I (finish) my homework early.

➡ _____

[09~11] 다음 글을 읽고 물음에 답하시오.

> Dear Eric,
> It's a beautiful spring in Seoul. The last winter vacation was a great time for me. I made two <u>person</u> changes during the vacation. One is my new hobby. It's making cupcakes. Making my own cupcakes is a lot of fun. The other change is breaking one of my bad habits. In the past, I often bit my nails. Now I don't anymore. I feel great about the changes I made. If you try to make some changes, I'm sure you'll feel great like me. I hope to hear from you soon.
> Your friend, Junho.

09 위 글의 밑줄 친 person을 알맞은 형으로 고치시오.

➡ _____

10 적절한 대명사를 이용하여 다음 물음에 답하시오.

> **Q:** How does Junho feel about the changes he made?

➡ _____

11 위 글의 내용을 참고하여 대화의 빈칸을 알맞게 채우시오.

> **Jason:** How did you spend your last winter vacation?
> **Junho:** I spent my vacation _____ two personal changes.
> **Jason:** Oh, really? What was that?
> **Junho:** _____ is making cupcakes and ____ ____ is ____ my bad habit.
> **Jason:** That sounds great.

➡ _____

[12~13] 다음 글을 읽고 물음에 답하시오.

> Dear Junho,
> In Sydney, it's fall in March. You talked about your changes in your email. Now, it's time to talk about my new changes. These days, I'm into 3D printing. I printed two things with a 3D printer. One is a model of my dream car. (A)<u>교통이 혼잡하면, 그것은 날 수 있는 차로 바뀌어.</u> The other is a special cup for my grandfather. He can't hold his cup well because he's sick. My special cup has three handles, so it is easy to hold. My grandfather is very happy. By the way, I want to try your cupcakes some day, Junho.
> Take care.
> Best wishes,
> Eric.

12 주어진 단어를 이용하여 밑줄 친 우리말 (A)를 영어로 쓰시오.

> (if / heavy / change)

➡ _____

13 위 글의 내용에 맞게 다음 물음에 완전한 문장의 영어로 답하시오.

> **Q:** How does Eric's cup look?

➡ _____

창의사고력 서술형 문제

01 다음 대화의 내용과 일치하도록 Jack의 일기를 완성하시오.

> **Sue:** You know what? Jenny's family is going to move to Japan.
>
> **Jack:** Is that right? Jenny didn't tell me about it.
>
> **Sue:** She learned about it just last week and she's very upset now.
>
> **Jack:** I can understand her feelings. I am going to miss her so much.
>
> **Sue::** Me, too. She said she would keep in touch with us.

> Monday, April 1st, 2019
>
> Today, I heard that (A)_____. I was so surprised because Jenny did not tell me about it at all. Sue said that (B)_____ because her family didn't tell her about it until last week. I understood how she felt. Anyway, I'll miss her so much and (C)_____ with her.

02 다음 <보기>와 같이 두 가지 사물이나 사람을 설명하는 문장을 쓰시오.

> ┤ 보기 ├
>
> There are two people at the table. One is a man. The other is a woman.

(1) _____

(2) _____

(3) _____

(4) _____

(5) _____

03 다음 단어를 이용하여 <보기>와 같이 내일 계획을 쓰시오.

> ┤ 보기 ├
>
> If it is cloudy tomorrow, I will cancel my appointment.
> sunny   windy   rainy   hot

(1) _____

(2) _____

(3) _____

(4) _____

단원별 모의고사

01 다음 짝지어진 단어의 관계가 같도록 빈칸에 알맞은 말을 쓰시오.

> clean : dirty = _____ : true

02 다음 영영풀이에 해당하는 말을 고르시오.

> a part that is designed especially to be grasped by the hand

① barrier   ② handle
③ hold   ④ grip
⑤ container

03 다음 주어진 우리말과 일치하도록 빈칸을 완성하시오.

(1) 그들이 무엇이라 이야기하든 그것은 진실이다.
➡ It is the _____ no matter what they say.

(2) 손톱은 네게 건강에 관한 많은 것을 이야기해 줄 수 있다.
➡ The _____ can tell you many things about your health.

(3) 제가 개인적인 의견을 드려도 될까요?
➡ Can I give you my _____ opinion?

04 다음 문장의 빈칸에 들어갈 말을 보기에서 골라 알맞은 형태로 쓰시오.

> ┤ 보기 ├
> break a bad habit / come true / not ~ anymore / take a class

(1) I believe your dreams _____ _____.
(2) I decided to _____ a yoga _____.
(3) They are _____ children _____.
(4) She started to keep a diary to _____ _____ _____.

[05~08] 다음 대화를 읽고 물음에 답하시오.

Emily: You know (A)[what / why], Junsu? (a) 나는 미술 수업을 들을 생각이야.

Junsu: Really? Why did you decide to take a painting class, Emily?

Emily: (B)[Because of / Because] I want to go to an art high school.

Junsu: Are you thinking of becoming an (C)_____ in the future?

Emily: I hope so. I'm (D)[interested / interesting] in painting pictures.

Junsu: That's great. I hope your wish comes true.

Emily: Thanks. I'll do my best.

05 위 대화의 괄호 (A), (B) 및 (D)에 들어갈 말로 바르게 짝지어진 것은?

	(A)	(B)	(D)
①	what	Because of	interested
②	what	Because	interested
③	what	Because of	interesting
④	why	Because	interesting
⑤	why	Because of	interesting

06 위 대화의 빈칸 (C)에 다음 영영 풀이가 가리키는 말을 쓰시오.

> a person who creates works of art, especially paintings or drawings

➡ _____

07 위 대화의 밑줄 친 (a)의 우리말을 영작하시오.

➡ _____

08 위 대화의 내용과 일치하지 <u>않는</u> 것은?

① Emily는 미술 수업을 들으려고 생각 중이다.
② Emily는 예술 고등학교에 가고 싶어 한다.
③ Emily는 그림 그리는 것에 관심이 있다.
④ Junsu는 Emily가 최선을 다하기를 바란다.
⑤ Emily는 미래에 미술가가 되기를 희망한다.

[09~10] 다음 대화를 읽고 물음에 답하시오.

> Jane: Minsu, Sujin and I are thinking of starting a club.
> Minsu: Really? What kind of club?
> Jane: We want to learn about stars and planets. So, we're thinking of starting a space science club.
> Minsu: Sounds good. How often are you going to meet?
> Jane: Maybe once a week.
> Minsu: I see. Where will you meet?
> Jane: In Room 101. Minsu, do you want to join our club?
> Minsu: Yes, ⓐ나도 우주에 관심이 있어.

09 위 대화의 밑줄 친 ⓐ의 우리말을 영작하시오.

➡ _____

10 How often are the members of the space science club going to meet?

➡ _____

[11~12] 다음 대화를 읽고, 물음에 답하시오.

> Sue: (A) You know what? Jenny's family is going to move to Japan.
> Jack (B) Is that right? Jenny didn't tell me about it.
> Sue: (C) She learned about it just last week and she's very upset now.
> Jack: (D) I am going to miss her so much.
> Sue: (E) Me, too. She said she would keep in touch with us.

11 위 대화의 (A)~(E) 중 주어진 문장이 들어가기에 가장 적절한 곳은?

> I can understand her feelings.

① (A)　② (B)　③ (C)　④ (D)　⑤ (E)

12 위 대화를 통해 대답할 수 <u>없는</u> 것은?

① Why is Jenny upset now?
② Where is Jenny's family going to move?
③ When did Jenny learn about her move?
④ Who will keep in touch with Jenny?
⑤ Why does Jenny's family want to move?

13 다음 중 어법상 바르지 <u>않은</u> 것은?

① There were two pears on the table, and one is here. Where is the other?
② Unless you don't use soap, your clothes won't get clean.
③ I'm not sure if they will want me to teach them.
④ If you wake up early, will you wake me up?
⑤ A student left alone. The other students went home.

14 다음 빈칸에 가장 적절한 것은?

> I have two candy bars. I want only one of them. Would you like _____?

① other one
② another one
③ the other one
④ the others
⑤ others

15 주어진 단어를 사용하여 다음 우리말을 영어로 쓰시오.

> Kevin은 나머지 다른 소년들과는 달라요.
> (different from)

➡ _____

16 주어진 어구를 바르게 배열하여 다음 우리말을 영어로 쓰시오. (하나의 단어를 두 번 쓸 것)

> 만약 네가 택시를 탄다면, 10분밖에 안 걸릴 거야.
> (10 minutes / if / only / you / take / will / it / a taxi)

➡ _____

17 다음 중 어법상 바르지 않은 것은?

> Emily bought two dresses. ①One is red, and ②another is blue. She really ③likes the dresses, so she wants ④to buy ⑤ another one.

[18~21] 다음 글을 읽고 물음에 답하시오.

> Dear Eric,
> It's a beautiful spring in Seoul. The last winter vacation was a great time for me. I made two personal changes during the vacation. One is my new hobby. It's ⓐmaking cupcakes. Making my own cupcakes is a lot of fun. ⓑ The other is breaking one of my bad habits. In the past, I often bit my nails. Now I don't anymore. I feel great about the changes I made. If you try to make some changes, I'm sure you'll feel great like me. I hope to hear from you soon.
> Your friend, Junho.

18 밑줄 친 ⓐ와 쓰임이 다른 것은?

① Computers play an important role in making films.
② By making conversation, people become friends.
③ The girl is making a box.
④ My goal is making a cake for her birthday present.
⑤ I want you to stop making trouble now.

19 위 글을 읽고 답할 수 없는 것은?

① How did Junho spend his last winter vacation?
② When did Junho write the letter?
③ How many changes did Junho make?
④ What did Junho use to bite?
⑤ How does Junho feel about Eric?

20 밑줄 친 ⓑ가 의미하는 것을 구체적으로 쓰시오.

➡ _____

21 위 글의 내용에 맞게 빈칸에 알맞은 말을 쓰시오.

In the email, Junho is mainly talking about _____ _____ _____ _____.

[22~25] 다음 글을 읽고 물음에 답하시오.

Dear Junho,
In Sydney, it's fall in March. You talked about your changes in your email. Now, it's time ⓐ_____ about my new changes. These days, I'm into 3D printing. I printed two things with a 3D printer. One is a model of my dream car. If the traffic is heavy, it will change into a ⓑ_____ car. The other is a special cup for my grandfather. He can't hold his cup well ⓒ_____ he's sick. My special cup has three handles, so it is easy to hold. My grandfather is very happy. By the way, I want to ⓓtry your cupcakes some day, Junho.
Take care.
Best wishes,
Eric.

22 주어진 동사를 어법에 맞게 빈칸 ⓐ와 ⓑ에 각각 쓰시오.

(talk / fly)

➡ ⓐ: _____ ⓑ: _____

23 다음 중 빈칸 ⓒ에 들어갈 말과 같은 말이 들어가는 것은?

① Some people like juice, _____ others don't.
② He is quite strong _____ he is old.
③ I wonder _____ he is at home.
④ You will miss the bus _____ you walk more quickly.
⑤ I couldn't sleep last night _____ I was so afraid.

24 다음 중 밑줄 친 ⓓ의 의미로 가장 적절한 것은?

① test   ② taste   ③ wear
④ see   ⑤ attempt

25 다음 중 위 글의 내용과 일치하는 것의 개수는?

ⓐ Junho lives in Sydney.
ⓑ Eric wrote the email in fall.
ⓒ Eric wrote about 3D printing.
ⓓ Eric bought a car.
ⓔ Junho talked about his cupcakes in his email.

① 1개   ② 2개   ③ 3개
④ 4개   ⑤ 5개

Lesson 2

Better Safe Than Sorry

 의사소통 기능

- 걱정 표현하기
  I'm worried about my leg.

- 충고하기
  You should clean your room.

 언어 형식

- 의문사 + to부정사
  I don't know **what to do**.

- 관계대명사
  Here are some tips **which** can be helpful.

Words & Expressions

Key Words

- **amazing** [əméiziŋ] 형 놀라운
- **avoid** [əvɔ́id] 동 방지하다, 막다, 피하다
- **break** [breik] 동 깨다, 부수다, 부서지다
- **by** [bai] 전 ~까지
- **cover** [kʌ́vər] 동 씌우다, 덮다
- **dangerous** [déindʒərəs] 형 위험한
- **decide** [disáid] 동 결정하다, 결심하다
- **disaster** [dizǽstər] 명 재난, 재해
- **earthquake** [ə́ːrθkweik] 명 지진
- **elevator** [éləvèitər] 명 승강기
- **empty** [émpti] 형 비어 있는, 빈
- **escape** [iskéip] 동 탈출하다
- **fall** [fɔːl] 동 넘어지다
- **floor** [flɔːr] 명 바닥, 마루
- **follow** [fálou] 동 따르다, 따라가다
- **forget** [fərgét] 동 잊어버리다
- **hurt** [həːrt] 동 다치게 하다, 아프게 하다
- **injury** [índʒəri] 명 상처, 부상
- **knife** [naif] 명 칼
- **low** [lou] 형 낮은
- **medicine** [médisn] 명 약
- **might** [mait] 조 ~할 수 있다
- **natural disaster** 자연 재해

- **prepare** [pripέər] 동 준비하다, 대비하다
- **pole** [poul] 명 기둥, 장대
- **program** [próugræm] 명 (방송) 프로그램
- **protect** [prətékt] 동 보호하다
- **rule** [ruːl] 명 법칙, 규칙
- **safety** [séifti] 명 안전
- **scary** [skέəri] 형 두려운, 무서운
- **serious** [síəriəs] 형 심각한
- **shake** [ʃeik] 명 흔들림, 떨림 동 흔들다
- **situation** [sìtʃuéiʃən] 명 상황
- **slip** [slip] 동 미끄러지다
- **slippery** [slípəri] 형 미끄러운
- **solve** [sɑlv] 동 해결하다
- **sore** [sɔːr] 형 아픈
- **space** [speis] 명 공간
- **stair** [stεər] 명 계단
- **strange** [streindʒ] 형 이상한, 낯선
- **strike** [straik] 동 발생하다
- **survive** [sərváiv] 동 살아남다, 생존하다
- **throat** [θrout] 명 목구멍
- **wet** [wet] 형 젖은
- **wipe** [waip] 동 닦다
- **worry** [wə́ːri] 명 걱정, 근심 동 걱정하다

Key Expressions

- **a little** 약간, 좀
- **be worried about** ~에 대해 걱정하다
- **feel better** (기분이) 나아지다
- **get out of** (~에서) 나가다, 떠나다
- **hold on to** ~을 꼭 잡다
- **keep ~ in mind** ~을 기억하다

- **one by one** 하나씩, 차례차례
- **stay away from** ~에서 떨어져 있다
- **take a rest** 휴식을 취하다
- **take cover** 숨다
- **these days** 요즘
- **Why don't you** ~? ~하는 것이 어때?

Word Power

※ 서로 반대되는 뜻을 가진 어휘

□ **empty** 비어 있는 ↔ **full** 가득 찬

□ **prepared** 준비된 ↔ **unprepared** 준비되지 않은

□ **low** 낮은 ↔ **high** 높은

□ **wet** 젖은 ↔ **dry** 건조한

□ **forget** 잊어버리다 ↔ **remember** 기억하다

□ **cover** 덮다, 씌우다 ↔ **uncover** 덮개를 벗기다

□ **safe** 안전한 ↔ **dangerous** 위험한

□ **strange** 낯선 ↔ **familiar** 친근한, 친숙한

※ 자연 재해를 가리키는 어휘

□ **earthquake** 지진

□ **flood** 홍수

□ **hurricane** 허리케인

□ **drought** 가뭄

□ **storm** 폭풍

□ **typhoon** 태풍

□ **tsunami** 쓰나미

□ **tornado** 토네이도

English Dictionary

□ **avoid** 방지하다, 막다, 피하다
→ to stay away from; to prevent the occurrence of something bad, unpleasant, etc.
떨어져 있다; 나쁘거나 좋지 않은 무언가가 발생하는 것을 막다

□ **break** 깨다, 부수다
→ to separate something into parts or pieces often in a sudden and forceful or violent way, to cause to separate into two or more pieces
두 개 또는 그 이상의 조각들로 분리되도록 하기 위해 갑자기 강압적인 또는 폭력적인 방식으로 무언가를 조각나게 하거나 분리시키다

□ **disaster** 재난, 재해
→ something such as a flood, tornado, fire, plane crash, etc. that happens suddenly and causes much suffering or loss to many people
갑자기 일어나 많은 사람들에게 많은 고통이나 손실을 야기하는 홍수, 토네이도, 화재, 비행기 사고 등과 같은 것

□ **earthquake** 지진
→ a shaking of a part of the Earth's surface that often causes great damage
종종 큰 피해를 야기하는 지구 표면의 한 부분의 흔들림

□ **empty** 비어 있는, 빈
→ not having any people, and not occupied; containing nothing
어떤 사람도 있지 않고, 점유되지 않은; 아무것도 포함하지 않은

□ **fall** 넘어지다
→ to come or go down suddenly from a standing position
서 있는 자세에서 갑자기 밑으로 가다

□ **follow** 따르다
→ to move behind someone or something and go where they go
어떤 사람이나 어떤 것의 뒤에서 움직이며 그들이 가는 곳으로 가다

□ **forget** 잊어버리다
→ to be unable to think of or remember something
무언가를 생각해 내지 못하거나 기억하지 못하다

□ **hurt** 다치게 하다
→ to cause pain or injury to yourself, someone else, or a part of your body
당신 자신이나 다른 누군가 또는 자신의 신체의 한 부분에 상처를 입히거나 고통을 야기시키다

□ **injury** 상처, 부상
→ harm or damage; an act or event that causes someone or something to no longer be fully healthy or in good condition
해 또는 손상; 누군가나 무언가가 더 이상 건강하거나 좋은 상태가 되지 못하도록 하는 행동이나 사건

□ **pole** 기둥, 막대
→ a long, thin stick made of wood or metal, used to hold something up
무언가를 떠받치기 위해 사용되는 나무나 금속으로 만들어진 길고 가는 막대

□ **protect** 보호하다
→ to keep someone or something from being harmed, lost, etc.
누군가나 무언가를 손상되거나 상실되는 것으로부터 막다

□ **safety** 안전
→ the state of not being dangerous or harmful
위험하거나 해롭지 않은 상태

□ **shake** 흔들림, 떨림
→ short, quick movement back and forth or up and down
앞뒤로 또는 위아래로 짧고 빠른 움직임

01 다음 짝지어진 단어의 관계가 같도록 빈칸에 알맞은 말을 쓰시오.

> low: high = _____ : full

02 다음 우리말에 맞게 빈칸에 알맞은 말을 쓰시오.

(1) 건강이 재산보다 낫다는 것을 기억해라.

➡ _____ _____ _____ that good health is above wealth.

(2) 나는 장난감을 하나씩 상자에 넣었다.

➡ I put the toys into the box _____ _____ _____.

(3) 나는 이것보다 약간 더 긴 것을 원해요.

➡ I want _____ _____ longer than this one.

(4) 큰 개에게서 떨어져 있어라.

➡ _____ _____ _____ the big dog.

03 다음 중 밑줄 친 부분의 뜻풀이가 바르지 <u>않은</u> 것은?

① <u>Shake</u> the bottle before you drink it.
흔들다

② He was disappointed with an <u>empty</u> box.
비어 있는

③ Minho is suffering from a <u>serious</u> illness.
경미한

④ This village was damaged by a powerful <u>earthquake</u>. 지진

⑤ I was worried about the <u>injury</u> on my head. 상처

04 다음 문장의 빈칸에 들어갈 말을 보기에서 골라 쓰시오.

> ┤ 보기 ├
> slip / shake / escape / follow

(1) She was lucky to _____ from the burning car.

(2) You should _____ the safety rules.

(3) Be careful not to _____ on the ice.

(4) Suddenly, her hands began to _____.

05 다음 주어진 문장의 밑줄 친 pole의 의미와 같은 의미로 쓰인 것은? (2개)

> Hold on to the <u>pole</u> or the tree.

① We will soon reach the North <u>Pole</u>.

② Walk straight until you see a <u>pole</u> with a sign.

③ The man is locking his bike to the <u>pole</u>.

④ Do you know who is the first person to discover the South <u>Pole</u>?

⑤ A compass shows the magnetic <u>pole</u>.

06 다음 영영풀이가 가리키는 것을 고르시오.

> something such as a flood, tornado, fire, plane crash, etc. that happens suddenly and causes much suffering or loss to many people

① drought   ② disaster

③ earthquake   ④ volcano

⑤ tsunami

01 다음 짝지어진 단어의 관계가 같도록 빈칸에 알맞은 말을 쓰시오.

wet : dry = _____ : dangerous

02 다음 우리말과 일치하도록 주어진 어구를 모두 배열하여 영작하시오.

(1) 나는 영어 시험을 걱정하고 있다.
(about / the / exam / I'm / English / worried)
➡ _____

(2) 너는 계단에서 걸어야 한다.
(walk / stairs / on / you / should / the)
➡ _____

(3) 차에서 나올 때, 네 머리를 조심해라.
(the car / of / head / watch / you / your / get / when / out)
➡ _____
_____

(4) 너는 문을 닫을 때 손을 조심해야 한다.
(should / the / door / when / you / close / your / hand / you / watch)
➡ _____
_____

03 다음 대화의 (A)~(C)에 들어갈 말을 고르시오.

Sujin: It's raining. I'm worried (A)[about / of] our picnic in the afternoon.
Mom: It is going to rain (B)[from / until] late afternoon today. You should go (C)[one / another] day.
Sujin: You're right, Mom. I'll call my friend and choose another day.

➡ (A) _____, (B) _____, (C) _____

04 다음 문장의 빈칸에 들어갈 말을 순서대로 쓰시오.

• Keep his advice (A)_____ your mind.
• You should stay away (B)_____ wild animals.
• I called their names one (C)_____ one

➡ (A) _____ (B) _____ (C) _____

05 다음 우리말에 맞게 빈칸에 알맞은 말을 쓰시오.

(1) 나는 이 곡을 좋아해, 왜냐하면 이 곡은 나의 기분이 나아지게 만들기 때문이야.
➡ I like this song because it makes me _____ _____.

(2) 비가 오기 시작했을 때, 나는 나무 아래로 숨었다.
➡ When it started to rain, I _____ _____ under the tree.

(3) 지진은 자연 재해의 한 형태이다.
➡ An _____ is one type of the _____ _____.

06 다음 문장의 빈칸에 들어갈 말을 〈보기〉에서 골라 쓰시오.

┌─ 보기 ─┐
hold on to / stay away from / get out of / take cover / feel better

(1) _____ _____ _____ the fireplace.
(2) _____ _____ _____ _____ the pole not to fall down.
(3) I decided to move to _____ _____ _____ the city.
(4) The thieves tried to _____ _____ behind the tree.

Conversation

① 걱정 표현하기

I'm worried about my leg. 나는 내 다리가 걱정돼.

- 'I'm worried about ~'은 걱정을 나타내는 표현으로 '나는 ~을 걱정하고 있다'라는 뜻이다. about 다음에는 걱정에 해당하는 명사 형태의 표현을 사용한다. 걱정을 나타낼 때, 'I'm concerned about ~' 또는 'I'm anxious about ~'으로 나타낼 수 있다.

걱정 표현하기

I'm worried about the exam. (나는 시험을 걱정하고 있어.)

I'm anxious about my sore throat. (나는 아픈 목이 걱정이야.)

I'm concerned about my red eyes. (나는 충혈된 눈이 걱정이야.)

핵심 Check

1. 다음 우리말과 일치하도록 빈칸에 알맞은 말을 쓰시오.

   A: _____ _____ _____ my bad cold. (나는 심한 감기를 걱정하고 있어.)

   B: I think you need to take some medicine. (나는 네가 약을 좀 먹을 필요가 있다고 생각해.)

2. 다음 우리말과 일치하도록 빈칸에 알맞은 말을 쓰시오.

   A: _____ _____ _____ because I'll be with you. (내가 너와 함께 있을 테니 걱정 마.)

   B: Thank you so much. (정말 고마워요.)

3. 다음 우리말과 일치하도록 빈칸에 알맞은 말을 쓰시오.

   A: _____ _____ _____ pimples on my face. (나는 얼굴에 여드름이 나서 걱정이에요.)

   B: Why don't you go see a doctor? (의사에게 가보는 게 어때?)

충고하기

You should clean your room. 너는 네 방을 청소해야 해.

■ 충고하기
'You should ~'는 충고를 할 때 쓰는 표현으로 '너는 ~해야 해'라는 뜻이다. 'Why don't you ~?',
'How[What] about ~ing?' 또는 'You'd better ~'와 바꿔 쓸 수 있다.

충고하기

You should exercise. (너는 운동을 해야 해.)

Why don't you wear a helmet? (헬멧을 쓰는 게 어때?)

How about walking on the stairs? (계단에서는 걷는 게 어때?)

You'd better watch your step. (발밑을 조심하는 게 좋아.)

He advised her to take an umbrella. (그는 그녀에게 우산을 가져가라고 조언했다.)

I think you need to go see a doctor. (나는 네가 의사에게 가 볼 필요가 있다고 생각해.)

핵심 Check

4. 다음 우리말과 일치하도록 빈칸에 알맞은 말을 쓰시오.

A: It's snowing a lot outside. (밖에 눈이 많이 오고 있어.)

B: _____ _____ wear a heavy coat. (너는 두꺼운 코트를 입어야 해.)

5. 다음 우리말과 일치하도록 빈칸에 알맞은 말을 쓰시오.

A: I'm going to ride my bike. (나는 자전거를 타려고 해.)

B: _____ _____ _____ wear a helmet? (헬멧을 쓰는 게 어때?)

6. 다음 우리말과 일치하도록 빈칸에 알맞은 말을 쓰시오.

A: I hurt my leg, so I can't walk. (다리를 다쳐서 걸을 수가 없어요.)

B: _____ _____ _____ _____ _____ call an ambulance. (나는 우리가 구급
차를 불러야 할 필요가 있다고 생각해.)

Conversation 교과서 대화문 익히기

A. Listen and Speak 1-B

Brian: What are you watching?

Jane: It's a program about earthquakes.

Brian: ❶Sounds interesting. ❷I'm worried about earthquakes ❸these days.

Jane: Me, too. This program has some helpful tips.

Brian: Really? What does it say?

Jane: When things start to shake, you need to ❹take cover under a table.

Brian: Oh, I didn't know ❺that.

Brian: 무엇을 시청하고 있니?
Jane: 지진에 관한 프로그램이야.
Brian: 그거 재미있겠다. 나는 요즘 지진이 걱정돼.
Jane: 나도 그래. 이 프로그램에는 도움이 되는 몇 가지 조언이 있어.
Brian: 그래? 뭐라고 하는데?
Jane: 물건들이 흔들리기 시작하면 탁자 아래에 숨어야 해.
Brian: 아, 그건 몰랐어.

❶ (That) Sounds interesting.: 재미있겠네. sound 다음에는 형용사가 보어로 와서 '~처럼 들리다'라는 뜻을 갖는다.
❷ I'm worried about ~: ~을 걱정하고 있다
❸ these days: 요즘
❹ take cover: 숨다
❺ that은 흔들리기 시작할 때, 탁자 아래로 숨을 필요가 있다는 것을 가리킨다.

Check(√) True or False

(1) Jane got helpful tips from the program about earthquakes.　　T ☐ F ☐

(2) When things start to shake, people should take cover under a table.　　T ☐ F ☐

B. Real Life Communication

Brian: There was ❶a big fire at the city library yesterday.

Mina: Yes, I heard about it. I was worried about the people ❷there.

Brian: Don't worry. Everybody was okay. ❸They all followed the safety rules.

Mina: Really? What are the rules?

Brian: You need to cover your nose and mouth with a wet towel. Then ❹ stay low and escape.

Mina: Oh, I didn't know that.

Brian: You should ❺keep that in mind. It might be helpful some day.

Brian: 어제 시립 도서관에 큰 불이 났어.
Mina: 응, 그것에 대해 들었어. 거기 있었던 사람들이 걱정 됐어.
Brian: 걱정하지 마. 모두들 무사했어. 사람들이 모두 안전 규칙을 따랐대.
Mina: 정말? 그게 뭔데?
Brian: 젖은 수건으로 코와 입을 가려야 해. 그 다음, 몸을 낮게 유지하고 탈출하는 거야.
Mina: 아, 그건 몰랐어.
Brian: 넌 그것을 명심해야 해. 언젠가 도움이 될 수도 있어.

❶ a big fire: 큰 화재, fire는 셀 수 없는 명사이지만 사건이나 사고를 나타낼 때는 하나의 사건으로 보아 단수로 취급할 수 있다.
❷ there=at the city library
❸ They all: 그들은 모두(They와 all은 동격) / safety rules: 안전 규칙
❹ stay는 be동사와 같이 불완전동사로 형용사 low를 보어로 취하고 있다.
❺ keep ~ in mind: ~을 기억하다

Check(√) True or False

(3) Brian tells Mina what to do during a fire.　　T ☐ F ☐

(4) Many people were hurt because of a big fire at the city library yesterday.　　T ☐ F ☐

Listen and Speak 1-A

Tom: Yujin, ❶what's wrong?

Yujin: ❷I'm worried about my leg. It hurts a lot.

Tom: ❸Why don't you ❹go see a doctor?

Yujin: I'm going to go after school today.

Tom: I hope you ❺feel better soon.

Yujin: ❻I hope so, too.

❶ what's wrong?: 무슨 일이니?(= what's the matter?)
❷ I'm worried about ~: 나는 …에 관해 걱정이다
❸ Why don't you ~?: ~하는 것이 어때?
❹ go see a doctor 의사에게 가 보다 (= go and see a doctor)
❺ feel better: 나아지다
❻ I hope so= I hope (that) I feel better

Listen and Speak 2-B

Emily: What time is the movie?

Tom: It starts at 4:30.

Emily: Oh, no. We only ❶have 20 minutes left. Let's run!

Tom: No! You ❷might fall and ❸hurt yourself. You should walk on the stairs.

Emily: You're right. We can be ❹a little late.

Tom: Yes. ❺Better safe than sorry.

❶ have 20 minutes left: 20분 남다(left는 leave의 과거분사)
❷ might는 조동사로 '~일지도 모른다'를 뜻한다. may보다 약한 가능성을 나타낼 때 쓰인다
❸ hurt oneself: 다치다
❹ a little: 약간
❺ 후회하는 것보다는 안전한 것이 더 낫다.

Listen and Speak 2-A

Jack: Dad, I'm going out to play basketball with Minu.

Dad: Did you ❶finish cleaning your room?

Jack: No, not yet. Can I do it later?

Dad: No. ❷You should clean your room first.

Jack: Okay. I'll clean my room and then play basketball.

Dad: Good. ❸Don't forget to be home ❹by six o'clock.

Jack: Okay.

❶ finish는 동명사를 목적어로 취한다.
❷ 'You should ~'는 '너는 ~해야 한다'의 뜻으로 충고하는 표현이다.
❸ 'Don't forget'은 Remember와 같은 의미로 '~할 것을 잊지 마'라는 의미이다. / be home: 집에 오다
❹ by: ~까지는(not later than a specified time)

Let's Check

Sujin: It's raining. ❶I'm worried about our picnic in the afternoon.

Mom: It is going to rain ❷until late afternoon today. ❸You should go another day.

Sujin: You're right, Mom. I'll call my friend and choose another day.

❶ 오후의 소풍에 대해 걱정을 나타낸다.
❷ until: ~까지
❸ 다른 날로 소풍 갈 것을 충고한다.

● 다음 우리말과 일치하도록 빈칸에 알맞은 말을 쓰시오.

Listen & Speak 1 A

Tom: Yujin, what's wrong?

Yujin: _____ _____ _____ my leg. It hurts a lot.

Tom: _____ _____ _____ go see a doctor?

Yujin: I'm going to go after school today.

Tom: I hope _____ _____ _____ soon.

Yujin: I hope so, too.

해석

Tom: 유진아, 무슨 일이야?
Yujin: 내 다리가 걱정돼서. 많이 아프거든.
Tom: 병원에 가보는 게 어때?
Yujin: 오늘 방과 후에 갈 거야.
Tom: 곧 괜찮아지기를 바라.
Yujin: 나도 그러길 바라.

Listen & Speak 1 B

Brian: What are you watching?

Jane: It's a program about _____.

Brian: _____ _____. _____ _____ _____ _____ these days.

Jane: Me, too. This program has some _____ _____.

Brian: Really? What does it say?

Jane: When things start to _____, you need to _____ _____ under a table.

Brian: Oh, I didn't know that.

Brian: 무엇을 시청하고 있니?
Jane: 지진에 관한 프로그램이야.
Brian: 그거 재미있겠다. 나는 요즘 지진이 걱정돼.
Jane: 나도 그래. 이 프로그램에는 도움이 되는 몇 가지 조언이 있어.
Brian: 그래? 뭐라고 하는데?
Jane: 물건들이 흔들리기 시작하면 탁자 아래에 숨어야 해.
Brian: 아, 그건 몰랐어.

Listen & Speak 2 A

Jack: Dad, I'm going out to play basketball with Minu.

Dad: Did you _____ _____ _____ _____?

Jack: No, _____ _____. Can I do it later?

Dad: No. _____ _____ _____ _____ _____ _____ _____.

Jack: Okay. I'll clean my room and then play basketball.

Dad: Good. _____ _____ to be home by six o'clock.

Jack: Okay.

Jack: 아빠, 저 민우와 농구하러 나갈 거예요.
Dad: 네 방 청소는 끝냈니?
Jack: 아니요, 아직 안했어요. 나중에 해도 돼요?
Dad: 아니. 너는 네 방을 먼저 청소해야 해.
Jack: 알았어요. 방을 청소하고 농구 할게요.
Dad: 착하구나. 6시까지 집에 오는 것 잊지 마라.
Jack: 알겠어요.

Listen & Talk 2 B

Emily: What time is the movie?

Tom: It starts at 4:30.

Emily: Oh, no. We only have 20 minutes _____. Let's run!

Tom: No! _____ _____ _____ _____ _____ _____.

    You should walk _____ _____ _____.

Emily: You're right. We can be _____ _____ _____.

Tom: Yes. _____ _____ _____ _____.

Real Life Communication

Brian: There was _____ _____ _____ at the city library yesterday.

Mina: Yes, I heard about it. _____ _____ _____ _____ _____ _____ _____.

Brian: Don't worry. Everybody was okay. They all followed the _____ rules.

Mina: Really? What are the rules?

Brian: You need to _____ your nose and mouth _____ _____ _____ _____. Then _____ _____ and _____.

Mina: Oh, I didn't know that.

Brian: You should _____ _____ _____ _____. It might be helpful some day.

Let's Check

Sujin: It's raining. I'm worried about _____ _____ in the afternoon.

Mom: It is going to rain _____ _____ _____ today. _____ _____ _____ _____ _____.

Sujin: You're right, Mom. I'll call my friend and _____ _____ _____.

Conversation 시험대비 기본평가

01 다음 대화의 밑줄 친 (A)와 바꾸어 쓸 수 있는 것을 <u>모두</u> 고르시오.

> A: (A)I'm worried about my sore throat.
> B: Why don't you take some medicine?
> A: Okay. I'll try.

① I'm surprised at my sore throat.
② I'm relieved due to my sore throat.
③ I'm concerned about my sore throat.
④ I'm satisfied with my sore throat.
⑤ I'm anxious about my sore throat.

02 다음 대화가 자연스럽게 이어지도록 배열하시오.

Tom: Yujin, what's wrong?

> (A) I hope so, too.
> (B) I'm going to go after school today.
> (C) Why don't you go see a doctor?
> (D) I hope you feel better soon.
> (E) I'm worried about my leg. It hurts a lot.

➡ _____

[03~04] 다음 대화를 읽고 물음에 답하시오.

Emily: What time is the movie?
Tom: It starts at 4:30.
Emily: Oh, no. We only have 20 minutes left. Let's run!
Tom: No! You might fall and hurt yourself. You should walk on the stairs.
Emily: You're right. We can be a little late.
Tom: Yes. (A)후회하는 것보다 안전한 게 낫지.

03 다음 주어진 영영풀이가 가리키는 말을 위 대화에서 찾아 쓰시오.

> to come or go down suddenly from a standing position

➡ _____

04 위 대화의 밑줄 친 (A)의 우리말을 4 단어를 사용하여 영어로 쓰시오.

➡ _____

[01~03] 다음 대화를 읽고 물음에 답하시오.

Tom: Yujin, (A)_____

Yujin: I'm worried about my leg. It hurts a lot.

Tom: (B)Why don't you go see a doctor?

Yujin: I'm going to go after school today.

Tom: I hope you feel better soon.

Yujin: I hope so, too.

01 위 대화의 빈칸 (A)에 들어갈 말로 <u>어색한</u> 것은?

① what happened?

② what's the matter?

③ what's wrong?

④ what's the matter with you?

⑤ what are you doing?

02 위 대화의 밑줄 친 (B)와 바꾸어 쓸 수 <u>없는</u> 것은?

① What about going to see a doctor?

② You had better go see a doctor.

③ I think you should see a doctor.

④ How about going to see a doctor?

⑤ Why didn't you go see a doctor?

03 위 대화에서 Yujin의 심경으로 적절한 것은?

① calm   ② nervous

③ anxious   ④ pleased

⑤ lonely

[04~06] 다음 대화를 읽고 물음에 답하시오.

Brian: What are you watching?

Jane: It's a program about earthquakes.

Brian: Sounds interesting. I'm worried about earthquakes these days.

Jane: (A)Me, too. This program has some helpful tips.

Brian: Really? What does it say?

Jane: When things start to shake, (B)_____.

Brian: Oh, I didn't know that.

04 위 대화의 밑줄 친 (A)와 바꾸어 쓸 수 있는 것은?

① So am I.   ② So do I.

③ Neither did I.   ④ Neither am I.

⑤ Neither do I.

서답형

05 위 대화의 빈칸 (B)에 들어갈 말을 보기에 주어진 어구를 모두 배열하여 완성하시오.

┌─ 보기 ┐

cover   need   a table   take

you   to   under

→ _____

중요

06 위 대화의 내용과 일치하지 <u>않는</u> 것은?

① Jane은 지진에 관한 프로그램을 보고 있다.

② Brian과 Jane은 요즘 지진에 대해 걱정하고 있다.

③ Jane은 프로그램에서 지진에 관한 유용한 정보를 얻었다.

④ 지진 발생시, 탁자 아래에 숨어야 한다.

⑤ 물건이 흔들리기 시작할 때, 물건을 탁자 아래로 옮겨야 한다.

[07~09] 다음 대화를 읽고 물음에 답하시오.

Jack: Dad, I'm going out to play basketball with Minu.
Dad: Did you finish cleaning your room?
Jack: No, not yet. Can I do it later?
Dad: No. You should clean your room first.
Jack: Okay. I'll clean my room and then play basketball.
Dad: Good. Don't forget to be home by six o'clock.
Jack: Okay.

서답형
07 What is Jack going to do with Minu?

➡ _____

서답형
08 What did Jack's dad tell him to do before going out?

➡ _____

서답형
09 By what time should Jack return home?

➡ _____

[10~11] 다음 대화를 읽고 물음에 답하시오.

Emily: What time is the movie?
Tom: It starts at 4:30.
Emily: Oh, no. We only have 20 minutes left. Let's run!
Tom: No! You might fall and hurt yourself. You should walk on the stairs.
Emily: You're right. We can be a little late.
Tom: Yes. (A)_____

10 위 대화의 빈칸 (A)에 들어갈 말로 적절한 것은?

① Will is power.
② Better safe than sorry.
③ A sound mind in a sound body.
④ A friend in need is a friend indeed.
⑤ No smoke without fire.

11 위 대화의 내용과 일치하지 <u>않는</u> 것은?

① The movie will start at 4:30.
② It's 4:10 now.
③ Emily is in a hurry not to be late for the movie.
④ Tom advises Emily not to run on the stairs.
⑤ Tom prefers being on time to being safe.

[12~13] 다음 대화를 읽고 물음에 답하시오.

Brian: There was a big fire at the city library yesterday.
Mina: Yes, I heard about it. I was worried about the people there.
Brian: Don't worry. Everybody (A)[was / were] okay. They all followed the safety rules.
Mina: Really? What are the rules?
Brian: You need (B)[covering / to cover] your nose and mouth with a wet towel. Then (C)[stay / staying] low and escape.
Mina: Oh, I didn't know that.
Brian: You should keep that in mind. It might be helpful some day.

서답형
12 위 대화의 괄호 (A)~(C)에서 적절한 것을 골라 쓰시오.

➡ (A) _____ (B) _____ (C) _____

13 위 대화의 내용과 일치하지 <u>않는</u> 것은?

① 어제 시립 도서관에서 큰 불이 있었다.
② Mina는 도서관에 있던 사람들을 걱정했다.
③ 도서관에 있던 사람들은 모두 안전 규칙을 따랐다.
④ 화재 시 젖은 수건으로 코와 입을 가려야 한다.
⑤ 화재 시 똑바로 서서 탈출해야 한다.

01 다음 대화가 자연스럽게 이어지도록 순서대로 배열하시오.

Dad, I'm going out to play basketball with Minu.

> (A) No, not yet. Can I do it later?
> (B) No. You should clean your room first.
> (C) Did you finish cleaning your room?
> (D) Good. Don't forget to be home by six o'clock.
> (E) Okay. I'll clean my room and then play basketball.

➡ _____

[02~03] 다음 대화를 읽고 물음에 답하시오.

Emily: What time is the movie?
Tom: It starts at 4:30.
Emily: Oh, no. We only have 20 minutes left. Let's run!
Tom: No! You might fall and hurt yourself. (A)You should walk on the stairs. (why)
Emily: You're right. We can be a little late.
Tom: Yes. Better safe than sorry.

☆02 위 대화의 밑줄 친 (A)와 의미가 같도록 주어진 표현을 이용하여 다시 쓰시오.

➡ _____

03 Why did Tom tell Emily not to run on the stairs?

➡ _____

[04~07] 다음 대화를 읽고 물음에 답하시오.

Brian: There was a big fire at the city library yesterday.
Mina: Yes, I heard about it. I was worried about the people there.

Brian: Don't worry. Everybody was okay. They all followed the safety rules.
Mina: Really? What are the rules?
Brian: You need to cover your nose and mouth with a wet towel. Then stay low and escape.
Mina: Oh, I didn't know that.
Brian: You should keep (A)that in mind. It might be helpful some day.

04 What happened at the city library yesterday?

➡ _____

☆05 Why didn't everyone get hurt at the big fire?

➡ _____

06 위 대화의 밑줄 친 (A)가 가리키는 내용을 우리말로 간략히 설명하시오.

➡ _____

☆07 다음 대화의 빈칸에 들어갈 말을 보기에 주어진 어구를 모두 배열하여 완성하시오.

> A: I heard about your accident. I was worried about you.
> B: Thanks. I hurt my hand, but it's not serious. I'll be okay.
> A: Good. _____
> B: You're right. I will.

> ─┤ 보기 ├─
> the door / watch / your / hands /
> you / close / should / you / when

➡ _____

_____

Grammar

1 의문사+to부정사

> • I don't know **what to do**. 나는 무엇을 해야 할지 모르겠어.
> • She asked me **how to make** the cake. 그녀는 나에게 그 케이크를 만드는 법을 물었다.

■ '의문사+to부정사'는 문장 속에서 명사구로 주어, 목적어, 보어 역할을 한다. 해당하는 의문사는 what, when, where, how, which, who, whom 등이 있으며, 'where to go'는 '어디로 가야 할지'와 같이 의문사와 동사의 의미를 넣어 해석한다.

- Can you tell me **where to find** the hotel? 어디에서 그 호텔을 찾을지 말해줄래?
- **How to teach** students is important. 학생들을 가르치는 방법은 중요하다.
- Did you decide **whom to invite**? 누구를 초대할지 결정했니?
- I didn't tell you **when to sleep**. 네가 언제 자야 할지 나는 말하지 않았어.

■ '의문사+to부정사'는 '의문사+주어+should+동사원형'으로 바꾸어 쓸 수 있다.

- Julia told me **what to do**. (= Julia told me what I should do.) Julia는 내게 무엇을 해야 할지 말해주었다.
- Let me show you **how to do** it. (= Let me show you how you should do it.) 네가 그것을 어떻게 해야 하는지 내가 보여줄게.
- Let's choose **what to eat** for lunch. (= Let's choose what we should eat for lunch.) 점심으로 무엇을 먹을지 선택하자.

핵심 Check

1. 다음 우리말과 같도록 빈칸에 알맞은 말을 쓰시오.

(1) 나는 자동차를 운전하는 방법을 몰라.

➡ I don't know ＿＿＿＿ ＿＿＿＿ ＿＿＿＿ a car.

= I don't know ＿＿＿＿ ＿＿＿＿ ＿＿＿＿ ＿＿＿＿ a car.

(2) 우리는 언제 떠날지 몰라.

➡ We don't know ＿＿＿＿ ＿＿＿＿ ＿＿＿＿.

= We don't know ＿＿＿＿ ＿＿＿＿ ＿＿＿＿ ＿＿＿＿.

(3) 나는 누구를 믿어야 할지 모르겠어.

➡ I don't know ＿＿＿＿ ＿＿＿＿ ＿＿＿＿.

= I don't know ＿＿＿＿ ＿＿＿＿ ＿＿＿＿ ＿＿＿＿.

② 관계대명사

> • Bradley is my friend **who** lives in Mexico. Bradley는 멕시코에 사는 내 친구이다.
> • The woman you saw yesterday is my aunt. 네가 어제 본 그 여자는 내 숙모야.

■ 관계대명사는 두 개의 문장을 하나로 이어주는 접속사 역할을 하면서 동시에 명사 역할을 한다. 본래 문장에서 주격으로 쓰인 명사는 주격 관계대명사로, 소유격으로 쓰인 명사는 소유격 관계대명사로, 목적격으로 쓰인 명사는 목적격 관계대명사로 바꾸어준다.

• I thanked the woman. She found me my wallet.
= I thanked the woman **who** found me my wallet.

• The pants were on the bed. I washed them.
= The pants **which** I washed were on the bed.

■ 선행사에 따라서 사용되는 관계대명사의 종류는 다음과 같으며, 목적격 관계대명사와 '주격 관계대명사+be동사'는 생략 가능하다.

	주격	소유격	목적격
사람	who	whose	whom[who]
사물	which	whose[of which]	which

• Tell me about the famous people **who[whom]** you became friends with in Yale.
네가 예일 대학에 있을 때 친구가 된 유명한 사람들에 대해 말해줘.

• I know a dentist **whose** daughters are twins. 나는 쌍둥이 딸을 가진 치과의사를 안다.

• The movie **which** we booked yesterday was canceled. 우리가 어제 예약한 영화는 취소되었다.

■ 관계대명사 that은 who와 which를 대신하여 사용될 수 있으며 소유격은 없다. 단, 선행사가 '사람+사물'인 경우에는 반드시 that을 쓰며, 선행사가 'the+최상급', 'the+서수', 'the only', 'the very', 'the same'의 수식을 받거나, 선행사가 '-thing', '-body', '-one'으로 끝나는 경우 관계대명사 that을 쓰는 경우가 많다.

• The woman **that[who/whom]** I called yesterday had a nice voice. 내가 어제 통화했던 여자는 예쁜 목소리를 가졌다.

• Cathy is the only friend **that** I can tell my secrets. Cathy는 내 비밀을 말할 수 있는 유일한 친구이다.

핵심 Check

2. 다음 우리말과 같도록 빈칸에 알맞은 말을 쓰시오.

(1) 경주에서 진 그 소녀는 비참했다.
➡ The girl _____ lost the race was miserable.

(2) 나는 그의 누나가 매우 키가 큰 남자를 안다.
➡ I know the man _____ _____ is very tall.

01 다음 문장에서 어법상 <u>어색한</u> 부분을 바르게 고쳐 쓰시오.

composer: 작곡가

(1) Some people don't know when quit.

_____ ➡ _____

(2) I stayed in the room and which was very beautiful.

_____ ➡ _____

(3) I'm not sure which way to going.

_____ ➡ _____

(4) Do you know the song who the famous composer wrote?

_____ ➡ _____

02 다음 주어진 단어를 어법에 맞게 빈칸에 쓰시오.

(1) They taught me _____ _____ _____. (how / read)

(2) Look at the boys who _____ playing the guitar on the stage. (be)

(3) Jimmy took care of a dog _____ tail was hurt. (who)

(4) I don't know _____ _____ _____ the question. (who / ask)

03 다음 우리말에 맞게 주어진 어구를 바르게 배열하시오. (필요하면 단어를 추가하거나 변형할 것)

(1) 언제 오실지 알려 드리겠습니다.

   (come / I / when / you / let / will / know)

   ➡ _____

(2) 갖고 싶은 것이 있어?

   (have / there / to / is / you / anything / that / want)

   ➡ _____

(3) 나는 그 기계를 사용하는 방법을 몰라.

   (the machine / I / use / know / how / don't)

   ➡ _____

(4) 나는 어느 유명한 작가가 쓴 책을 읽었다.

   (write / read / I / a famous writer / a book / which)

   ➡ _____

01 다음 빈칸에 들어갈 말로 가장 적절한 것은?

> • I don't know _____ to submit.
> 어느 것을 제출해야 할지 모르겠어.

① when   ② how   ③ which

④ who   ⑤ where

02 다음 중 빈칸에 들어갈 말이 나머지 넷과 다른 하나는?

① She is a woman _____ lives in Tokyo.
② I don't know _____ to talk to.
③ I know a girl _____ goal is to win the race.
④ There lived a boy _____ thought himself an angel.
⑤ The girl _____ hates to be alone is happy now.

03 다음 주어진 우리말을 영어로 바르게 옮긴 것은?

> 나는 어디서부터 시작해야 할지 모르겠어.

① I don't know when to start.
② I don't know how to do.
③ I don't know who to start.
④ I don't know where to start.
⑤ I don't know what to do.

서답형
04 다음 두 개의 문장을 하나의 문장으로 만드시오.

> The man lives here. He is cleaning the house.

➡ _____

05 다음 문장과 같은 의미의 문장은?

> Tell me where I should park this car.

① Would you tell her where to park this car?
② Can you tell me where to park this car?
③ Will you tell him how to park this car?
④ Could you tell me when to park this car?
⑤ Tell me whose car to park.

06 다음 빈칸에 알맞은 말을 모두 고르시오.

> Yesterday, I met the boy _____ you were interested in.

① that   ② whose   ③ which

④ who   ⑤ whom

07 다음 빈칸에 들어갈 말이 바르게 짝지어진 것은?

> • Let me know _____ to begin.
> • Do you know the boy _____ is wearing a blue shirt?

① when – whom   ② that – that

③ who – who   ④ when – that

⑤ how – whose

서답형
08 주어진 문장과 같은 의미의 문장을 쓰시오.

> Let me know where I should get off.

➡ _____

09 다음 빈칸에 공통으로 들어갈 말은?

> • Helen advised me _____ to buy.
> • This is the box _____ Jason was looking for.

① that ② of which ③ who
④ which ⑤ whose

10 다음 중 나머지 넷과 쓰임이 <u>다른</u> 하나는?

① Please tell me <u>that</u> it doesn't matter.
② Why do you think <u>that</u> he did it?
③ It is a fact <u>that</u> she can dance.
④ It is said <u>that</u> time is money.
⑤ There was a boy <u>that</u> had a beautiful voice.

11 ⭐중요 다음 중 어법상 옳은 것을 바르게 묶은 것은?

> ⓐ Do you know how make an apple pie?
> ⓑ They were invited to the party which was very boring.
> ⓒ The man who is singing on the stage is my boyfriend.
> ⓓ Did you find the key was on the sofa?
> ⓔ I'm not sure what to do next.

① ⓐ, ⓒ, ⓓ   ② ⓑ, ⓓ, ⓔ
③ ⓐ, ⓑ, ⓓ   ④ ⓑ, ⓒ, ⓔ
⑤ ⓒ, ⓓ, ⓔ

서답형
12 다음 문장을 같은 의미가 되도록 빈칸에 알맞은 말을 쓰시오.

> • The pen is mine. It is on the desk.
> = The pen _____ is mine.

➡ _____

13 다음 중 어법상 바르지 <u>않은</u> 것은?

> The man ①who ②is standing over there ③tell me ④to do something. But I don't know ⑤what to do first.

14 ⭐중요 다음 중 어법상 옳은 문장은?

① They are not sure when should ask him.
② Jason is the only friend which I trust.
③ You didn't tell me where go.
④ The woman who I saw was your teacher.
⑤ I have a puppy that are three years old.

15 다음 밑줄 친 부분 중 생략할 수 <u>없는</u> 것은?

① Do you use the pen <u>that</u> you borrowed from me?
② The movie <u>that</u> you talked about is very interesting.
③ You can tell me anything <u>that</u> you want to talk about.
④ Julia has four books <u>that</u> are very interesting.
⑤ The tip of the brush <u>that</u> you gave me is very soft.

서답형
16 to부정사와 주어진 단어를 활용하여 다음 우리말을 영어로 쓰시오.

> 무엇을 주문해야 할지 모르겠어.
> (order)

➡ _____

17 다음 빈칸에 들어갈 말이 바르게 짝지어진 것은?

> The film _____ made people all over the
> world surprised _____ made by a famous
> director.

① that – are
② who – were
③ whose – is
④ whom – was
⑤ which – was

18 다음 주어진 문장과 같은 의미의 문장을 고르시오.

> He doesn't know how he should behave.

① He wants to know what to behave.
② He doesn't know how to behave.
③ He can't know when to behave.
④ He doesn't know where to behave.
⑤ He wants to know which to behave.

19 다음 빈칸에 공통으로 들어갈 말은?

> • Did you kick the ball _____ was in my
>   room?
> • Have you seen the girls _____ always
>   do something together?

① who
② that
③ which
④ whose
⑤ whom

20 다음 우리말을 영어로 옮길 때 빈칸에 알맞은 말을 쓰시오.

> • 나에게 공원으로 가는 길을 물어본 그 남자는 어
>   디로 가야 할지 몰랐어.
> = The man _____ _____ _____ the way to
>   the park didn't know _____ _____ _____.

➡ _____

21 다음 중 밑줄 친 관계대명사의 쓰임이 바른 것은?

① Jenny liked the movie <u>whom</u> she saw
   with her friends.
② The cake <u>whose</u> he made was really
   delicious.
③ The pants <u>that</u> she is wearing are new.
④ Do you know that man <u>whom</u> swims so
   well?
⑤ We eat the vegetables <u>who</u> we grew in the
   yard.

22 다음 우리말을 영어로 옮길 때 빈칸에 알맞은 말을 쓰시오.

> 어디에서 만날지 결정하자.
> = Let's decide _____ .

➡ _____

23 다음 두 문장을 한 문장으로 만들 때 빈칸에 알맞은 것을 <u>모두</u> 고르시오.

> I bought a book from the boy. He was
> talking with my sister.
> = I bought a book from the boy _____
> _____

① whose was talking with my sister.
② he was talking with my sister.
③ which was talking with my sister.
④ talking with my sister.
⑤ who was talking with my sister.

24 빈칸에 알맞은 말을 쓰시오.

> I don't know _____ to do.
> = I don't know what I _____ .

➡ _____

01 〈보기〉의 문장과 관계대명사를 이용하여 빈칸을 알맞게 채우시오. (that은 쓰지 말 것)

┌─ 보기 ─┐
- They were painted by your mom.
- They want to be rich.
- It is very useful for you.
- The person is visiting a place for pleasure and interest.

(1) A tourist is someone _____
_____.
(2) What happened to the pictures _____
_____?
(3) There are many people _____.
(4) She will give you a tip _____
_____.

02 다음 문장이 서로 같은 의미가 되도록 빈칸에 알맞은 말을 쓰시오.

(1) She asked me where she should find the bathroom.
= She asked me _____.
(2) It's up to you to decide what you should do next.
= It's up to you to decide _____
_____.
(3) I haven't decided which class I should sign up for.
= I haven't decided _____
_____.

03 다음 우리말을 주어진 단어를 이용하여 영어로 쓸 때 빈칸을 알맞게 채우시오.

┌─────────────────────────────┐
나는 졸업 후에 무엇을 해야 할지 확실히 모르겠어.
(to / graduation)
└─────────────────────────────┘

➡ I'm not sure _____

04 다음 빈칸에 공통으로 들어갈 말을 쓰시오.

┌─────────────────────────────┐
- I don't know _____ to speak to.
- He is the man _____ everyone respects.
└─────────────────────────────┘

➡ _____

05 주어진 단어를 바르게 배열하여 다음 우리말을 영어로 쓰시오. 필요하다면 단어를 변형하시오.

┌─────────────────────────────┐
안녕이라고 말하는 방식은 문화마다 다르다.
(cultures / how / different / hello / in / to / vary / say)
└─────────────────────────────┘

➡ _____

06 다음 두 문장을 하나의 문장으로 쓰시오.

┌─────────────────────────────┐
- There are children.
- They are playing in the garden.
└─────────────────────────────┘

➡ _____

07 다음 대화의 빈칸을 어법에 맞게 채우시오.

┌─────────────────────────────┐
A: Do you know _____ _____ _____?
B: Yes, I do. Mom said we should go to the park.
└─────────────────────────────┘

➡ _____

08 다음 중 서로 관련 있는 문장을 연결하여 하나의 문장으로 쓰시오. 관계대명사 that은 사용하지 마시오.

> • The apartment is no longer available.
> • The boy is now in the hospital.
> • Do you want to buy the pictures?
> • Bruno Mars is a singer.
> • I must thank the people.
> • An artist is a person.

> • They are very expensive.
> • He is very popular all over the world.
> • He cut his finger.
> • He or she draws or paints pictures as a job.
> • It was empty.
> • They congratulated me.

➡ _____

➡ _____

➡ _____

➡ _____

➡ _____

➡ _____

09 다음 빈칸에 알맞은 말을 쓰시오.

> A: I don't know what I should do for the project.
> B: Do you see the man _____ is writing something? He is the manager. He will tell you _____ _____ _____.

10 다음 빈칸에 알맞은 말을 쓰시오.

> • There are many people.
> • They are doing their best.
> = There are many people _____ _____ _____ _____ their best.
> = There are many people _____ their best.

11 다음 우리말을 영어로 옮길 때 빈칸에 알맞은 말을 쓰시오.

> • 이 책은 그것을 읽는 사람들에게 어떻게 생각해야 할지를 가르쳐 줘.
> =This book teaches people _____ _____ _____ _____ _____ _____ .

12 다음 대화의 빈칸에 알맞은 말을 쓰시오.

> Carrie: A police officer helped you. Did you thank her?
> Jason: Yes, I thanked the police officer _____ _____ _____ .

13 적절한 관계대명사와 주어진 단어를 이용하여 다음 우리말을 영어로 쓰시오.

> 읽고 있던 책을 다 읽었니? (finish)

➡ _____

14 다음 우리말을 두 가지의 영어 문장으로 쓰시오.

> 나는 뭐라고 말해야 할지 모르겠어.

➡ _____

➡ _____

Reading

교과서

Prepare for the shake

Do you know <u>what to do</u> when an earthquake strikes? Take this quiz
'의문사+to부정사'로 know의 목적어

and think about <u>how to be safe</u> <u>during</u> this kind of natural disaster.
'의문사+to부정사'로 about의 목적어   while (×)

1. When things <u>start to</u> shake, run outside quickly. (O / ×)
~하기 시작하다

2. <u>Stay away from</u> windows. (O / ×)
~에서 떨어져 있다

3. Use the stairs to <u>get out of</u> buildings. (O / ×)
~에서 나가다

4. When you <u>are outside</u>, <u>hold on to</u> a pole or a tree. (O / ×)
밖에 있다   ~을 꼭 잡다

How did you do on the quiz? Can you survive an earthquake safely?

<u>Here are</u> some safety tips <u>which</u> can be helpful in an earthquake. Let's
Here is/are ~ : 여기에 ~이 있다   주격 관계대명사(that으로 바꿔 쓸 수 있다)

check them <u>one by one</u> and learn <u>what to do.</u>
하나씩   무엇을 할지(=what we should do)

---

shake: 흔들림, 떨림
earthquake: 지진
strike: 발생하다
disaster: 재난
stay away from: ~에서 떨어져 있다
stair 계단
hold on to: ~을 꼭 잡다
pole: 기둥
survive: 살아남다
safely: 안전하게
safety: 안전

📎 확인문제

● 다음 문장이 본문의 내용과 일치하면 T, 일치하지 <u>않으면</u> F를 쓰시오.

1 The passage is about how to be safe in an earthquake. ☐

2 There are some safety tips to survive in all kinds of natural disasters. ☐

3 We can learn what we should do during an earthquake. ☐

4 The following passage will be about people who survived an earthquake. ☐

Don't run outside when things are shaking. Find a table or a desk and

때를 나타내는 부사절로 'things are shaking'은 현재진행형이 사용되어 '물건들이 흔들리고 있을 때'라는 뜻이다.

take cover under it. You can hold on to the legs to protect yourself.

to부정사의 부사적 용법 '~하기 위해서' 재귀대명사의 재귀적 용법(주어와 목적어가 같을 때 목적어로 재귀대명사 사용)

Also, stay away from windows. They can break during an earthquake

~에서 떨어져 있어라 =Windows

and hurt you.

You can go outside when the shaking stops. To get out of buildings,

to부정사의 부사적 용법 '~하기 위해서'

don't use the elevator. Take the stairs. It's much safer.

부정명령문 비교급 강조 부사 '훨씬'

Once you are outside, find an empty space that is far from buildings.

일단 ~하면 주격 관계대명사 ~에서 멀다

There may be people who want to hold on to a pole or a tree, but think

추측을 나타내는 조동사 주격 관계대명사(that으로 바꿔 쓸 수 있다)

again. That's a bad idea because it can fall on you.

=To hold on to a pole or a tree

Earthquakes can strike anytime. They can be scary experiences for

언제든지

everyone. So learn how to be safe in an earthquake. You can avoid

'how+to부정사' 안전할 방법

injuries and protect yourself. Follow these tips and be safe!

take cover: 숨다
protect: 보호하다
break: 깨다, 부수다, 부서지다
hurt: 다치다
once: 한 번; 일단 ~하면
outside: 밖에, 밖으로
empty: 비어 있는
space: 공간, 공터
avoid: 방지하다
pole: 기둥
scary: 무서운
experience: 경험
injury: 상처, 부상

확인문제

● 다음 문장이 본문의 내용과 일치하면 T, 일치하지 않으면 F를 쓰시오.

1 If things are still shaking, you should run outside as fast as possible. ☐

2 When things are shaking, it is good to take cover under a table or a desk. ☐

3 Staying close to the window is not a good idea. ☐

4 When the shaking stops, we should be indoors. ☐

5 Holding on to a pole or a tree is a bad idea. ☐

● 우리말을 참고하여 빈칸에 알맞은 말을 쓰시오.

_____ for the shake

1 Do you know _____ _____ _____ when an earthquake _____?

2 _____ this quiz and think about _____ _____ _____ safe _____ this kind of natural disaster.

3 When things start _____ _____, run outside _____. (o / x)

4 _____ _____ from windows. (o / x)

5 _____ the stairs _____ _____ _____ _____ buildings. (o / x)

6 _____ you are outside, _____ _____ _____ a pole or a tree. (o / x)

7 _____ did you do _____ the quiz?

8 Can you _____ _____ _____ _____ _____?

9 _____ _____ some safety tips _____ can be _____ in an earthquake.

10 Let's check _____ _____ _____ _____ and learn _____ _____.

11 Don't run outside _____ _____ _____ _____.

12 _____ a table or a desk and _____ _____ under it.

13 You can hold on to the legs _____ _____ _____.

14 Also, _____ _____ _____ windows.

15 _____ can break _____ an earthquake and hurt you.

16 You can _____ _____ when _____ _____ _____.

<table>
<tr><td colspan="2">지진을 대비하라</td></tr>
<tr><td>1</td><td>지진이 발생할 때 해야 할 일을 알고 있습니까?</td></tr>
<tr><td>2</td><td>이 퀴즈를 풀며 이러한 종류의 자연 재해가 발생하는 동안 어떻게 해야 안전할 수 있는지를 생각해 보세요.</td></tr>
<tr><td>3</td><td>물건들이 흔들리기 시작하면, 빨리 밖으로 뛰어나가세요.</td></tr>
<tr><td>4</td><td>창문으로부터 멀리 떨어지세요.</td></tr>
<tr><td>5</td><td>건물에서 나갈 때는 계단을 이용하세요.</td></tr>
<tr><td>6</td><td>밖에 나가서는 기둥이나 나무를 붙들고 있으세요.</td></tr>
<tr><td>7</td><td>퀴즈가 어떠셨나요?</td></tr>
<tr><td>8</td><td>당신은 지진에서 안전하게 살아남을 수 있나요?</td></tr>
<tr><td>9</td><td>여기에 지진 발생 시 도움이 될 수 있는 안전 지침이 있습니다.</td></tr>
<tr><td>10</td><td>하나하나 확인하면서 무엇을 해야 하는지를 배워 봅시다.</td></tr>
<tr><td>11</td><td>물건들이 흔들리기 시작할 때 밖으로 뛰어나가지 마세요.</td></tr>
<tr><td>12</td><td>탁자나 책상을 찾아서 그 밑에 숨으세요.</td></tr>
<tr><td>13</td><td>자신을 보호하기 위해 탁자나 책상 다리를 붙들고 있으세요.</td></tr>
<tr><td>14</td><td>또한, 창문으로부터 멀리 떨어지세요.</td></tr>
<tr><td>15</td><td>지진이 일어나는 동안 창문들이 깨져 다칠 수 있으니까요.</td></tr>
<tr><td>16</td><td>흔들림이 멈추었을 때 밖으로 나가도 됩니다.</td></tr>
</table>

17 _____ _____ _____ _____ buildings, don't use the elevator.

18 _____ the stairs.

19 It's _____ _____.

20 _____ you are outside, _____ _____ _____ _____ that _____ far _____ buildings.

21 There may be people _____ _____ _____ _____ _____ _____ a pole or a tree, _____ think again.

22 That's a bad idea _____ _____ can _____ _____ you.

23 _____ can strike _____.

24 _____ can be _____ _____ for everyone.

25 So learn _____ _____ _____ _____ _____ in an earthquake.

26 You can _____ _____ and _____ _____.

27 _____ these tips and _____ safe!

17 건물에서 나가기 위해 엘리베이터를 이용하지 마세요.

18 계단을 이용하세요.

19 그것이 훨씬 더 안전합니다.

20 일단 밖으로 나가면, 건물로부터 멀리 떨어진 공터를 찾으세요.

21 기둥이나 나무를 꼭 잡고 있으려는 사람들이 있을 수 있지만, 다시 생각해 보세요.

22 그것이 당신 위로 넘어질 수 있으므로 그것은 좋지 않은 생각입니다.

23 지진은 언제든지 발생할 수 있습니다.

24 지진은 모두에게 무서운 경험일 것입니다.

25 따라서 지진이 날 때 안전을 지키는 법을 배우세요.

26 부상을 방지하고 자신을 보호할 수 있습니다.

27 이 지침을 따르고 안전을 지키세요!

● 우리말을 참고하여 본문을 영작하시오.

1 지진이 발생할 때 해야 할 일을 알고 있습니까?
➡ _____

2 이 퀴즈를 풀며 이러한 종류의 자연 재해가 발생하는 동안 어떻게 해야 안전할 수 있는지를 생각해 보세요.
➡ _____

3 물건들이 흔들리기 시작하면, 빨리 밖으로 뛰어나가세요.
➡ _____

4 창문으로부터 멀리 떨어지세요.
➡ _____

5 건물에서 나갈 때는 계단을 이용하세요.
➡ _____

6 밖에 나가서는 기둥이나 나무를 붙들고 있으세요.
➡ _____

7 퀴즈가 어떠셨나요?
➡ _____

8 당신은 지진에서 안전하게 살아남을 수 있나요?
➡ _____

9 여기에 지진 발생 시 도움이 될 수 있는 안전 지침이 있습니다.
➡ _____

10 하나하나 확인하면서 무엇을 해야 하는지를 배워 봅시다.
➡ _____

11 물건이 흔들리기 시작할 때 밖으로 뛰어나가지 마세요.
➡ _____

12 탁자나 책상을 찾아서 그 밑에 숨으세요.
➡ _____

13 자신을 보호하기 위해 탁자나 책상 다리를 붙들고 있으세요.
➡ _____

14 또한, 창문으로부터 멀리 떨어지세요.
➡ _____

15 지진이 일어나는 동안 창문들이 깨져 다칠 수 있으니까요.
➡ _____

16 흔들림이 멈추었을 때 밖으로 나가도 됩니다.
➡ _____

17 건물에서 나가기 위해 엘리베이터를 이용하지 마세요.

➡ _____

18 계단을 이용하세요.

➡ _____

19 그것이 훨씬 더 안전합니다.

➡ _____

20 일단 밖으로 나가면, 건물로부터 멀리 떨어진 공터를 찾으세요.

➡ _____

21 기둥이나 나무를 꼭 잡고 있으려는 사람들이 있을 수 있지만, 다시 생각해 보세요.

➡ _____

22 그것이 당신 위로 넘어질 수 있으므로 그것은 좋지 않은 생각입니다.

➡ _____

23 지진은 언제든지 발생할 수 있습니다.

➡ _____

24 지진은 모두에게 무서운 경험일 것입니다.

➡ _____

25 따라서 지진이 날 때 안전을 지키는 법을 배우세요.

➡ _____

26 부상을 방지하고 자신을 보호할 수 있습니다.

➡ _____

27 이 지침을 따르고 안전을 지키세요!

➡ _____

01 자연스러운 글이 되도록 (A)~(D)를 바르게 나열한 것은?

> Here are some safety tips which can be helpful in an earthquake.

(A) You can hold on to the legs to protect yourself. Also, stay away from windows.

(B) Don't run outside when things are shaking. Find a table or a desk and take cover under it.

(C) They can break during an earthquake and hurt you.

(D) Let's check them one by one and learn what to do.

① (B)-(D)-(A)-(C)   ② (B)-(A)-(C)-(D)

③ (C)-(B)-(A)-(D)   ④ (D)-(A)-(B)-(C)

⑤ (D)-(B)-(A)-(C)

[02~05] 다음 글을 읽고 물음에 답하시오.

> Do you know ⓐwhat you should do when an earthquake strikes? Take this quiz and think about how to be safe ⓑ_____ this kind of natural disaster.
> 1. When things start to shake, run outside quickly. (O / ×)
> 2. Stay away from windows. (O / ×)
> 3. Use the stairs to get out of buildings. (O / ×)
> 4. When you are outside, hold on to a pole or a tree. (O / ×)

[서답형]
02 밑줄 친 ⓐ를 대신하여 쓸 수 있는 말을 다음 빈칸에 쓰시오.

➡ _____ _____ _____

[중요]
03 다음 중 빈칸 ⓑ에 들어갈 말로 가장 적절한 것은?

① at   ② during   ③ by

④ on   ⑤ for

[서답형]
04 다음과 같이 풀이되는 단어를 위 글에서 찾아 쓰시오.

> short, quick movement back and forth or up and down

➡ _____

05 What is the quiz about?

① when to go if you are in trouble

② where to go when you feel alone

③ what to do when you feel scared

④ how to go to the safest place in the world

⑤ what to do when an earthquake strikes

[06~10] 다음 글을 읽고 물음에 답하시오.

> How did you do on the quiz? Can you ⓐsurvive an earthquake safely? Here ⓑ____ some safety tips ⓒ____ can be helpful in an earthquake. Let's check them one ⓓ____ one and learn what to do.

06 다음 중 밑줄 친 ⓐ의 의미로 가장 적절한 것은?

① find a hiding place

② affect someone in a bad way

③ remain alive

④ keep someone from being harmed

⑤ break something into parts

[서답형]
07 be동사의 알맞은 형태를 빈칸 ⓑ에 쓰시오.

➡ _____

중요

08 빈칸 ⓒ에 들어갈 말로 적절한 것을 <u>모두</u> 고르시오.

① who ② whom ③ that
④ which ⑤ whose

09 다음 중 빈칸 ⓓ에 들어갈 말과 같은 말이 들어가는 것은?

① We left _____ 3 o'clock.
② Are you interested _____ painting?
③ I know that she traveled _____ bus.
④ The shop is crowded _____ tourists.
⑤ They look forward _____ seeing each other again.

서답형

10 다음은 위 글의 앞에 나온 내용을 설명한 문장이다. 빈칸에 알맞은 말을 쓰시오. (2단어)

• Before the passage, there was _____ which we should take.

➡ _____

[11~16] 다음 글을 읽고 물음에 답하시오.

Here are some safety tips which can be helpful in an earthquake. Let's check them ⓐ _____ and learn what to do. ① Don't run outside when things are shaking. ② Find a table or a desk and take cover under ⓑit. ③ You can hold on to the legs ⓒto protect yourself. ④ They can break during an earthquake and hurt you. ⑤

11 빈칸 ⓐ에 들어갈 말로 가장 적절한 것은?

① case by case ② side by side
③ little by little ④ day by day
⑤ one by one

서답형

12 밑줄 친 ⓑ가 가리키는 것을 위 글에서 찾아 쓰시오.

➡ _____

중요

13 ①~⑤ 중 다음 주어진 문장이 들어가기에 가장 적절한 곳은?

Also, stay away from windows.

① ② ③ ④ ⑤

서답형

14 위 글의 내용을 참고하여 다음 빈칸에 알맞은 말을 어법에 맞게 쓰시오.

To protect yourself, you should find a table or a desk _____ _____ you can hold on to and take cover _____ _____.

15 다음 중 밑줄 친 ⓒ와 쓰임이 같은 것은?

① I want you to come back to me.
② Is it possible to be safe during an earthquake?
③ Emilia went out to buy some snacks.
④ They hoped to visit there again.
⑤ Do you have something to write with?

중요

16 다음 중 글의 내용과 일치하는 것은?

① Running outside during an earthquake is helpful.
② It is good to stand still when things are shaking.
③ You should hold on to your legs.
④ Putting your things under a table or a desk is important.
⑤ Standing near the window can hurt you.

[17~21] 다음 글을 읽고 물음에 답하시오.

You can go outside when the shaking stops. (A)[Getting / To get] out of buildings, don't use the elevator. Take the stairs. It's (B)[very / much] safer. Once you are outside, find an empty space that is far from buildings. There may be people ⓐ_____ want to hold on to a pole or a tree, but think again. That's a bad idea (C)[because of / because] it can fall on you.

17 빈칸 ⓐ에 들어갈 말로 적절한 것을 모두 고르시오.

① which   ② whom   ③ who
④ that   ⑤ whose

18 중요 (A)~(C)에서 어법상 옳은 것끼리 바르게 짝지은 것은?

① Getting – very – because of
② To get – very – because
③ Getting – much – because of
④ To get – much – because
⑤ Getting – much – because

19 서답형 위 글의 내용에 맞게 다음 대화의 빈칸에 알맞은 말을 쓰시오.

A: Now, we can get out of this building.
B: What makes you think so?
A: It's because _____ _____ _____.

20 다음 중 위 글의 내용과 일치하지 <u>않는</u> 것은?

① If the shaking stops, we can go outside.
② It is not a good idea to use the elevator.
③ You should stand still near the building.
④ It is possible that a pole falls on you.
⑤ The empty space should be far from buildings.

21 서답형 다음과 같이 풀이되는 단어를 위 글에서 찾아 쓰시오.

not having any people; containing nothing

➡ _____

[22~26] 다음 글을 읽고 물음에 답하시오.

(A)_____.
Here are some tips. Let's learn (B)what to do and be (C)_____!
A wet floor can be dangerous. People might slip and fall. So you should wipe up the water on the floor. Broken glass can be also dangerous. You should clean up the broken glass because people might step on the broken glass.

22 서답형 다음 두 문장을 하나의 문장으로 만들어 빈칸 (A)에 쓰시오.

• There are many situations.
• They can be dangerous.

➡ _____

23 밑줄 친 (B)를 대신하여 쓸 수 있는 것은?

① what you do
② what we learn
③ what we should do
④ what you have
⑤ what we should get

24 서답형 빈칸 (C)에는 본문에 있는 한 단어의 반의어가 들어간다. (C)에 들어갈 알맞은 말을 쓰시오.

➡ _____

25 서답형 According to the writer, what can be dangerous to people? Answer in English with a full sentence.

➡ _____

_____

26 중요 위 글의 내용과 일치하는 것은?

① People like to slip on the floor.
② If a floor is wet, you should wipe it up.
③ It is hard to say that a wet floor is dangerous.
④ People can fall on broken glass.
⑤ We should be careful about glass.

[27~32] 다음 글을 읽고 물음에 답하시오.

You can go outside when the shaking stops. To get out of buildings, don't use the elevator. Take the stairs. It's much ①safer. Once you are ②outside, find an empty space that is far from buildings. There may be people who want to hold (A)_____ to a pole or a tree, but think again. That's a ③fine idea because it can fall (B)_____ you.

Earthquakes can strike anytime. They can be ④scary experiences for everyone. So learn (C)_____ to be safe in an earthquake. You can avoid injuries and protect yourself. Follow these tips and ⑤be safe!

27 빈칸 (A)와 (B)에 공통으로 들어갈 말로 가장 적절한 것은?

① in   ② toward   ③ on
④ by   ⑤ with

28 중요 다음 중 빈칸 (C)에 들어갈 말과 같은 것은?

① _____ time is it now?
② _____ beautiful the flower is!
③ _____ do you do for a living?
④ _____ a scary moment it was!
⑤ _____ makes you say so?

29 중요 ①~⑤ 중 글의 흐름상 어색한 것은?

①   ②   ③   ④   ⑤

30 다음 중 위 글에서 반의어를 찾을 수 없는 것은?

① inside   ② full   ③ close to
④ dangerous   ⑤ prevent

31 서답형 위 글의 내용에 맞게 다음 대화의 빈칸을 알맞게 채우시오.

A: I don't know _____ _____
   out of the building.
B: We'd better _____ _____ .
   I heard that it is safer than using the elevator.

32 서답형 Once you are outside, what should you look for? Answer in English with a full sentence.

➡ _____

[01~04] 다음 글을 읽고 물음에 답하시오.

Do you know what to do when an earthquake strikes? Take this quiz and think about ⓐ_____ during ⓑthis kind of natural disaster.

1. When things start ⓒ_____, run outside quickly. (○ / ✕)
2. Stay away from windows. (○ / ✕)
3. Use the stairs to get out of buildings. (○ / ✕)
4. When you are outside, hold on to a pole or a tree. (○ / ✕)

01 주어진 단어를 어법에 맞게 활용하여 빈칸 ⓐ에 쓰시오.

(how / safe)

➡ _____

02 밑줄 친 ⓑ가 가리키는 것을 위 글에서 찾아 쓰시오.

➡ _____

03 주어진 동사를 어법에 맞게 빈칸 ⓒ에 쓰시오.

shake

➡ _____

04 다음과 같이 풀이되는 단어를 위 글에서 찾아 쓰시오.

to affect someone or something suddenly in a bad way, to cause damage or harm to someone or something

➡ _____

[05~07] 다음 글을 읽고 물음에 답하시오.

How did you do on the quiz? Can you survive an earthquake safely? ⓐHere are some safety tips which can be helpful in an earthquake. Let's check ⓑthem one by one and learn ⓒwhat to do.

05 밑줄 친 ⓐ를 두 개의 문장으로 풀어 쓰시오.

➡ _____
➡ _____

06 밑줄 친 ⓑ가 가리키는 것을 위 글에서 찾아 쓰시오.

➡ _____

07 적절한 조동사를 이용하여 밑줄 친 ⓒ와 같은 의미의 문장을 쓰시오.

➡ _____

[08~10] 다음 글을 읽고 물음에 답하시오.

Here ⓐ_____ some safety tips which can be helpful in an earthquake. Let's check them one by one and ⓑ_____ what to do.

Don't run outside when things are shaking. Find a table or a desk and take cover under it. You can hold on to the legs ⓒ_____ yourself. ⓓAlso, stay away from windows. They can break during an earthquake and hurt you.

08 주어진 동사를 문맥과 어법에 맞게 빈칸 ⓐ, ⓑ, ⓒ에 쓰시오.

(protect / learn / be)

➡ ⓐ _____ ⓑ _____ ⓒ _____

09 적절한 관계대명사를 이용하여 밑줄 친 ⓓ를 하나의 문장으로 쓰시오.

➡ _____

_____

10 주어진 단어를 바르게 배열하여 다음 물음에 답하시오.

Q: Why is taking cover under a table helpful?
A: (things / and / tables / fall / because / desks / us / when / protect / can)

➡ _____

[11~17] 다음 글을 읽고 물음에 답하시오.

You can go outside when the shaking stops. To get out of buildings, don't use the elevator. Take the stairs. It's much safer. Once you are outside, (A)_____. There may be people who want to hold on to a pole or a tree, but think again. That's a bad idea because it can fall on you.

Earthquakes can strike anytime. They can be scary experiences for everyone. So learn how to be safe in an earthquake. You can avoid injuries and protect yourself. Follow these tips and be safe!

11 다음 두 문장을 하나의 문장으로 연결하여 빈칸 (A)에 쓰시오.

• Find an empty space.
• It is far from buildings.

➡ _____

12 글의 내용에 맞게 다음 빈칸에 알맞은 말을 쓰시오.

Q: When can you go outside?
A: _____, we can go outside.

➡ _____

13 글의 내용에 맞게 빈칸에 알맞은 말을 쓰시오.

_____ _____ _____ is much safer than _____ _____ _____.

14 글의 내용에 맞게 다음 물음에 답하시오.

Q: Why is holding on to a pole or a tree a bad idea?
A: It's because _____.

➡ _____

15 지진으로 인한 흔들림이 멈춘 후 하지 말아야 할 두 가지 행동을 주어진 단어를 이용하여 쓰시오.

don't

➡ _____
➡ _____

16 주어진 단어를 활용하여 위 글의 주제를 쓰시오.

(how / to / during)

➡ _____

17 위 글의 내용에 맞게 다음 빈칸에 알맞은 말을 쓰시오.

Because earthquakes can be scary experiences for everyone, we must _____ _____ _____ _____ _____ _____ _____ .

Real Life Communication B

A: I heard about your accident. I was worried about you.
~에 대해 들었다   ~에 대해 걱정하다 (= be anxious about = be concerned about)

B: Thanks. I hurt my hand, but it's not serious. I'll be okay.
다치다

A: Good. You should watch your hands when you close the door.
충고 표현 '너는 ~해야 한다'   ~할 때

B: You're right. I will.
=That's right.

구문해설 • accident: 사고 • serious: 심각한 • close: 닫다

Culture & Life

When an earthquake struck in Italy in 2016, people found Georgia thanks to
넓은 장소와 연도 앞에 전치사 in

Leo, a dog. Leo found the eight-year-old girl 16 hours after the earthquake
동격 (Leo라는 개)   ~한지 16시간이 지나

struck.

구문해설 • strike: (일이) 발생하다 • thanks to: ~ 덕분에 • find: 발견하다

2016년 이탈리아에 지진이 발생했을 때, 사람들은 Leo 라는 개 덕분에 Georgia를 발견했다. Leo는 지진 발생 후 16시간이 지나 그 8살짜리 소녀를 발견했다.

Culture & Life Project

Here are the items for our survival bag. We packed some food and water. We
여기에 ~이 있다   약간의

need them to survive. We also packed some matches that might be helpful in
=food and water to부정사의 부사적 용법 중 목적(~하기 위해서)   주격 관계대명사

disasters. We put medicine in the bag, too. We might need it for injuries.
또한   ~일지도 모르다   medicine

구문해설 • survival bag: 생존 가방 • pack: ~을 싸다 • match: 성냥 • disaster: 재난 • injury: 부상

여기 우리의 생존 가방에 들어갈 물품이 있습니다. 우리는 약간의 음식과 물을 챙겼습니다. 우리는 생존하기 위해서 그것들이 필요합니다. 우리는 또한 재난 발생 시 유용할 수 있는 성냥을 챙겼습니다. 가방에 약품도 넣었습니다. 부상 당했을 때 필요할 수 있습니다.

Words & Expressions

01 다음 중 나머지 네 개의 단어들을 포함할 수 있는 것은?

① flood   ② drought

③ earthquake   ④ disaster

⑤ storm

02 다음 영영풀이가 가리키는 것을 고르시오.

> the state of not being dangerous or harmful

① safety   ② pole   ③ hazard

④ elevator   ⑤ occasion

03 다음 중 밑줄 친 부분의 뜻풀이가 바르지 <u>않은</u> 것은?

① The floor is wet and <u>slippery</u>.
                       부드러운

② I have a really <u>sore</u> throat. 아픈

③ There is not enough <u>space</u> between the desk and the bed.   공간

④ I heard about the news of the <u>disaster</u>.
                            재난

⑤ You should always wear a helmet for the <u>safety</u>. 안전

04 다음 문장에 공통으로 들어갈 말을 고르시오.

> • My parents worked hard to _____ my tuition fee.
> • Jack _____ed his mouth with his hands.
> • Emma designed the _____ of this book.

① cost   ② avoid   ③ head

④ fix   ⑤ cover

05 다음 문장의 빈칸에 들어갈 말을 보기에서 골라 쓰시오

> ┤ 보기 ├
> take a rest / keep in mind / one by one / why don't you

(1) _____ _____ _____ that it's better to be safe than sorry.

(2) Children are getting off the bus
_____ _____ _____ .

(3) You'd better _____ _____ _____ during the break time.

(4) _____ _____ _____ go see a doctor?

06 다음 우리말을 주어진 단어를 이용하여 영작하시오.

(1) 너는 네 모자를 꼭 잡아야 한다. (should / hold / hat / to)

➡ _____

(2) 나는 혼잡한 장소에서 떨어져 있기 위해 노력했다. (stay / places / away / crowded)

➡ _____

(3) 내 남동생은 자동차 뒤에 숨었다. (younger / behind / took)

➡ _____

Conversation

[07~08] 다음 대화를 읽고 물음에 답하시오.

Tom: Yujin, what's wrong?

Yujin: (A) It hurts a lot.

Tom: (B) Why don't you go see a doctor?

Yujin: (C) I'm going to go after school today.

Tom: (D) I hope you feel better soon.

Yujin: (E) I hope so, too.

07 위 대화의 (A)~(E) 중 다음 문장이 들어가기에 적절한 곳은?

> I'm worried about my leg.

① (A)　② (B)　③ (C)　④ (D)　⑤ (E)

08 위 대화를 읽고 대답할 수 없는 것은?

① What's the matter with Yujin?
② Where does Yujin hurt?
③ What is Yujin going to do after school?
④ What does Tom hope for now?
⑤ Why didn't Yujin go see a doctor?

[09~11] 다음 대화를 읽고 물음에 답하시오.

Jack: Dad, I'm going out to play basketball with Minu.

Dad: Did you finish cleaning your room?

Jack: No, not yet. Can I do it later?

Dad: No. (A)_____

Jack: Okay. I'll clean my room and then play basketball.

Dad: Good. (B)Don't forget to be home by six o'clock. (remember)

Jack: Okay.

09 위 대화의 빈칸 (A)에 들어갈 말로 나머지와 의도가 다른 것은?

① You should clean your room first.
② I think you ought to clean your room first.
③ You'd better clean your room first.
④ If I were you, I'd clean your room first.
⑤ Why didn't you clean your room first?

10 위 대화의 밑줄 친 (B)와 의미가 같도록 주어진 표현을 사용하여 다시 쓰시오.

➡ _____

11 위 대화의 내용과 일치하지 <u>않는</u> 것은?

① Jack은 Minu와 농구하기 위해 외출할 예정이다.
② Jack은 방청소를 끝내지 않았다.
③ Jack의 아버지는 Jack에게 방청소부터 할 것을 충고하였다.
④ Jack은 6시까지 귀가할 것이다.
⑤ Jack은 Minu와 농구를 한 후 방청소를 하기로 아버지와 약속하였다.

[12~14] 다음 대화를 읽고 물음에 답하시오.

Brian: What are you watching?

Jane: It's a program about earthquakes.

Brian: Sounds (A)[interesting / interested]. I'm (B)[worrying / worried] about earthquakes these days.

Jane: Me, too. This program has some helpful tips.

Brian: Really? What does it say?

Jane: When things start to shake, you need to take (C)[cover / to cover] under a table.

Brian: Oh, I didn't know that.

12 위 대화의 (A)~(C)에 들어갈 알맞은 말을 고르시오.

➡ (A) _____, (B) _____, (C) _____

13 What are Brian and Jane worried about these days?

➡ _____

14 According to the program, what should you do when the earthquake occurs?

➡ _____

[15~16] 다음 대화를 읽고 물음에 답하시오.

> Emily: What time is the movie?
> Tom: (A) It starts at 4:30.
> Emily: (B) Oh, no. We only have 20 minutes left. Let's run!
> Tom: (C) You should walk on the stairs.
> Emily: (D) You're right. We can be a little late.
> Tom: (E) Yes. Better safe than sorry.

15 위 대화의 (A)~(E) 중 주어진 문장이 들어가기에 적절한 곳은?

> No! You might fall and hurt yourself.

① (A) ② (B) ③ (C) ④ (D) ⑤ (E)

16 위 대화의 내용과 일치하도록 빈칸을 완성하시오.

> Although Tom and Emily were late a little for the movie, they agreed that there was nothing more important than _____.

Grammar

17 다음 빈칸에 적절하지 <u>않은</u> 것은?

> The man _____ is sitting there.

① for whom I was looking
② whom I was looking for
③ I was looking for
④ that I was looking for
⑤ for I was looking

18 다음 중 우리말을 영어로 바르게 옮기지 <u>않은</u> 것은?

① Julie는 그 열쇠를 어디에 두어야 할지 확신하지 못해.
   → Julie isn't sure where to put the key.
② 나는 기타 치는 방법을 배우고 싶어.
   → I want to learn how to play the guitar.
③ 친구가 유명한 배우인 그 여자를 아니?
   → Do you know the woman who friend is a famous actor?
④ 많은 학생들이 존경하는 그 선생님은 나의 아버지이다.
   → The teacher whom in many students look up to is my father.
⑤ 나는 그곳에 언제 갈지 결정 못하겠어.
   → I can't decide when to go there.

19 다음 대화의 밑줄 친 ⓑ와 같은 표현을 빈칸 ⓐ에 쓰시오.

> A: Did you answer the question?
> B: No, I didn't. I don't know ⓐ_____. Do you have any idea ⓑ<u>what I should say</u>?

➡ _____

20 다음 빈칸에 들어갈 말이 바르게 짝지어진 것은?

> • What is the title of the book _____ cover is colorful?
> • What is the title of the book _____ you bought last week?

① which – that   ② that – which
③ whose – which   ④ whose – whose
⑤ whose – whom

21 다음 중 어법상 바르지 <u>않은</u> 것은?

> The man ①<u>who</u> ②<u>was</u> wearing a blue suit ③<u>showed me</u> ④<u>where</u> I should ⑤<u>to wash</u> my hands.

22 다음 빈칸에 공통으로 들어갈 말로 가장 적절한 것은?

> • The chair _____ you made is very comfortable.
> • I can't decide _____ dress to buy.

① that ② who ③ whose
④ which ⑤ what

23 다음 빈칸에 적절한 말로 옳은 것을 <u>모두</u> 고르시오.

> The people _____ gathered together are the guests of the party.

① which ② who ③ that
④ whose ⑤ whom

24 주어진 단어와 to부정사를 활용하여 다음 우리말을 영어로 쓰시오.

> 너는 너의 돈을 현명하게 쓰는 법을 알아야 해.
> (should / know / use / to / wisely)

➡ _____

25 다음 중 밑줄 친 부분의 쓰임이 <u>다른</u> 하나는?

① He is not the man <u>who</u> will betray us.
② The boys <u>who</u> took my class are noisy.
③ Do you know the girl <u>who</u> Kevin likes?
④ Jake is the child <u>who</u> had lunch with my son.
⑤ I don't know <u>who</u> he is.

26 적절한 관계사를 이용하여 다음 두 문장을 하나의 문장으로 쓰시오.

> • Where is the ketchup?
> • It was in the refrigerator.

➡ _____

27 빈칸에 공통으로 들어갈 말로 가장 적절한 것은?

> • Mike, _____ do you think about learning it?
> • Please inform me _____ to do next.

① who ② when ③ where
④ how ⑤ what

28 다음 빈칸에 알맞은 말을 쓰시오.

> I can't decide _____ _____ _____ _____.
> 나는 무엇에 대하여 쓸지 결정할 수 없어.

Reading

[29~31] 다음 글을 읽고 물음에 답하시오.

Do you know what to do when an earthquake strikes? Take this quiz and think about ⓐ _____ to be safe during this kind of natural disaster.
1. When things start to shake, run outside quickly. (o / x)
2. Stay away from windows. (o / x)
3. Use the stairs to get out of buildings. (o / x)
4. When you are outside, hold on to a pole or a tree. (o / x)

ⓑ _____ did you do on the quiz? Can you survive an earthquake safely? Here are some safety tips which can be helpful in an earthquake. Let's check them one by one and learn what to do.

29 다음 중 ⓐ와 ⓑ에 공통으로 들어갈 말로 가장 적절한 것은? (대·소문자 무시)

① when   ② what   ③ how
④ where   ⑤ who

30 다음 중 위 글의 내용과 일치하는 것은?

① The passage is about living without natural disasters.
② The quiz is not helpful at all.
③ The writer wants to talk about some safety tips.
④ The quiz is about how to plant trees.
⑤ We can survive an earthquake easily.

31 다음 우리말에 맞게 빈칸에 알맞은 말을 쓰시오.

> • 글쓴이가 우리와 함께 확인하기를 원하는 안전 지침은 지진 발생 시 도움이 될 수 있다.
> = Some _____ _____ _____ the writer wants to check with us _____ _____ _____ in an earthquake.

[32~33] 다음 글을 읽고 물음에 답하시오.

Here are some safety tips which can be helpful in an earthquake. Let's check them one by one and learn what to do.

Don't run outside when things are shaking. Find a table or a desk and take cover under it. You can hold on to the legs to protect yourself. ⓐ_____, stay away from windows. They can break during an earthquake and hurt you.

32 빈칸 ⓐ에 들어갈 말로 가장 적절한 것은?

① However   ② Therefore
③ Moreover   ④ Likewise
⑤ On the other hand

33 다음 중 글의 내용과 일치하지 <u>않는</u> 것은?

① The writer gives us a few safety tips for an earthquake.
② The writer wants readers to check the tips one by one.
③ When things are shaking, we should find a table or a desk.
④ We should jump on the table in an earthquake.
⑤ The writer tells us not to run outside in an earthquake.

[34~35] 다음 글을 읽고 물음에 답하시오.

You can go outside when the shaking stops. ⓐ <u>To get</u> out of buildings, don't use the elevator. Take the stairs. It's much safer. Once you are outside, find an empty space that is far from buildings. There may be people who want to hold on to a pole or a tree, but think again. That's a bad idea because it can fall on you.

34 다음 중 밑줄 친 ⓐ와 쓰임이 같은 것은?

① I want <u>to have</u> some pizza.
② Julia came here <u>to meet</u> me.
③ Do you need anything <u>to wear</u>?
④ It is nice <u>to see</u> you again.
⑤ They encouraged me <u>to try</u> it again.

35 다음 중 글의 내용과 일치하는 것은?

① We can go out anytime we want.
② Using the elevator is safe when we get out of buildings.
③ Taking the stairs is not as safe as using the elevator.
④ When we are outside, we'd better be in an empty space.
⑤ We should not think twice when we want to hold on to something.

출제율 90%

01 다음 대화가 자연스럽게 이어지도록 순서대로 배열하시오.

> (A) You're right. I will.
> (B) I heard about your accident. I was worried about you.
> (C) Thanks. I hurt my hand, but it's not serious. I'll be okay.
> (D) Good. You should watch your hands when you close the door.

➡ _____

출제율 90%

02 주어진 단어를 바르게 배열하여 문장을 완성하시오. 필요하다면 단어를 추가하시오.

> A director of a film _____.
> (what / is / a person / do / who / the actors / tells)

➡ _____

[03~04] 다음 대화를 읽고 물음에 답하시오.

> Tom: Yujin, what's wrong?
> Yujin: (A)내 다리가 걱정돼. It hurts a lot.
> Tom: Why don't you go see a doctor?
> Yujin: I'm going to go after school today.
> Tom: (B)_____
> Yujin: I hope so, too.

출제율 85%

03 위 대화의 우리말 (A)를 영작하시오.

➡ _____

출제율 90%

04 위 대화의 빈칸 (B)에 들어갈 말을 보기에 주어진 단어를 모두 배열하여 완성하시오.

┌─ 보기 ─┐
hope / feel / I / soon / better / you
└────────┘

➡ _____

[05~06] 다음 대화를 읽고 물음에 답하시오.

> Brian: What are you watching?
> Jane: It's a program about earthquakes.
> Brian: Sounds interesting. I'm worried about earthquakes these days.
> Jane: Me, too. This program has some (A) helpful tips.
> Brian: Really? What does it say?
> Jane: When things start to shake, you need to take cover under a table.
> Brian: Oh, I didn't know that.

출제율 100%

05 위 대화의 밑줄 친 (A)와 바꾸어 쓸 수 있는 것은?

① useful   ② handy
③ friendly   ④ generous
⑤ convenient

출제율 90%

06 위 대화의 내용과 일치하도록 Jane의 일기를 완성하시오.

> Mon, April 29th. 2019.
> Today, I watched a program about (A)_____. Because I was concerned about (A)_____ these days, it was so interesting. While I was watching the program, I talked with Brian and gave him (B)_____ for the earthquake safety. The program said that when things around us start to shake, (C)_____.

➡ (A) _____
➡ (B) _____
➡ (C) _____

[07~08] 다음 대화를 읽고 물음에 답하시오.

Jack: Dad, I'm going out ⓐto play basketball with Minu.

Dad: Did you finish ⓑto clean your room?

Jack: No, ⓒnot yet. Can I do it later?

Dad: No. You should clean your room first.

Jack: Okay. I'll clean my room and then ⓓplay basketball.

Dad: Good. Don't forget ⓔto be home by six o'clock.

Jack: Okay.

✏️ 출제율 95%

07 위 대화의 밑줄 친 ⓐ~ⓔ 중 어법상 **틀린** 것을 찾아 바르게 고치시오.

➡ _____

✏️ 출제율 90%

08 위 대화를 읽고 대답할 수 **없는** 것은?

① What is Jack going to do with Minu?
② What does Jack's dad ask him to do before going out?
③ Why does Jack want to clean his room later?
④ What should Jack remember to do?
⑤ By when should Jack be home?

[09~10] 다음 대화를 읽고 물음에 답하시오.

Brian: There was a big fire at the city library yesterday.

Mina (A) Yes, I heard about it. I was worried about the people there.

Brian: (B) Don't worry. Everybody was okay. They all followed the safety rules.

Mina (C) Really? What are the rules?

Brian: (D) Then stay low and escape.

Mina (E) Oh, I didn't know that.

Brian: ⓐ_____ It might be helpful some day.

✏️ 출제율 85%

09 위 대화의 빈칸 ⓐ에 들어갈 말을 보기에 주어진 단어를 모두 배열하여 완성하시오.

┌─ 보기 ─┐
should / keep / mind / in / you / that

➡ _____

✏️ 출제율 90%

10 위 대화의 (A)~(E) 중 주어진 문장이 들어가기에 적절한 곳은?

You need to cover your nose and mouth with a wet towel.

① (A)　② (B)　③ (C)　④ (D)　⑤ (E)

✏️ 출제율 100%

11 빈칸에 공통으로 들어갈 말은?

• The problem is not _____ easy.
• Everything _____ you cooked for me is very delicious.
• I think _____ he wants you to take the taxi.

① what　② who　③ that
④ which　⑤ whom

✏️ 출제율 90%

12 다음 중 뜻이 같은 문장이 **아닌** 것은?

① The girl is showing him where to dig.
　= The girl is showing him where he should dig.
② I know the man. I admire his goal.
　= I know the man who I admire.
③ Tell me when to stand up.
　= Tell me when I should stand up.
④ He called the girl. She lives in Canada.
　= He called the girl who lives in Canada.
⑤ Susan met a girl. Her name is Linda.
　= Susan met a girl whose name is Linda.

13 다음 대화의 빈칸에 알맞은 말을 쓰시오. 출제율 95%

> A: I don't know where I should go.
> B: Don't worry. I will explain to you _____ _____ _____.

14 다음 중 어법상 옳은 것을 바르게 묶은 것은? 출제율 90%

> ⓐ The music which I listened to last night was popular in the 2000s.
> ⓑ The dress Amelia is wearing is mine.
> ⓒ In our town, there are people don't have their own gardens.
> ⓓ Thomas actually enjoyed playing the game we did it together.
> ⓔ Mr. Thomson teaches a subject which I am really into.

① ⓐ, ⓑ, ⓓ   ② ⓐ, ⓑ, ⓔ
③ ⓑ, ⓒ, ⓓ   ④ ⓑ, ⓒ, ⓔ
⑤ ⓒ, ⓓ, ⓔ

15 다음 중 어법상 바르지 않은 것은? 출제율 100%

① The man is holding a mug that is expensive.
② People who do taekwondo wear white uniforms.
③ Bradley wanted me to tell him where to park the car.
④ It teaches you how you to protect yourself.
⑤ The students who won the group jump rope felt excited.

16 다음 빈칸에 공통으로 들어갈 말은? 출제율 95%

> • The couple _____ adopted the child are happy now.
> • The goldfish _____ is in the fishbowl looks so cute.

① which   ② that   ③ whom
④ what   ⑤ whose

17 주어진 단어를 활용하여 다음 우리말을 영어로 쓰시오. 출제율 90%

> 나와 함께 대화를 나눈 그 사람은 내게 좋은 조언을 해주었다.
> (talk with / give / advice)

➡ _____

_____

[18~20] 다음 글을 읽고 물음에 답하시오.

> How did you do on the quiz? Can you survive an earthquake safely? Here are some safety tips ⓐ_____ can be helpful in an earthquake. Let's check (A)[it / them] one by one and learn what to do.
>
> Don't run outside when things are shaking. Find a table or a desk and take cover under it. You can hold on to the legs to protect (B)[you / yourself]. Also, stay away from windows. They can break (C)[during / while] an earthquake and hurt you.

18 다음 중 빈칸 ⓐ에 들어갈 말과 다른 것은? 출제율 90%

① The key _____ you put on the table is lost.
② He bought a bike _____ is similar to mine.
③ Bony is the girl _____ I like most.
④ Do you know the car _____ handle is broken?
⑤ Cathy has a dog _____ looks very cute.

✏️ 출제율 100%

19 (A)~(C) 중 어법상 옳은 것끼리 바르게 짝지은 것은?

① it – you – during
② them – you – while
③ them – yourself – during
④ them – yourself – while
⑤ it – you – while

✏️ 출제율 90%

20 다음 대화의 빈칸에 해당하는 말을 위 글에서 찾아 쓰시오.

> A: Things start to shake. I think an earthquake strikes. I don't know where to hide.
>
> B: _____.

[21~25] 다음 글을 읽고 물음에 답하시오.

> You can go outside when the shaking stops. To get out of buildings, don't use the elevator. ① Take the stairs. ⓐIt's much safer. Once you are outside, find an empty space ⓑthat is far from buildings. ② There ⓒmay be people who want to ⓓhold on to a pole or a tree, but think again. ③ That's a bad idea (A)because it can fall on you. ④
>
> Earthquakes can strike ⓔanytime. ⑤ So learn how to be safe in an earthquake. You can avoid injuries and protect yourself. Follow these tips and be safe!

✏️ 출제율 95%

21 ①~⑤ 중 주어진 문장이 들어가기에 가장 적절한 곳은?

> They can be scary experiences for everyone.

①   ②   ③   ④   ⑤

✏️ 출제율 90%

22 밑줄 친 (A)를 대신하여 쓰일 수 있는 것을 모두 고르시오.

① since   ② when   ③ although
④ as   ⑤ while

✏️ 출제율 90%

23 다음 중 위 글을 읽고 답할 수 없는 것은?

① When can we go outside?
② How can we get out of buildings safely?
③ Why do people hold on to something?
④ Why is holding on to a tree a bad idea?
⑤ What should we do first once we are outside?

✏️ 출제율 85%

24 위 글의 내용에 맞게 다음 빈칸에 알맞은 말을 쓰시오.

> A: I don't know _____ _____ _____ myself when an earthquake strikes.
>
> B: You can protect yourself by following some tips.

✏️ 출제율 90%

25 ⓐ~ⓔ에 대한 설명 중 바른 것은?

① ⓐ: 엘리베이터를 이용하는 것을 의미한다.
② ⓑ: 주격 관계대명사로 쓰였으므로 who로 대체 가능하다
③ ⓒ: '~해도 좋다'는 허가를 의미한다.
④ ⓓ: '~을 고수하다'는 의미이다.
⑤ ⓔ: 'at any time'으로 바꾸어 쓸 수 있다.

[01~03] 다음 대화를 읽고 물음에 답하시오.

> **Tom:** Yujin, what's @wrong?
>
> **Yujin:** I'm ⓑworrying about my leg. It hurts a lot.
>
> **Tom:** Why don't you go ©see a doctor?
>
> **Yujin:** I'm going to go after school today.
>
> **Tom:** I hope you feel ⓓbetter soon.
>
> **Yujin:** I hope ⓔso, too.

01 위 대화의 밑줄 친 @~ⓔ 중 어법상 틀린 것을 찾아 바르게 고치시오.

➡ _____

02 What is Yujin concerned about?

➡ _____

03 What is Yujin going to do after school?

➡ _____

04 주어진 단어를 바르게 배열하여 다음 우리말을 영어로 쓰시오.

> 나는 나와 함께 일하는 사람들을 좋아해.
> (with / like / work / I / the people / I / whom)

➡ _____

05 주어진 어구를 이용하여 다음 우리말을 두 가지의 영어 문장으로 쓰시오.

> 졸업 후에 무엇을 해야 할지 나는 잘 모르겠어.
> (graduation)

➡ I'm not sure _____

➡ I'm not sure _____

06 〈보기〉와 같이 하나의 문장을 두 개의 문장으로 쓰시오.

> ┤ 보기 ├
> The people who moved in our apartment enjoy talking loudly in the morning.
> ➡ The people enjoy talking loudly in the morning.
> ➡ They moved in our apartment.

(1) I want to have the cheese cake which is sold only online.

➡ _____

➡ _____

(2) Where is the cap that was in the closet?

➡ _____

➡ _____

07 다음 대화의 우리말을 주어진 단어를 사용하여 영작하시오.

> **A:** I heard about your accident.
> (A)나는 네가 걱정돼. (worried)
> **B:** Thanks. I hurt my hand, but it's not serious. I'll be okay.
> **A:** Good. (B)너는 칼을 사용할 때 손을 조심해야 해. (should, watch, hands, when)

➡ (A) _____

➡ (B) _____

08 다음 빈칸에 알맞은 말을 쓰시오.

> **A:** Can you teach me _____ _____ _____ step by step? Because I am not good at dancing.
> **B:** Oh, sure. I will teach you how you should dance.

You can go outside when the shaking stops. To get out of buildings, don't use the elevator. Take the stairs. It's much safer. Once you are outside, find an empty space that is far from buildings. (A)There may be people who want to hold on to a pole or a tree, but think again. (B)That's a bad idea because it can fall on you.

Earthquakes can (C)_____ anytime. They can be scary experiences for everyone. So learn how to be safe in an earthquake. You can (D)_____ injuries and (E)_____ yourself. (F)_____ these tips and be safe!

09 밑줄 친 (A)를 두 개의 문장으로 나누어 쓰시오.

➡ _____

➡ _____

10 밑줄 친 (B)가 의미하는 것을 우리말로 쓰시오.

➡ _____

11 주어진 동사를 어법과 문맥에 맞게 빈칸 (C)~(F)에 각각 쓰시오.

| follow / protect / strike / avoid |

➡ (C) _____ (D) _____
(E) _____ (F) _____

12 주어진 단어를 바르게 배열하여 다음 물음에 답하시오.

Q: When the shaking stops, how should you get out of buildings?
A: (safer / we / much / is / it / should / because / stairs / the / use)

➡ _____

13 위 글에서 다음 물음에 대한 답을 찾아 완전한 문장의 영어로 답하시오.

Q: What can we learn from the passage?

➡ _____

Here are some safety tips which can be helpful in an earthquake. Let's check them one by one and learn what to do.

Don't run outside when things are shaking. Find a table or a desk and take cover under it. You can hold on to the legs to protect yourself. ⓐ_____, stay away from windows. They can break during an earthquake and hurt you.

14 Write the reason why we need to stay away from windows.

➡ _____

15 위 글의 내용에 맞게 빈칸에 알맞은 말을 위 글에서 찾아 쓰시오.

The tips _____ the writer gives to readers are _____.

➡ _____

01 다음 대화의 내용과 일치하도록 Mina의 일기를 완성하시오.

> Brian: There was a big fire at the city library yesterday.
> Mina: Yes, I heard about it. I was worried about the people there.
> Brian: Don't worry. Everybody was okay. They all followed the safety rules.
> Mina: Really? What are the rules?
> Brian: You need to cover your nose and mouth with a wet towel. Then stay low and escape.
> Mina: Oh, I didn't know that.
> Brian: You should keep that in mind. It might be helpful some day.

> Tue, May 7th, 2019
> I heard that there was a big fire at the city library yesterday. I talked about it with Brian. I was concerned about (A)_____. Brian told me that everybody was safe because (B)_____. Frankly speaking, I didn't know what to do in the event of a fire. Brian told me that I should (C)_____, then stay low and escape. I kept that in mind. Moreover, I decided to study more about the safety rules.

02 주어진 동사와 '의문사+to부정사'를 이용하여 문장을 만드시오.

> prepare / cook / go / meet / buy

(1) _____
(2) _____
(3) _____
(4) _____
(5) _____

03 〈보기〉와 같이 관계대명사를 이용하여 다음 직업을 설명하는 문장을 쓰시오.

> ▍보기 ▍
> A carpenter is a person who makes and repairs wooden things.
> pilot / nurse / architect / dentist / farmer

(1) _____
(2) _____
(3) _____
(4) _____
(5) _____

단원별 모의고사

01 다음 영영풀이가 가리키는 것을 고르시오.

> short, quick movement back and forth or up and down

① protect   ② hurt   ③ shake
④ cover   ⑤ change

02 다음 주어진 문장의 밑줄 친 fall과 같은 의미로 쓰인 것은?

> Be careful! You might <u>fall</u> and hurt yourself.

① The leaves were starting to <u>fall</u>.
② I visited Canada in the <u>fall</u> of 2018.
③ Do you love the weather of <u>fall</u>?
④ The <u>fall</u> term just started in the United States.
⑤ Have you ever seen Niagara <u>Falls</u>?

03 다음 문장에 공통으로 들어갈 말을 고르시오.

> • Let's take a _____. We need to get some rest.
> • If you drop the cup, it'll _____ into pieces.
> • Do you think he can _____ a record at the Olympics?

① escape   ② solve   ③ break
④ slip   ⑤ strike

04 다음 대화가 자연스럽게 이어지도록 순서대로 배열하시오.

> (A) It starts at 4:30.
> (B) You're right. We can be a little late.
> (C) What time is the movie?
> (D) Oh, no. We only have 20 minutes left. Let's run!
> (E) No! You might fall and hurt yourself. You should walk on the stairs.

➡ _____

05 다음 주어진 단어를 이용하여 우리말을 영작하시오.

(1) 어떻게 우리는 자연 재해에 대비할 수 있을까요? (how / prepare / natural)

➡ _____

(2) 지진이 발생할 때, 건물들이 흔들리거나 무너질 수 있다. (strikes / down)

➡ _____

(3) 계단에서 뛰지 마세요. 넘어지거나 다칠 수 있어요. (on / might / get)

➡ _____

[06~08] 다음 대화를 읽고 물음에 답하시오.

Brian: What are you watching?
Jane: It's a program about earthquakes.
Brian: Sounds interesting. I'm worried about earthquakes these days.
Jane: Me, too. This program has some helpful (A)<u>tips</u>.
Brian: Really? What does it say?
Jane: When things start to shake, you need to take cover under a table.
Brian: Oh, I didn't know (B)<u>that</u>.

06 위 대화에서 다음 영영풀이가 가리키는 말을 찾아 쓰시오.

> a shaking of a part of the Earth's surface that often causes great damage

➡ _____

07 위 대화의 밑줄 친 (A)와 바꾸어 쓸 수 있는 것을 모두 고르시오.

① data ② information
③ guidance ④ report
⑤ material

08 위 대화의 밑줄 친 (B)가 가리키는 것을 우리말로 20자 이내로 설명하시오.

➡ _____

09 다음 대화의 내용과 일치하도록 빈칸을 완성하시오.

> Jack: Dad, I'm going out to play basketball with Minu.
> Dad: Did you finish cleaning your room?
> Jack: No, not yet. Can I do it later?
> Dad: No. You should clean your room first.
> Jack: Okay. I'll clean my room and then play basketball.
> Dad: Good. Don't forget to be home by six o'clock.
> Jack: Okay.

⬇

> Jack was supposed to (A)_____. His dad told him to (B)_____ first before going out, but he wanted to put it off. But his dad requested him to do it first, so Jack decided to clean his room. Going out to play basketball, Jack promised to (C)_____.

➡ (A) _____
  (B) _____
  (C) _____

10 다음 대화의 내용과 일치하지 않는 것은?

> Sujin: It's raining. I'm worried about our picnic in the afternoon.
> Mom: It is going to rain until late afternoon today. You should go another day.
> Sujin: You're right, Mom. I'll call my friend and choose another day.

① 수진은 오후에 있을 소풍을 걱정하고 있다.
② 오늘 오후 늦게까지 비가 올 것이다.
③ 엄마는 다른 날 소풍 가는 것이 좋을 것이라고 충고하였다.
④ 수진은 엄마의 충고를 받아들였다.
⑤ 수진은 친구에게 전화해서 오후에 소풍을 갈 것이다.

11 다음 밑줄 친 ⓐ~ⓔ 중 어색한 것을 골라 바르게 고치시오.

> A: I heard about your ⓐaccidental. I was ⓑworried about you.
> B: Thanks. I hurt my hand, but it's not ⓒserious. I'll be okay.
> A: Good. You should ⓓwatch your hands when you ⓔclose the door.
> B: You're right. I will.

➡ _____

12 다음 중 짝지어진 대화가 어색한 것은?

① A: It's raining a lot outside.
  B: I think you should take an umbrella.
② A: The floor is slippery.
  B: I like your bed slippers.
③ A: I'm going to ride my bike.
  B: How about bring your helmet?
④ A: I have a bad cold.
  B: Why don't you go see a doctor?
⑤ A: I'm worried about the storm.
  B: You'd better stay inside.

13 주어진 문장의 빈칸에 들어갈 말과 <u>다른</u> 하나는?

> There were many children _____ knew what to do in the public place.

① Look at the house _____ has large windows.

② Shakespeare wrote many plays _____ are read all over the world.

③ I have two sisters _____ I should take care of.

④ That is the boy _____ sister won the first prize.

⑤ There was a dog _____ was looking after its babies.

14 다음 우리말을 바르게 영작한 것을 <u>모두</u> 고르시오.

> 나는 눈이 큰 저 소녀를 안다.

① I know the girl which has big eyes.

② I know the girl whose eyes are big.

③ I know the girl who is big eyes.

④ I know the girl that eyes are big.

⑤ I know the girl who has big eyes.

15 다음 우리말에 맞게 빈칸에 알맞은 말을 쓰시오.

> 무엇을 먹을지 결정하는 건 쉬운 일이 아니다.
> It is not easy to _____ _____ _____ .

16 주어진 단어를 바르게 배열하여 다음 문장을 완성하시오.

> Monday _____ Tuesday.
> (before / that / the / comes / day / is)

➡ _____

17 다음 빈칸에 적절한 관계대명사를 바르게 배열한 것은?

> • I met a boy _____ could speak many languages.
> • This is a picture of my brother _____ life is full of adventure.

① that – whom   ② who – that

③ that – whose   ④ whose – whose

⑤ what – that

[18~20] 다음 글을 읽고 물음에 답하시오.

> Do you know what to do when an earthquake strikes? Take this quiz and think about how to be safe during this kind of natural disaster.
> 1. When things start to shake, run outside (A) [quick / quickly]. (o / x)
> 2. Stay away (B)[from / in] windows. (o / x)
> 3. Use the stairs (C)[getting / to get] out of buildings. (o / x)
> 4. When you are outside, hold on to a pole or a tree. (o / x)
> How did you do on the quiz? Can you survive an earthquake safely? Here are some safety tips which can be helpful in an earthquake. Let's check them one by one and learn what to do.

18 (A)~(C) 중 어법상 옳은 것끼리 바르게 짝지어진 것은?

① quick – from – getting

② quickly – in – getting

③ quick – in – to getting

④ quickly – from – to get

⑤ quick – in – to get

19 위 글의 내용에 맞게 다음 빈칸에 알맞은 말을 쓰시오.

> _____ the quiz helps us think about
>
> _____ _____ _____ _____
>
> when an earthquake _____.

20 다음 중 위 글의 내용과 일치하지 <u>않는</u> 것은?

① An earthquake is a natural disaster.

② The writer will talk about some safety tips in an earthquake.

③ Safety tips can be useful to readers.

④ The quiz is about safety rules in school.

⑤ By checking the tips, readers can learn what they should do in an earthquake.

[21~23] 다음 글을 읽고 물음에 답하시오.

Don't run outside when things are shaking. Find a table or a desk and take cover under it. You can hold on to the legs to protect yourself. (A)_____, stay away from windows. They can break during an earthquake and hurt you.

You can go outside when the shaking stops. To get out of buildings, don't use the elevator. Take the stairs. It's much safer. Once you are outside, find an empty space that is far from buildings. There may be people who want to hold on to a pole or a tree, but think again. That's a bad idea because it can fall on you.

21 다음 중 빈칸 (A)에 들어갈 말로 가장 적절한 것은?

① However   ② Therefore

③ In addition   ④ In other words

⑤ Otherwise

22 다음 중 위 글의 내용과 일치하는 것의 개수는?

> ⓐ Although things stop shaking, you should stay inside.
> ⓑ When things are shaking, we should find a table or a desk.
> ⓒ Windows can be dangerous during an earthquake.
> ⓓ After getting out of buildings, we stay close to the buildings.
> ⓔ Finding an empty place is the first thing to do when we are outside.

① 1개   ② 2개   ③ 3개

④ 4개   ⑤ 5개

23 위 글의 내용에 맞도록 다음 물음에 완전한 문장의 영어로 답하시오.

> Q: To protect yourself under a table, what can you hold on to?

➡ _____

[24~25] 다음 글을 읽고 물음에 답하시오.

Darlene Etienne, a 16-year-old girl, survived the earthquake that hit Haiti in 2010. People found her 15 days after the earthquake struck. They think that she possibly survived by (A) _____ bath water.

24 주어진 단어를 어법에 맞게 빈칸 (A)에 쓰시오.

> drink

➡ _____

25 위 글의 내용과 일치하지 <u>않는</u> 것은?

① There was an earthquake in Haiti in 2010.

② Darlene was 16 years old in 2010.

③ Darlene was not found for more than two weeks.

④ Darlene is a survivor from an earthquake.

⑤ The earthquake continued for 15 days.

Happy Others, Happier Me

의사소통 기능

- 도움 제안하기
  Let me help you.
- 칭찬에 답하기
  I'm glad you like(d) it.

언어 형식

- 목적격 관계대명사
  Here are two stories **which** I read yesterday.
- to부정사를 목적격보어로 취하는 동사
  She **asked** him **to do** the job.

Words & Expressions

Key Words

- **activity** [æktívəti] 명 활동
- **arrow** [ǽrou] 명 화살, 화살표
- **avoid** [əvɔ́id] 동 피하다
- **basket** [bǽskit] 명 바구니
- **bus stop** 버스 정류장
- **children's center** 아동 센터
- **coin** [kɔin] 명 동전
- **confusing** [kənfjúːziŋ] 형 혼란스러운
- **danger** [déindʒər] 명 위험
- **decide** [disáid] 동 결심하다
- **different** [dífərənt] 형 다른
- **disappear** [dìsəpíər] 동 사라지다
- **effort** [éfərt] 명 노력
- **explain** [ikspléin] 동 설명하다
- **few** [fjuː] 형 몇몇의
- **forget** [fərɡét] 동 잊어버리다
- **frame** [freim] 명 틀, 테
- **free** [friː] 형 무료의
- **glad** [ɡlæd] 형 기쁜
- **hear** [hiər] 동 듣다
- **map** [mæp] 명 지도
- **mentee** [mentíː] 명 멘티

- **mentor** [méntɔːr] 명 멘토
- **need** [niːd] 동 필요로 하다
- **outside** [áutsàid] 형 바깥의, 외부의
- **pay phone** 공중전화
- **plan** [plæn] 동 …하려고 계획하다
- **plastic bag** 비닐봉지
- **possible** [pásəbl] 형 가능한
- **refrigerator** [rifrídʒərèitər] 명 냉장고
- **rest** [rest] 동 쉬다, 휴식하다
- **say** [sei] 동 (글·글씨 등이) 쓰이다
- **secret** [síːkrit] 명 비밀, 비결 형 비밀의
- **sign** [sain] 명 표지판
- **soap** [soup] 명 비누
- **solution** [səlúːʃən] 명 해결책
- **solve** [sɑlv] 동 해결하다
- **start** [stɑːrt] 동 시작하다
- **sticker** [stíkər] 명 딱지, 스티커
- **street** [striːt] 명 거리
- **success** [səksés] 명 성공
- **trash** [træʃ] 명 쓰레기
- **volunteer club** 자원 봉사 동아리
- **wonderful** [wʌ́ndərfəl] 형 훌륭한, 굉장한

Key Expressions

- **come up with** (생각을) 찾아내다, 제시하다
- **during the day** 낮 동안
- **give it a try** 시도하다, 한번 해 보다
- **give out** …을 나누어 주다
- **have to** …해야 한다
- **on one's own** 자기 스스로

- **one day** (과거의) 어느 날
- **put up** 설치하다, 세우다
- **stop -ing** …하는 것을 멈추다
- **thanks to** … 덕분에
- **the other day** 며칠 전에, 지난번, 요전에
- **waste one's time** …의 시간을 낭비하다

Word Power

※ 서로 반대되는 뜻을 가진 어휘

- ☐ **mentor** 멘토 ↔ **m** ☐ **same** 같은 ↔ **different** 다른
- ☐ **forget** 잊어버리다 ↔ **remember** 기억하다
- ☐ **success** 성공 ↔ **failure** 실패
- ☐ **start** 시작하다 ↔ **finish** 끝내다
- ☐ **danger** 위험 ↔ **safety** 안전

- ☐ **outside** 바깥의 ↔ **inside** 안쪽의
- ☐ **possible** 가능한 ↔ **impossible** 불가능한
- ☐ **free** 한가한 ↔ **busy** 바쁜

※ 동사 – 명사

- ☐ **succeed** 성공하다 — **success** 성공
- ☐ **fail** 실패하다 — **failure** 실패

- ☐ **advise** 충고하다 — **advice** 충고
- ☐ **solve** 해결하다 — **solution** 해결

English Dictionary

☐ **activity** 활동
→ something that is done as work for a particular purpose 특별한 목적을 위한 일로 이루어지는 것

☐ **arrow** 화살표
→ a mark that is shaped like an arrow and that is used to show direction
화살과 같은 모양으로 방향을 보여주기 위해 사용되는 표시

☐ **confusing** 혼란스러운
→ difficult to understand 이해하기 어려운

☐ **disappear** 사라지다
→ to stop being visible 보여지는 것이 멈추다

☐ **few** 몇몇의
→ not many, but some 많지 않은, 그러나 약간 있는

☐ **free** 무료의
→ not costing any money 어떠한 돈도 들지 않는

☐ **hear** 듣다
→ to be aware of sounds with your ears
당신의 귀로 소리를 인식하다

☐ **map** 지도
→ a drawing or plan of the earth's surface or part of it, showing countries, town, rivers, etc.
국가, 마을, 강 등을 보여주는 지구의 표면 또는 그것의 일부의 그림이나 도면

☐ **mentee** 멘티
→ a person who is advised and helped by a more experienced person
좀 더 경험이 있는 사람에 의해 조언을 받거나 도움을 받는 사람

☐ **montor** 멘토
→ someone who teaches or gives help and advice to a less experienced and often younger person
경험이 별로 없거나 종종 어린 사람에게 도움이나 조언을 주거나 가르치는 사람

☐ **refrigerator** 냉장고
→ a device or room that is used to keep things cold
사물들을 차갑게 유지하기 위해 사용되는 장치나 공간

☐ **secret** 비밀의
→ kept hidden from others 다른 사람들로부터 숨겨진

☐ **sign** 표지판
→ a piece of paper, wood, etc., with words or pictures on it that gives information about something
어떤 것에 관한 정보를 제공하는 글귀나 사진들이 위에 있는 종이, 나무 등의 조각

☐ **success** 성공
→ the correct or desired result of an attempt
어떤 시도의 정확하거나 바람직한 결과

☐ **start** 시작하다
→ to begin doing or using something
무언가를 하거나 사용하기 시작하다

01 다음 영영풀이가 나타내는 말을 고르시오.

> a drawing or plan of the earth's surface or part of it, showing countries, towns, rivers, etc.

① arrow   ② map
③ effort   ④ soap
⑤ activity

02 다음 문장에 공통으로 들어갈 말을 고르시오.

> • What does the card _____?
> • Will you _____ what you mean simply?
> • I disagree with what you _____.

① tell   ② write
③ say   ④ hear
⑤ listen

03 중요 다음 중 밑줄 친 부분의 뜻풀이가 바르지 <u>않은</u> 것은?

① The <u>sign</u> in the store window says 'OPEN'. 서명
② The moon <u>disappeared</u> behind a cloud.
             사라졌다
③ Nobody else knows about this place because it's our <u>secret</u> place.
        비밀의
④ The <u>arrow</u> on the sign points north.
        화살표
⑤ We did a fun <u>activity</u> at an English camp.
        활동

04 서답형 다음 짝지어진 단어의 관계가 같도록 빈칸에 알맞은 말을 쓰시오.

> low: high = _____ : safety

05 다음 주어진 문장의 밑줄 친 free와 같은 의미로 쓰인 것은?

> • Hojun and I planned to give out <u>free</u> stickers today.

① I was so happy because I received <u>free</u> tickets.
② Each student has a <u>free</u> choice of course.
③ What do you like to do in your <u>free</u> time?
④ <u>Free</u> speech is one of the features of democracy.
⑤ Let's set <u>free</u> a bird from a cage.

06 서답형 다음 문장의 빈칸에 들어갈 말을 보기에서 골라 쓰시오.

> ┤ 보기 ├
> confusing / secret / soap / decide

(1) The road sign was really _____.
(2) You can _____ if you'll stay here or not.
(3) My sister made the _____ using the natural oil.
(4) The _____ to my health is to exercise regularly.

01 다음 짝지어진 단어의 관계가 같도록 빈칸에 알맞은 말을 쓰시오.

success : failure = possible : _____

02 다음 대화의 빈칸에 보기에 주어진 단어를 알맞게 채워 넣으시오.

┤ 보기 ├
help / try / glad / good / tip

A: I'm not (A)_____ at science. What can I do?
B: Let me (B)_____ you. Why don't you start with easier books?
A: Okay, I'll give it a (C)_____. Thanks for the (D)_____.
B: No problem. I'm (E)_____ you like it.

03 다음 주어진 우리말과 일치하도록 주어진 단어를 모두 배열하여 문장을 완성하시오.

(1) 그는 집 앞에 'For Sale' 표지판을 세웠다.
(a 'For Sale' / put / in / of / his / he / house / up / sign / front)
➡ _____

(2) 나는 그의 도움 덕택에 이 일을 일찍 끝냈다.
(thanks / this / work / earlier / finished / I / his / to / help)
➡ _____

(3) 우리는 우리 스스로 숙제를 해야 한다.
(on / we / own / our / homework / do / our / have / to)
➡ _____

04 다음 우리말에 맞게 빈칸에 알맞은 말을 쓰시오.

(1) 네 도움 덕분에 우리는 그 일을 마칠 수 있었다.
➡ _____ _____ your help, we could finish the work.

(2) 며칠 전에 엄마는 내게 쿠키를 구워 주셨다.
➡ My mother baked cookies for me _____ _____ _____ _____.

(3) 우리 견본을 좀 나누어 주는 게 어때?
➡ Why don't we _____ _____ some samples?

05 다음 문장의 빈칸에 들어갈 말을 보기에서 골라 쓰시오.

┤ 보기 ├
give out / come up with / put up / one day

(1) We'll _____ free umbrellas on a rainy day.
(2) She will _____ a new idea for our club.
(3) We _____ the poster on the window.
(4) _____, all dinosaurs disappeared completely.

06 다음 영영풀이가 나타내는 말을 찾아 쓰시오.

a piece of paper, wood, etc., with words or pictures on it that gives information about something

➡ _____

1 도움 제안하기

> **Let me help you.** 내가 도와줄게.

■ 상대방에게 도움을 제안하고자 할 때 'Let me help you.', 'I'll help you.' 또는 'I'll give you a hand.' 등으로 표현할 수 있다.

도움 요청하기

- Would you help me out? (나를 좀 도와주시겠어요?)
- Could you do something for me? (저를 좀 도와주시겠습니까?)
- Would you give me a hand? (저 좀 도와주시겠어요?)
- Would you mind helping me? (좀 도와주시겠습니까?)

도움 제안하기

- Let me help you. (내가 도와줄게.)
- Would you like me to help you? (내가 너를 도와주길 원하니?)
- Do you need any help? (도움이 필요하세요?)
- Can I give you a hand? (도와 드릴까요?)
- May I help you? (제가 도와드릴까요?)
- How can I help you? (무엇을 도와드릴까요?)
- I'll help you. (제가 도와드릴게요.)

핵심 Check

1. 다음 우리말과 일치하도록 빈칸에 알맞은 말을 쓰시오.

   A: I don't have a bottle-opener. I can't open the bottle.

   B: Let _____ _____ _____. (내가 도와드릴게요.)

2. 다음 우리말과 일치하도록 빈칸에 알맞은 말을 쓰시오.

   A: _____ _____ _____ _____ _____? (도움이 필요하신가요?)

   B: Yes. I can't fix the light. It's too high.

3. 다음 우리말과 일치하도록 빈칸에 알맞은 말을 쓰시오.

   A: I can't swim here. It's too _____. (여기서 수영을 못하겠어요. 너무 깊어요.)

   B: _____ _____. I'll _____ _____. (걱정 마세요. 제가 도와드릴게요.)

② 칭찬에 답하기

I'm glad you like it. 네가 그것을 좋아한다니 나도 기뻐.

■ 'I'm glad you like(d) it.'은 '네가 그것을 좋아한[했]다니 나도 기뻐.' 라는 뜻으로 자신이 상대방에게 해 준 일에 관해 칭찬의 말을 들었을 때 답하는 표현이다.

칭찬에 답하기

- My pleasure. (저도 기뻐요.)
- Not at all. (별 말씀을요.)
- You're welcome. (천만에요.)
- Don't mention it. (별 말씀을요.)
- I'm glad[happy, pleased] to hear that. (그 말을 들으니 기쁩니다.)
- You're so kind to say that. (그렇게 말해 주시다니 참 친절하시군요.)
- Thank you for saying so. (그렇게 말해 주셔서 감사합니다.)

핵심 Check

4. 다음 우리말과 일치하도록 빈칸에 알맞은 말을 쓰시오.

   A: It's a wonderful picture. I like it. (훌륭한 그림이야. 나는 그게 마음에 들어.)

   B: I'm _____ _____ _____ _____. (네가 그것을 좋아한다니 나도 기뻐.)

5. 다음 우리말과 일치하도록 빈칸에 알맞은 말을 쓰시오.

   A: How nice! I really like this scarf. (멋지다! 나 이 스카프가 정말 마음에 들어.)

   B: _____ _____. (저도 기뻐요.)

6. 다음 우리말과 일치하도록 빈칸에 알맞은 말을 쓰시오.

   A: What a great story! (정말 훌륭한 이야기예요!)

   B: Thank you _____ _____ _____. (그렇게 말해 주시니 감사합니다.)

A. Listen and Speak 1 A

Tom: Hojun and I planned to ❶give out free stickers today, but I think he forgot.

Sora: Really? ❷Let me help you then. Why are you going to give out stickers?

Tom: It's part of our ❸volunteer club activity.

Sora: ❹I see. What does this sticker mean?

Tom: It means that when we smile at ❺each other, the world will become a better place.

Sora: That's a wonderful idea.

Tom: 호준이와 나는 오늘 무료 스티커를 나눠주기로 계획 했는데 호준이가 잊어버린 것 같아.

Sora: 그래? 그럼 내가 도와줄 게. 너희는 스티커를 왜 나 눠주려고 하니?

Tom: 그건 우리 자원봉사 동아 리 활동의 일부야.

Sora: 그렇구나. 이 스티커는 무 엇을 의미하니?

Tom: 그건 우리가 서로에게 미 소 지을 때, 세상이 더 좋 은 곳이 될 거라는 의미야.

Sora: 그거 멋진 아이디어구나.

❶ give out: ~을 나누어 주다
❷ Let me help you then.: 그러면 내가 도와줄게.
❸ volunteer club: 자원봉사 동아리
❹ I see.: 알겠어.
❺ each other: 서로

Check(√) True or False

(1) Sora is going to help Tom.   T ☐   F ☐

(2) Sora already knew the meaning of the sticker.   T ☐   F ☐

B. Real Life Communication

Emily: Welcome back, Brian. Are you feeling better?

Brian: Yes, thanks. I tried to study ❶on my own in the hospital, but it was hard.

Emily: Let me help you. ❷Why don't you join my study group?

Brian: Did you start a ❸study group? That's wonderful.

Emily: Thanks. I think that we can learn better when we teach each other.

Brian: I agree. I'll try hard to be a good member. Thanks for helping me.

Emily: You're welcome. ❹I'm glad you like my idea.

Emily: 돌아온 걸 환영해, Brian. 좀 나아졌니?

Brian: 응, 고마워. 나는 병원에 서 혼자 공부하려고 했는 데, 어려웠어.

Emily: 내가 도와줄게. 우리 스 터디 모임에 함께 하는 게 어때?

Brian: 스터디 모임을 시작했 니? 그거 멋지다.

Emily: 고마워. 나는 우리가 서 로를 가르쳐주면 더 잘 배울 수 있을 거라고 생 각해.

Brian: 맞아. 나는 좋은 구성원 이 되려고 열심히 노력할 게. 도와줘서 고마워.

Emily: 천만에. 내 아이디어를 좋아해줘서 나도 기뻐.

❶ on one's own: 자기 스스로
❷ Why don't you ~?: 너는 ~하는 게 어때?
❸ study group: 공부 모임
❹ I'm glad you like my idea.: 상대방의 칭찬에 대답하는 표현이다.

Check(√) True or False

(3) Brian came back to school from the hospital.   T ☐   F ☐

(4) Brian isn't going to join Emily's study group.   T ☐   F ☐

Listen and Speak 1 B

Mike: Jimin, what are all these things in the box?

Jimin: They're for my ❶mentee at the ❷ children's center. I'm going to give her my old books today.

Mike: Do you teach ❸her every weekend?

Jimin: Yes. I feel happy when I teach her.

Mike: ❹You are a good mentor. Oh, the box looks heavy. Let me help you.

Jimin: Thanks.

❶ mentee (멘티) ↔ mentor (멘토)
❷ children's center: 아동 센터
❸ Jimin의 mentee를 가리킨다.
❹ Jimin을 칭찬하는 표현이다.

Listen and Speak 2 B

Yujin: I read a story about a special boy in India. Do you want to hear about ❶it?

Jack: Sure. Why is he special, Yujin?

Yujin: Many children in his town couldn't go to school and ❷had to work. So he taught ❸them in his house every day.

Jack: That's a great story.

Yujin: I'm glad you like it.

❶ a story about a special boy in India를 가리킨다.
❷ had to: ~해야 했다(have to의 과거형)
❸ many children in his town을 가리킨다.

Listen and Speak 2-A

Alex: Mom, ❶this is for you. I made it with plastic bags.

Mom: That's very cute, Alex. How did you know that I needed a new basket?

Alex: You talked about ❷it when we were having dinner ❸the other day.

Mom: ❹How nice! I really like this basket. It has many different colors.

Alex: I'm glad you like it.

❶ 'This is for you.'는 상대방에게 선물 등을 줄 때 쓰는 표현이다.
❷ a new basket을 가리킨다.
❸ the other day: 며칠 전, 요전날
❹ How nice!: '정말 마음에 든다!'라는 표현으로 감탄문 형식으로 쓰였다. 원래의 표현은 How nice this basket is!이며 '주어+동사' 뒷부분이 생략된 형태이다.

Let's Check

Henry: Your bag looks heavy. Let me help you.

Sujin: Thanks. Where is the ❶bus stop around here?

Henry: ❷It's over there. I'll carry your bag to the bus stop for you.

Sujin: ❸You're very kind.

Henry: ❹No problem. I am going that way, too.

❶ bus stop: 버스 정류장
❷ It's over there.: 그것은 저쪽에 있어.
❸ Henry의 도움에 칭찬하는 표현이다.
❹ '별말씀을요.'의 뜻으로 칭찬에 답하는 표현이다.

● 다음 우리말과 일치하도록 빈칸에 알맞은 말을 쓰시오.

Listen & Speak 1 A

Tom: Hojun and I planned to _____ _____ free stickers today, but I think he forgot.

Sora: Really? _____ _____ _____ _____ _____. Why are you going to give out stickers?

Tom: It's part of our _____ _____ _____.

Sora: I see. What does this sticker _____?

Tom: _____ _____ _____ when we smile at _____ _____, the world will become a _____.

Sora: That's a wonderful idea.

Listen & Speak 1 B

Mike: Jimin, what are all these things in the box?

Jimin: They're for _____ _____ at the children's center. I'm going to give her my old books today.

Mike: _____ _____ _____ _____ _____ _____ _____?

Jimin: Yes. I feel happy when I teach her.

Mike: _____ _____ _____ _____ _____. Oh, the box looks heavy. Let me help you.

Jimin: Thanks.

Listen & Speak 2 A

Alex: Mom, _____ _____ _____ _____. I made it with plastic bags.

Mom: That's very cute, Alex. _____ _____ _____ _____ I needed a new basket?

Alex: You talked about it when we were having dinner _____ _____.

Mom: _____ _____! I really like this basket. It has many different colors.

Alex: _____ _____ _____ _____ _____.

Listen & Talk 2 B

Yujin: _____ _____ _____ _____ _____ _____ _____ _____ _____ _____. Do you want to hear about it?

Jack: Sure. _____ _____ _____ _____ _____, Yujin?

Yujin: Many children in his town couldn't go to school and _____ _____ _____. So he taught them in his house every day.

Jack: That's a great story.

Yujin: _____ _____ _____ _____ _____ _____.

Real Life Communication

Emily: Welcome back, Brian. _____ _____ _____ _____?

Brian: Yes, thanks. I tried to study _____ _____ _____ in the hospital, but it was hard.

Emily: _____ _____ _____ _____. Why don't you _____ _____ _____ _____?

Brian: Did you start a study group? That's wonderful.

Emily: Thanks. I think that _____ _____ _____ _____ _____ _____ _____ _____ _____.

Brian: I agree. I'll try hard to be a good member. _____ _____ _____ _____.

Emily: You're welcome. I'm glad you like my idea.

Let's Check 1

Henry: Your bag _____ _____. _____ _____ _____ _____.

Sujin: Thanks. _____ _____ _____ _____ _____?

Henry: It's over there. I'll carry your bag to the bus stop for you.

Sujin: You're very kind.

Henry: _____ _____. I am going that way, too.

[01~02] 다음 대화를 읽고 물음에 답하시오.

Henry: Your bag looks heavy. (A)Let me help you.
Sujin: Thanks. Where is the bus stop around here?
Henry: It's over there. I'll carry your bag to the bus stop for you.
Sujin: You're very kind.
Henry: No problem. I am going that way, too.

01 위 대화의 밑줄 친 (A)의 의도로 적절한 것은?

① 도움 요청하기　　　② 도움 제안하기
③ 도움 거절하기　　　④ 충고 구하기
⑤ 선호 표현하기

02 위 대화의 내용과 일치하지 <u>않는</u> 것은?

① Sujin's bag looked heavy.
② Henry helped Sujin by carrying her bag.
③ Sujin was looking for the bus stop.
④ Henry was going to the taxi stop.
⑤ Sujin appreciated Henry's help.

[03~04] 다음 대화를 읽고 물음에 답하시오.

Alex: Mom, this is ⓐfor you. I made it ⓑwith plastic bags.
Mom: That's very cute, Alex. How did you know ⓒwhich I needed a new basket?
Alex: You talked about it when we were having dinner the ⓓother day.
Mom: ⓔHow nice! I really like this basket. It has many different colors.
Alex: I'm glad you like it.

03 위 대화의 밑줄 친 ⓐ~ⓔ 중 어법상 <u>틀린</u> 것을 찾아 바르게 고치시오.

➡ _____

04 위 대화의 내용과 일치하지 <u>않는</u> 것은?

① Alex는 엄마에게 바구니를 만들어 드렸다.
② Alex는 비닐봉지로 바구니를 만들었다.
③ Alex가 만든 바구니는 다양한 색을 갖고 있다.
④ Alex와 엄마는 며칠 전 저녁을 먹기 전 새 바구니를 구매했다.
⑤ 엄마는 Alex의 선물이 마음에 들었다.

01 다음 짝지어진 대화가 어색한 것은?

① A: I can't move the table. Can anybody help me?
　B: Let me help you.

② A: What's the matter with you?
　B: How can I help you?

③ A: It's hard for me to build the model airplane.
　B: I'll help you.

④ A: I can't open the window.
　B: Let me give you a hand.

⑤ A: I can't open the bottle.
　B: May I help you?

[02~04] 다음 대화를 읽고 물음에 답하시오.

Tom: Hojun and I planned to give out free stickers today, but I think he forgot.
Sora: Really? (A)내가 도와줄게.(let) Why are you going to give out stickers?
Tom: It's part of our volunteer club activity.
Sora: I see. What does this sticker mean?
Tom: It means that when we smile at each other, the world will become a better place.
Sora: (B)_____

02 위 대화의 밑줄 친 (A)의 우리말을 주어진 단어를 사용하여 영작하시오.

➡ _____

03 위 대화의 빈칸 (B)에 들어갈 말로 어색한 것은?

① What a great idea!
② That sounds good.
③ Excellent!
④ What a pity!
⑤ That's a wonderful idea.

04 위 대화의 내용과 일치하도록 빈칸을 완성하시오.

W: What does the sticker emphasize?
A: It emphasizes the importance of _____.

[05~06] 다음 대화를 읽고 물음에 답하시오.

Yujin: I read a story about a special boy in India. Do you want to hear about it? (A)
Jack: Sure. Why is he special, Yujin? (B)
Yujin: Many children in his town couldn't go to school and had to work. (C)
Jack: That's a great story. (D)
Yujin: I'm glad you like it. (E)

05 다음 (A)~(E) 중 주어진 문장이 들어가기에 적절한 곳은?

So he taught them in his house every day.

① (A)　② (B)　③ (C)　④ (D)　⑤ (E)

06 위 대화를 읽고 대답할 수 없는 것은?

① What did Yujin read?
② Why was the boy in India special?
③ What should many children in India do instead of going to school?
④ What did Jack think about the story about a special boy in India?
⑤ What did Yujin do to help many children in India?

서답형

07 다음 대화의 내용과 일치하도록 Mike의 일기를 완성하시오.

> Mike: Jimin, what are all these things in the box?
> Jimin: They're for my mentee at the children's center. I'm going to give her my old books today.
> Mike: Do you teach her every weekend?
> Jimin: Yes. I feel happy when I teach her.
> Mike: You are a good mentor. Oh, the box looks heavy. Let me help you.
> Jimin: Thanks.

> Mon, June 24th, 2019
> Today, I was impressed with Jimin. She teaches (A)_____ at the children's center every weekend. In addition, she was going to give (B)_____ to her mentee. She said that (C)_____ when she taught her. I thought (D)_____.
> The box looked heavy, so I helped her. I think that helping others makes the world a better place.

➡ (A) _____
　 (B) _____
　 (C) _____
　 (D) _____

[08~09] 다음 대화를 읽고 물음에 답하시오.

> Emily: Welcome back, Brian. Are you feeling better?
> Brian: Yes, thanks. I tried to study on my own in the hospital, but it was hard.
> Emily: Let me help you. Why don't you join my study group?
> Brian: Did you start a study group? That's wonderful.

> Emily: Thanks. I think that we can learn better when we teach each other.
> Brian: I agree. I'll try hard to be a good member. Thanks for helping me.
> Emily: You're welcome. I'm glad you like my idea.

서답형

08 What did Emily suggest to Brain?

➡ _____

서답형

09 Why did Emily start a study group?

➡ _____
　 _____

서답형

10 다음 대화가 자연스럽게 이어지도록 순서대로 배열하시오.

> (A) Okay, I'll give it a try. Thanks for the tip.
> (B) I'm not good at science. What can I do?
> (C) No problem. I'm glad you like it.
> (D) Let me help you. Why don't you start with easier books?

➡ _____

[11~12] 다음 대화를 읽고 물음에 답하시오.

> Aram: I'm very tired. What should I do?
> Jack: Let me help you. I can give you a massage.
> Aram: Thank you for your help.
> Jack: No problem. I'm glad you liked ⓐit.

서답형

11 위 대화의 밑줄 친 ⓐit이 가리키는 것을 영어로 쓰시오.

➡ _____

서답형

12 What did Jack do to make Aram feel better?

➡ _____

[01~02] 다음 대화를 읽고 물음에 답하시오.

Mike: Jimin, what are all these things in the box?

Jimin: They're for my mentee at the children's center. I'm going to give her my old books today.

Mike: Do you teach her every weekend?

Jimin: Yes. (A)_____

Mike: You are a good (B)m_____. Oh, the box looks heavy. Let me help you.

Jimin: Thanks.

01 다음 빈칸 (A)에 들어갈 말을 보기에 주어진 단어를 모두 배열하여 완성하시오.

┌─── 보기 ───┐
happy / when / I / her / teach / feel / I
└──────────┘

➡ _____

02 위 대화의 빈칸 (B)에 주어진 영영 풀이가 가리키는 말을 쓰시오.

someone who teaches or gives help and advice to a less experienced and often younger person

➡ m_____

[03~04] 다음 대화를 읽고 물음에 답하시오.

Yujin: I read a story about a special boy in India. Do you want to hear about it?

Jack: Sure. Why is he special, Yujin?

Yujin: Many children in his town couldn't go to school and had to work. So he taught (A)them in his house every day.

Jack: That's a great story.

Yujin: I'm glad you like it.

03 위 대화의 밑줄 친 (A)them이 가리키는 것을 영어로 쓰시오.

➡ _____

04 위 대화의 내용과 일치하도록 Jack의 담화를 완성하시오.

Jack: Today, Yujin told me a great story about (A)_____. I was wondering why she said that (B)_____. Yujin said the boy taught many children in his town who (C)_____ in his house every day. It was a great story.

➡ (A) _____
  (B) _____
  (C) _____

[05~06] 다음 대화를 읽고 물음에 답하시오.

Tom: Hojun and I planned to give out free stickers today, but I think he forgot.

Sora: Really? Let me help you then. Why are you going to give out stickers?

Tom: It's part of our volunteer club activity.

Sora: I see. What does this sticker mean?

Tom: It means that when we smile at each other, the world will become a better place.

Sora: That's a wonderful idea.

05 What is Sora going to do to help Tom?

➡ _____

06 Tom이 준비한 스티커의 의미를 우리말로 20자 내외로 서술하시오.

➡ _____

Grammar

① 목적격 관계대명사

> - I have a friend **whom** I want you to meet. 나는 네가 만나보기를 원하는 친구가 한 명 있어.
> - The chair **which** you gave to me was broken. 네가 나에게 준 의자가 망가졌어.

■ 관계대명사는 두 개의 문장을 하나로 이어주는 접속사 역할을 하면서 동시에 대명사 역할을 한다. 전치사의 목적어 혹은 동사의 목적어였던 대명사를 목적격 관계대명사로 만들어 문장을 하나로 이어준다.

- There were many people in the cafe **which** we visited last week. 〈동사의 목적어〉 우리가 지난주에 방문한 카페에는 사람이 많았어.
- Those boys **who(m)** the woman is looking after look very cute. 〈전치사의 목적어〉 그 여자가 돌보고 있는 저 소년들은 매우 귀여워 보인다.

■ 목적격 관계대명사 who(m), which는 that으로 대체할 수 있으며, 생략 가능하다. 관계대명사가 전치사의 목적어로 사용된 경우 전치사는 동사 뒤에 그대로 두거나, 전치사를 관계대명사 앞으로 보낼 수 있다.

- Mr. Pang **who(m)** the children love teaches how to swim to them. 그 아이들이 사랑하는 Pang씨는 그들에게 수영하는 방법을 가르친다.
- She never touched food **which** she didn't like. 그녀는 좋아하지 않는 음식에는 손도 대지 않았다.
- The i-pad **which** I got from my father was my birthday present. 내가 아버지로부터 받은 그 아이패드는 내 생일 선물이었어.
- The areas **which** you have mentioned have some problems. 네가 언급한 그 지역에는 몇 가지 문제점이 있어.
- The missing boy **who(m)** people were looking for came home last night. 사람들이 찾던 그 실종 소년이 어젯밤 집으로 왔다.
- Tell me about the people **who(m)** you cared for in the hospital. 네가 병원에서 돌봤던 사람들에 관해 말해줘.

핵심 Check

1. 다음 우리말과 같도록 빈칸에 알맞은 말을 쓰시오.

(1) 이것은 그가 작년에 산 집이다.

➡ This is the house _____ he bought last year.

(2) 나는 모두가 천재라고 생각하는 한 남자를 안다.

➡ I know a man _____ everyone thinks a genius.

② to부정사를 목적격보어로 취하는 동사

> • Dan **persuaded** me **to buy** the computer for him. Dan은 내가 그를 위해 컴퓨터를 사도록 설득했다.
>
> • Andrea **expected** us **to welcome** her. Andrea는 우리가 그녀를 환영하리라고 기대했다.

■ '동사+목적어+to V' 형태로 목적어가 to부정사의 주체가 되도록 해석한다.

- I don't **want** her **to see** my portfolio. 나는 그녀가 나의 포트폴리오를 보는 걸 원치 않아.
- Mom **persuaded** me **to do** my homework first. 엄마는 내가 숙제를 먼저 하도록 설득하셨다.

■ to부정사를 목적격보어로 취하는 동사에는 allow, ask, tell, advise, get, force, require, order, persuade, encourage, enable, cause, need, want, help, would like, teach, expect 등이 있다.

- Our teacher **encourages** us **to think** of others before us. 우리 선생님은 우리가 우리보다 타인을 먼저 생각하도록 권장하신다.
- We **would like** you **to have** a cup of tea. 우리는 당신이 차 한 잔 하길 원합니다.

■ to부정사 목적격보어의 부정형은 'not to V'로 표현한다.

- My lawyer **advised** me **not to say a word**. 나의 변호사는 내게 한마디도 하지 말라고 조언했다.
- Dad **ordered** me **not to go** out at night. 아빠는 내게 밤에 나가지 말라고 명령하셨다.

■ make, have, let은 원형부정사를 목적격보어로 취하는 사역동사이다. '목적어가 V하게 하다'로 해석한다.

- She **let** me **go** shopping with my friends. 그녀는 내가 친구들과 함께 쇼핑하러 가게 허락했다.
- What **made** you **break** the promise? 무엇이 너로 하여금 그 약속을 어기게 만든 거야?

핵심 Check

1. 다음 우리말과 같도록 빈칸에 알맞은 말을 쓰시오.

(1) Julia는 우리가 그와 악수하도록 설득했다.

➡ Julia _____ us _____ _____ hands with him.

(2) 나는 그들이 훨씬 더 많이 먹으리라고 예상한다.

➡ I _____ them _____ _____ much more.

(3) 그 여자는 그녀의 아들에게 늦지 말라고 말했다.

➡ The woman _____ her son _____ _____ _____ late.

Grammar 시험대비 기본평가

01 다음 문장에서 어법상 <u>어색한</u> 부분을 바르게 고쳐 쓰시오.

(1) The eggs who I bought are very fresh.

_____ ➡ _____

(2) The building which John built were huge.

_____ ➡ _____

(3) I believe that it will enable us continue this work together.

_____ ➡ _____

(4) Will you allow me to passing, please?

_____ ➡ _____

02 괄호 안에 주어진 단어를 어법에 맞게 빈칸에 쓰시오.

(1) The man whom I fell in love with _____ near my house now.
   (live)
(2) The race _____ you took part in was very successful. (which)
(3) The police told them _____ calm. (stay)
(4) We encouraged her _____ a new life. (start)

03 주어진 단어를 바르게 배열하여 다음 우리말을 영어로 쓰시오. 필요하다면 단어를 추가하거나 변형하시오.

(1) 이것은 그들이 필요로 했던 테이블이다. (need / this / is / the / they / table)

   ➡ _____

(2) 그녀는 내가 주관한 어떤 회의에 왔어요. (I / a meeting / she / come / that / run / to)

   ➡ _____

(3) 우리는 그들이 열심히 일하도록 강요할 수 없어. (hard / can't / them / we / work / force)

   ➡ _____

(4) 무엇이 네가 그렇게 생각하게 만들었니? (so / think / what / you / make)

   ➡ _____

01 다음 빈칸에 알맞은 말을 모두 고르시오.

> You can find the things _____ you need in the refrigerator.

① who   ② whom   ③ that
④ which   ⑤ whose

02 다음 빈칸에 들어갈 말로 적절한 것은?

> 이것은 어제 엄마가 내게 사주신 신발이다.
> = These are the shoes _____
>   yesterday.

① whom my mom bought for her
② which I bought for my mom
③ that was bought for my mom
④ which my mom bought for me
⑤ that was bought to me by mom

03 다음 빈칸에 적절하지 않은 것은?

> _____ to save time.

① The plan enabled us
② He wanted me
③ She encouraged us
④ Our boss made us
⑤ Mom advised us

04 주어진 단어와 적절한 관계대명사를 이용하여 다음 우리말을 영어로 쓰시오.

> 그는 내가 가진 모든 돈을 쓰도록 허락하지 않았다.
> (allow / use / all / have)

➡ _____

_____

05 다음 밑줄 친 부분 중 생략할 수 없는 것은?

① Is she the girl who you talked about?
② The milk which I bought went bad.
③ This is the letter that he sent me.
④ This is the jacket which you brought.
⑤ It is true that he spread the rumor.

06 다음 우리말을 영어로 바르게 옮긴 것은?

> 부산에 있는 작은 가게들은 사람들로 붐빈다.

① Small shops in Busan was crowded with people.
② There were small shops in Busan.
③ Small shops in Busan are crowded with people.
④ Busan has small shops which are run by many people.
⑤ There are small shops in Busan which many people run.

07 다음 중 빈칸에 들어갈 동사 'play'의 형태가 다른 하나는?

① Mom didn't allow me _____ the piano at night.
② My parents encouraged me _____ the flute in front of the guests.
③ We decided _____ soccer after school.
④ Many radio stations refused _____ the music.
⑤ Are you interested in _____ music on the stage?

서답형
08 다음 우리말에 맞게 빈칸에 알맞은 말을 쓰시오.

> 네가 해야 하는 다음 단계는 그것을 끓이는 것이다.
> The next step _____ _____ _____
> _____ is _____ _____ it.

09 다음 중 어법상 바르지 않은 것은?

① Some flowers which you picked are on the table.
② Would you like me to speak at the dinner?
③ My advice caused him stop smoking.
④ Is this the yogurt you brought?
⑤ I need you to sign for it.

10 다음 중 어법상 바른 문장의 개수는?

> ⓐ The toys in the room is not mine.
> ⓑ I don't think that she wanted me do the job.
> ⓒ Did you find the key that you were looking for?
> ⓓ The car he drives is very old.
> ⓔ Ms. Henderson requires us handing in the reports as soon as possible.

① 1개　　② 2개　　③ 3개
④ 4개　　⑤ 5개

11 다음 중 빈칸에 적절하지 않은 것은?

> The doctor _____ my dad to drink lots of water.

① advises　　② encourages　　③ tells
④ persuades　　⑤ has

서답형
12 다음 두 문장을 하나의 문장으로 만드시오.

> • Do you remember those people?
> • You met them on holiday.

➡ _____

_____

13 다음 중 보기의 밑줄 친 that과 쓰임이 같은 것은?

> ┤ 보기 ├
> Why aren't you wearing the watch that you borrowed from me?

① Did you know that he came back from Toronto?
② He doesn't know the fact that you don't want to believe it.
③ Most people think that the Beatles is the best pop group.
④ Kelly said that she made some mistakes.
⑤ She is using the pan that I gave to her.

14 다음 중 어법상 옳은 것끼리 바르게 짝지어진 것은?

> • A rabbit is an animal [who / which] every child loves.
> • Persuade him [tell / to tell] us what he knows.
> • He made me [pay / to pay] the bill at the restaurant.

① who – tell – pay
② which – tell – pay
③ who – to tell – to pay
④ which – to tell – pay
⑤ which – to tell – to pay

15 다음 빈칸에 공통으로 들어갈 말로 가장 적절한 것은?

- Have you noticed _____ many Italian foods have tomatoes in them?
- The coat _____ the girl is wearing does not look special.

① who　　② which　　③ that
④ whom　　⑤ whose

서답형

16 주어진 단어를 빈칸에 어법에 맞게 쓰시오.

I want you _____ _____ _____ _____ _____ because I need a mentor who can help me with math.
(help / with)

중요

17 다음 중 빈칸에 들어갈 관계대명사의 쓰임이 다른 하나는?

① The students _____ we chose are diligent and honest.
② The candies _____ the shop sells taste good.
③ The performance _____ he saw has been loved by many people.
④ The camera _____ many people love is too expensive.
⑤ A shampoo bottle _____ is in the bathroom is empty.

서답형

18 다음 우리말 의미에 맞게 빈칸에 알맞은 말을 쓰시오.

여기에 어제 내가 했던 두 가지 흥미로운 일이 있다.
Here are two interesting things _____ _____ _____ _____ .

서답형

19 주어진 단어를 활용하여 다음 빈칸에 알맞은 말을 쓰시오.

나가, 그렇지 않으면 우리가 너희를 나가게 만들 거야.
Get out, or _____ _____ _____ _____ _____ go out. (force)

서답형

20 주어진 어구를 바르게 배열하여 다음 우리말을 영어로 쓰시오.

네가 해서는 안 되는 유일한 것은 다른 사람들이 이야기하는 도중에 끼어드는 것이다.
(cut in / the only thing / you / while / are talking / others / that / should not do / is / to)

➡ _____

_____

21 다음 중 어법상 바르지 않은 것은?

Can you ①do me a favor? There ②is ③ one thing ④that I need you ⑤do for me.

중요

22 다음 중 빈칸에 들어갈 말로 가장 적절한 것은?

My parents would like me _____ with them.

① to living　　② living　　③ live
④ to live　　⑤ lives

서답형

23 다음 빈칸에 알맞은 말을 쓰시오.

그는 우리에게 삶을 사랑하도록 가르쳤어요.
He _____ _____ _____ _____ _____ life.

01 다음 주어진 동사를 문맥과 어법에 맞게 빈칸에 쓰시오.

> know / clean / be / believe / focus

> • The elderly are people who _____ old.
> • If you want to learn Hangul, let me _____. I will teach you.
> • Do you expect me _____ such a nonsense story?
> • Mom got me _____ my room.
> • The boss ordered us _____ on the job.

02 다음 대화를 읽고 주어진 단어를 활용하여 Hannah에 관하여 쓰시오.

> **Clark:** Do you know how to play the piano?
> **Hannah:** Yes, I do. My cousin taught me.

(teach / Hannah)

➡ _____

03 주어진 단어를 활용하여 다음 우리말을 영어로 쓰시오.

> 넌 내가 무엇을 하길 원하는 거야?
> (what / want / do)

➡ _____

04 다음 상황을 읽고 빈칸에 알맞은 말을 쓰시오.

> There was a girl who listened to music a little loudly in the library. So Peter said to the girl, "Would you turn down the music?"

➡ Peter asked _____

05 다음 보기와 같이 하나의 문장을 두 개의 문장으로 나누시오.

> ┤ 보기 ├
> Have you been to the place which Mary visited last year?
> ➡ Have you been to the place?
> ➡ Mary visited the place last year.

(1) Kyle has the money he found on the street.

➡ _____
➡ _____

(2) Is this the book that you are looking for?

➡ _____
➡ _____

06 주어진 단어를 활용하여 James와 Olivia의 대화 내용을 한 문장으로 요약하시오.

> **Olivia:** I have had a stomachache for a few days.
> **James:** Oh, I'm so sorry. Did you see a doctor?
> **Olivia:** No, I didn't.
> **James:** You should see a doctor.

(advise)

➡ _____

07 주어진 단어를 바르게 나열하여 다음 우리말을 영어로 쓰시오. 필요하다면 단어를 변형하시오.

> 내가 지원했던 그 일자리를 얻길 원해.
> (to / apply / I / I / that / the / for / job / get / want)

➡ _____

08 대화를 읽고 주어진 단어를 활용하여 빈칸에 알맞은 말을 쓰시오.

> **Jason:** I want to go shopping with Ann.
> **Mom:** You can go on Monday.

> allow

➡ Jason's mom _____

_____

09 주어진 문장과 같은 의미가 되도록 빈칸에 알맞은 말을 쓰시오.

> Emma asked me, "Can you play the guitar for me?"

➡ Emma asked me _____

10 주어진 단어를 바르게 배열하여 다음 우리말을 영어로 쓰시오. 필요하다면 단어를 추가하거나 변형하시오.

> 그들이 발달시킨 그 기술은 우리가 안전하게 자동차를 운전하는 것을 가능하게 한다.
> (safely / the / technology / a car / that / develop / they / enable / drive / us / have)

➡ _____

_____

11 주어진 단어를 활용하여 다음 우리말을 영어로 쓰시오. 필요하다면 단어를 변형하시오.

> 나는 John이 공원에서 발견했던 그 고양이를 좋아해.
> (like / find / at the park)

➡ _____

12 주어진 단어를 활용하여 빈칸에 알맞은 말을 쓰시오.

> 독감은 사람들에게 두통을 유발할 수 있다.
> The flu can _____
> (cause / have)

➡ _____

13 다음 두 개의 문장을 하나의 문장으로 연결하시오.

(1) Osaka is the city. My sister visited the city last week.

➡ _____

_____

(2) Robert is an actor. We like him very much.

➡ _____

(3) My dad gave me the wallet. I really wanted to have it.

➡ _____

_____

14 다음 우리말을 영어로 쓰시오.

> 내가 할 수 있는 유일한 것은 조용히 하는 거야.
> = The only thing _____ _____
> _____ _____ _____
> _____ _____.

15 주어진 단어를 바르게 배열하여 문장을 완성하시오.

> Sandra _____ _____ _____
> _____ a good vacation.
> (have / me / told / to)

Small but Great Ideas

Here are two stories which I read yesterday. Do you want to hear about
목적격 관계대명사(= that) 생략 가능 　　　　　　　　want의 목적어

them?
= two stories which I read yesterday

Call Someone You Love
Call someone. + You love someone.

New York had many pay phones on its streets. However, nobody really
부정주어로서 문장 전체를 부정의 뜻으로 만들며 '아무도 ~ 않다'라는 뜻

used them. One day, a man came up with an idea. He stuck coins to
어느 날 　　　　　　　　　　　　　　　stick - stuck - stuck

one of the phones. He also put up a sign that said, "Call Someone You
stick A to B: A를 B에 붙이다 　　He also put up a sign. + The sign said. "Call Someone (who(m)[that]

Love." Soon, many people were using the phone.
You Love." 　　　　　　　　　　　과거진행형

When they were talking to someone whom they loved, they didn't
= that

stop smiling. His idea became a big success. During the day, all the
stop+Ving: V하는 것을 멈추다

coins disappeared. The man was very happy because his small idea
이유를 나타내는 접속사

gave happiness to many people.
give ~ to ... : ~을 ···에게 주다 (3형식)

hear: 듣다
pay phone: 공중전화
one day: (과거의) 어느 날
come up with: (생각이) 떠오르다
put up: 세우다
say: (글·글씨 등이) 쓰이다
sign: 표지판
success: 성공
during the day: 낮 동안
disappear: 사라지다

📎 확인문제

● 다음 문장이 본문의 내용과 일치하면 T, 일치하지 <u>않으면</u> F를 쓰시오.

1 The first story is about what happened in New York. ☐

2 It was hard to see people using a pay phone. ☐

3 The man stuck a coin to some pay phones. ☐

4 People couldn't call someone they loved because they had no coins. ☐

5 It took several days for all the coins to disappear. ☐

The Red Arrow Man

A few years ago, the maps at bus stops in Seoul were very confusing.
몇 년 전에　　　　주어　　　　the maps 수식

They didn't have enough information. People had to ask others to
=The maps　　　　　　　　　　　　ask ~ to ... : ~에게 … 해 달라고 요청하다

explain the maps. "Where is this bus stop on the map? Does this bus

go to Gwanghwamun?" Many people often took the wrong bus and
버스를 잘못 탔다

wasted their time.

One day, a young man decided to solve this problem. He bought
(과거의) 어느 날　　　　　　decided의 목적어

lots of red arrow stickers. Every day he rode his bicycle around the
=many　　　　　　　　　　　ride–rode–ridden

city and stuck the stickers on the bus maps. Nobody asked him to do
stick-stuck-stuck

this. He just wanted to help others. Thanks to his effort, people could
버스 지도에 빨간 스티커를 붙이는 일　　=other people　　~ 덕분에

understand the maps easily and save time.

arrow: 화살, 화살표
few: 몇몇의
map: 지도
bus stop: 버스 정류장
confusing: 혼란스러운
waste one's time: ~의 시간을 낭비하다
thanks to: ~ 덕택에
understand: 이해하다
easily: 쉽게
save: 절약하다

확인문제

● 다음 문장이 본문의 내용과 일치하면 T, 일치하지 않으면 F를 쓰시오.

1 People in Seoul were confused by the bus maps. ☐

2 The bus maps had plenty of information in the past. ☐

3 There was someone who forced a young man to stick the stickers. ☐

4 What the man wanted to do was to help others. ☐

5 He borrowed some money to buy arrow stickers. ☐

● 우리말을 참고하여 빈칸에 알맞은 말을 쓰시오.

Small but Great Ideas

1   Here _____ two stories _____ I read yesterday.

2   Do you want _____ _____ about _____?

3   Call Someone _____ _____.

4   New York _____ many pay phones on its streets.

5   _____, _____ really used them.

6   One day, a man _____ _____ _____ an idea.

7   He _____ coins _____ one of the phones.

8   He also _____ _____ a sign _____ _____, "Call Someone You Love."

9   Soon, many people _____ _____ the phone.

10   _____ they were talking to someone _____ _____ _____, they didn't stop _____.

11   His idea became _____ _____ _____.

12   _____ the day, all the coins _____.

13   The man was very happy _____ his small idea gave _____ _____ many people.

작지만 위대한 아이디어

1   여기 내가 어제 읽은 이야기가 두 개 있어.

2   들어볼래?

3   당신이 사랑하는 누군가에게 전화하세요.

4   뉴욕에는 길거리에 공중전화가 많이 있었다.

5   그러나 아무도 그것들을 실제로 사용하지는 않았다.

6   어느 날, 한 남자에게 좋은 아이디어가 떠올랐다.

7   그는 공중전화 하나에 동전들을 붙였다.

8   그는 또한 "당신이 사랑하는 사람에게 전화하세요."라고 쓰인 표지판을 설치했다.

9   곧, 많은 사람들이 그 전화기를 사용하고 있었다.

10   그들이 사랑하는 누군가에게 전화하고 있을 때, 그들은 미소 짓기를 멈추지 않았다.

11   그의 아이디어는 커다란 성공이었다.

12   낮 동안, 모든 동전이 사라졌다.

13   그 남자는 자신의 작은 아이디어가 많은 사람에게 행복을 가져다주었기 때문에 매우 행복했다.

14 The Red _____ _____

15 _____ _____ _____ _____ , the maps at bus stops in Seoul _____ very _____ .

16 They didn't have _____ _____ .

17 People had to _____ _____ _____ _____ the maps.

18 "_____ is this bus stop _____ the map? Does this bus _____ _____ Gwanghwamun?"

19 Many people _____ _____ the wrong bus and _____ their time.

20 One day, a young man _____ _____ _____ this problem.

21 He bought _____ _____ _____ _____ _____ .

22 Every day he _____ his bicycle _____ the city and _____ the stickers _____ the bus maps.

23 Nobody _____ _____ _____ _____ this.

24 He just _____ _____ _____ others.

25 _____ _____ his effort, people could understand the maps _____ and _____ .

14 빨간 화살표 청년

15 몇 년 전에, 서울의 버스 정류장의 지도는 매우 혼란스러웠다.

16 지도에는 충분한 정보가 없었다.

17 사람들은 다른 사람들에게 지도를 설명해 달라고 요청해야 했다.

18 "이 버스 정류장은 지도의 어디에 있는 건가요? 이 버스가 광화문으로 가나요?"

19 많은 사람이 종종 버스를 잘못 타서 시간을 낭비하곤 했다.

20 어느 날, 한 젊은 청년이 이 문제를 해결해 보기로 했다.

21 그는 빨간 화살표 스티커를 많이 샀다.

22 매일 그는 자전거를 타고 서울 시내를 돌아다니며 버스 지도에 스티커를 붙였다.

23 아무도 그 청년에게 이 일을 하라고 요청하지 않았다.

24 그는 단지 다른 사람들을 돕고 싶었다.

25 그의 노력 덕분에, 사람들은 지도를 쉽게 이해하고 시간을 절약할 수 있었다.

● 우리말을 참고하여 본문을 영작하시오.

여기 내가 어제 읽은 이야기가 두 개 있어.

1 ➡ _____

들어볼래?

2 ➡ _____

당신이 사랑하는 누군가에게 전화하세요.

3 ➡ _____

뉴욕에는 길거리에 공중전화가 많이 있었다.

4 ➡ _____

그러나 아무도 그것들을 실제로 사용하지는 않았다.

5 ➡ _____

어느 날, 한 남자에게 좋은 아이디어가 떠올랐다.

6 ➡ _____

그는 공중전화 하나에 동전들을 붙였다.

7 ➡ _____

그는 또한 "당신이 사랑하는 사람에게 전화하세요."라고 쓰인 표지판을 설치했다.

8 ➡ _____

곧, 많은 사람들이 그 전화기를 사용하고 있었다.

9 ➡ _____

그들이 사랑하는 누군가에게 전화하고 있을 때, 그들은 미소 짓기를 멈추지 않았다.

10 ➡ _____

그의 아이디어는 커다란 성공이었다.

11 ➡ _____

낮 동안, 모든 동전이 사라졌다.

12 ➡ _____

그 남자는 자신의 작은 아이디어가 많은 사람에게 행복을 가져다주었기 때문에 매우 행복했다.

13 ➡ _____

14 빨간 화살표 청년

➡ _____

15 몇 년 전, 서울의 버스 정류장의 지도는 매우 혼란스러웠다.

➡ _____

16 지도에는 충분한 정보가 없었다.

➡ _____

17 사람들은 다른 사람들에게 지도를 설명해 달라고 요청해야 했다.

➡ _____

18 "이 버스 정류장은 지도의 어디에 있는 건가요? 이 버스가 광화문으로 가나요?"

➡ _____

19 많은 사람이 종종 버스를 잘못 타서 시간을 낭비하곤 했다.

➡ _____

20 어느 날, 한 젊은 청년이 이 문제를 해결해 보기로 했다.

➡ _____

21 그는 빨간 화살표 스티커를 많이 샀다.

➡ _____

22 매일 그는 자전거를 타고 서울 시내를 돌아다니며 버스 지도에 스티커를 붙였다.

➡ _____

23 아무도 그 청년에게 이 일을 하라고 요청하지 않았다.

➡ _____

24 그는 단지 다른 사람들을 돕고 싶었다.

➡ _____

25 그의 노력 덕분에, 사람들은 지도를 쉽게 이해하고 시간을 절약할 수 있었다.

➡ _____

[01~08] 다음 글을 읽고 물음에 답하시오.

Here are two stories which I read yesterday. Do you want to hear (A)[from / about] ⓐ them?

Call Someone You Love

New York had many pay phones on its streets. ⓑ_____, nobody really used (B)[it / them]. ① One day, a man came up with an idea. He stuck coins to one of the phones. ② He also put up a sign that said, "Call Someone You Love." ③ When they were talking to someone ⓒ_____ they loved, they didn't stop smiling. ④ His idea became a big success. (C)[During / While] the day, all the coins disappeared. ⑤ The man was very happy because his small idea gave happiness ⓓ_____ many people.

서답형
01 밑줄 친 ⓐ가 가리키는 것을 6단어의 영어로 쓰시오.

➡ _____

02 다음 중 빈칸 ⓑ에 들어갈 말로 가장 적절한 것은?

① Therefore   ② As a result
③ In addition   ④ For example
⑤ However

서답형
03 빈칸 ⓒ에 알맞은 말을 모두 쓰시오.

➡ _____

04 다음 중 빈칸 ⓓ에 들어갈 말로 가장 적절한 것은?

① in   ② to   ③ on
④ for   ⑤ by

05 ①~⑤ 중 주어진 문장이 들어가기에 가장 적절한 곳은?

Soon, many people were using the phone.

①   ②   ③   ④   ⑤

06 (A)~(C) 중 어법상 옳은 것끼리 짝지어진 것은?

① from – it – During
② about – it – During
③ from – them – While
④ about – them – During
⑤ from – it – while

07 다음 중 위 글을 읽고 답할 수 있는 것은?

① How many pay phones were there on New York streets?
② Why did nobody use the pay phones?
③ Who stuck coins to a pay phone?
④ How many coins were stuck to a pay phone?
⑤ How many coins did each person use?

서답형
08 주어진 단어를 이용하여 다음 질문에 완전한 문장의 영어로 답하시오.

Q: What did the sign say?
A: _____ (it)

➡ _____

[09~15] 다음 글을 읽고 물음에 답하시오.

The Red Arrow Man

(A)[A few / A little] years ago, the maps ⓐ_____ bus stops in Seoul were very (B)[confusing / confused]. They didn't have enough information. People had to ask others to explain the maps. "Where is this bus stop on the map? Does this bus go to Gwanghwamun?" Many people often took the wrong bus and ⓑ_____ (C)[its / their] time.

One day, a young man decided to solve this problem. He bought lots of red arrow stickers. Every day he rode his bicycle around the city and stuck the stickers on the bus maps. Nobody asked him ⓒto do this. He just wanted to help others. ⓓ_____ his effort, people could understand the maps easily and ⓔsave time.

09 다음 중 빈칸 ⓐ에 들어갈 말과 같은 것은?

① Did you turn _____ the light in the livingroom?
② I was surprised _____ the news.
③ Dad will pick you _____ at five.
④ Please take care _____ yourself.
⑤ Do you mind waiting _____ a little while?

서답형
10 빈칸 ⓑ에 밑줄 친 ⓔ의 반의어를 어법에 맞게 쓰시오.

➡ _____

서답형
11 밑줄 친 ⓒ가 의미하는 것을 우리말로 쓰시오.

➡ _____
_____

12 다음 중 빈칸 ⓓ에 들어갈 말로 가장 적절한 것은?

① Despite   ② Instead of
③ Thanks to   ④ At last
⑤ Depending on

중요
13 (A)~(C) 중 어법상 옳은 것끼리 짝지어진 것은?

① A few – confusing – its
② A little – confused – its
③ A few – confusing – their
④ A little – confused – their
⑤ A few – confused – their

서답형
14 Write the reason why people often took the wrong bus in Seoul. Use the words 'because', 'there', and 'on the maps.'

➡ _____
_____

15 다음 중 위 글의 내용과 일치하지 <u>않는</u> 것은?

① People needed some explanation about the maps.
② There were people who took the wrong bus because of the maps.
③ A young man had an idea to solve the problem of the maps.
④ Somebody wanted the young man to stick the stickers.
⑤ A young man used his bicycle in order to stick the stickers.

[16~22] 다음 글을 읽고 물음에 답하시오.

Here are two stories which I read yesterday. Do you want ⓐ_____ about them?

Call Someone You Love
New York had many pay phones ⓑ_____ its streets. However, nobody really used them. One day, a man came up with an idea. He stuck coins to one of the phones. He also put up a sign (A)that said, "Call Someone You Love." (B)Soon, many people were using (C)the phone. When they were ⓒ_____ to someone whom they loved, they didn't stop smiling. His idea became a big success. During the day, all the coins disappeared. The man was very happy because his small idea gave happiness to many people.

서답형
16 주어진 단어를 어법과 문맥에 맞게 빈칸 ⓐ와 ⓒ에 쓰시오.

| talk / hear |

➡ ⓐ _____ ⓒ _____

17 다음 중 빈칸 ⓑ에 들어갈 말과 같은 것은?

① Are you interested _____ studying English?
② She was not satisfied _____ the result.
③ Ms. Han wanted us to pay attention _____ her class.
④ He likes to take care _____ plants.
⑤ He is the person you can depend _____.

서답형
18 다음과 같이 풀이되는 단어를 위 글에서 찾아 쓰시오.

| to stop being visible |

➡ _____

19 다음 중 밑줄 친 (A)와 쓰임이 다른 하나는?

① Is he the boy that you talked with?
② The man and his dog that are running together look happy.
③ Do you remember the story that Miranda told you?
④ I want to say that he is my hero.
⑤ Kyle showed me the watch that was really expensive.

20 다음 중 밑줄 친 (B)를 대신하여 쓰일 수 있는 것은?

① For a long time   ② Before long
③ Hardly   ④ Still
⑤ Lately

서답형
21 다음은 밑줄 친 (C)를 설명하는 문장이다. 빈칸에 알맞은 말을 쓰시오.

| the phone _____ the man _____ _____ _____. |

22 다음 중 위 글의 내용과 일치하지 않는 것은?

① I read a couple of stories yesterday.
② Many pay phones were on the streets in New York.
③ Not everyone used pay phones.
④ A man stuck some coins to a pay phone.
⑤ All the coins were used during the day.

서답형

23 다음 주어진 문장과 자연스럽게 연결되도록 (A)~(C)를 바르게 나열하시오.

New York had many pay phones on its streets.

(A) He also put up a sign that said, "Call Someone You Love." Soon, many people were using the phone.

(B) However, nobody really used them. One day, a man came up with an idea. He stuck coins to one of the phones.

(C) When they were talking to someone whom they loved, they didn't stop smiling. His idea became a big success.

➡ _____

[24~30] 다음 글을 읽고 물음에 답하시오.

The Red Arrow Man
A few years ago, the maps at bus stops in Seoul were very ⓐ_____. They didn't have enough information. ⓑPeople had to ask others explain the maps. "Where is this bus stop ⓒ_____ the map? Does this bus go to Gwanghwamun?" Many people often took ①the wrong bus and wasted their time.
One day, a young man decided to ②solve this problem. He bought lots of red arrow stickers. Every day he rode his bicycle around the city and ③stuck the stickers ⓓ_____ the bus maps. ④Nobody asked him to do this. He just wanted to ⑤bother others. Thanks to his effort, people could understand the maps easily and save time.

24 다음 중 빈칸 ⓐ에 들어갈 말로 가장 적절한 것은?

① rare ② confusing
③ easy ④ familiar
⑤ common

서답형

25 밑줄 친 ⓑ에서 어법상 바르지 않은 것을 찾아 바르게 고쳐 쓰시오.

➡ _____

26 빈칸 ⓒ와 ⓓ에 공통으로 들어갈 말로 가장 적절한 것은?

① at ② by ③ on
④ under ⑤ about

중요

27 ①~⑤ 중 글의 흐름상 어색한 것은?

① ② ③ ④ ⑤

서답형

28 다음 질문에 완전한 문장의 영어로 답하시오.

Q: What was the problem with the bus maps in Seoul?

➡ _____

29 다음 중 위 글을 읽고 알 수 없는 것은?

① 서울 버스 정류장의 지도에 부족했던 것
② 사람들이 버스를 잘못 탄 이유
③ 광화문으로 가는 버스 번호
④ 청년이 산 스티커 모양
⑤ 청년이 자전거를 타고 돌아다니며 한 일

서답형

30 글의 내용에 맞게 다음 빈칸에 알맞은 말을 쓰시오.

Thanks to the young man's effort, people in _____ could take the _____ bus and _____ _____ _____.

[01~09] 다음 글을 읽고 물음에 답하시오.

ⓐHere are two stories which I read yesterday. Do you want to hear about them?

ⓑCall Someone You Love
New York had many pay phones on its streets. However, nobody really used ⓒthem. One day, a man came up with an idea. He stuck coins to one of the phones. He also put up a sign that said, "Call Someone You Love." Soon, many people were using the phone. When they were talking to someone whom they loved, ⓓthey didn't stop smiling. His idea became a big success. During the day, all the coins disappeared. The man was very (A)_____ because ⓔhis small idea gave (B)_____ to ⓕmany people.

01 주어진 단어를 어법에 맞게 빈칸 (A)와 (B)에 쓰시오.

happy

➡ (A) _____ (B)_____

02 적절한 대명사를 이용하여 밑줄 친 ⓐ를 두 개의 문장으로 나누어 쓰시오.

➡ _____

➡ _____

03 밑줄 친 ⓑ에는 생략된 단어가 있다. 생략하지 않은 문장으로 다시 쓰시오.

➡ _____

04 밑줄 친 ⓒ가 가리키는 것을 위 글에서 찾아 쓰시오.

➡ _____

05 주어진 동사를 이용하여 밑줄 친 ⓓ와 같은 의미의 문장을 쓰시오.

keep

➡ _____

06 다음은 밑줄 친 ⓔ의 의미를 영어로 쓴 것이다. 적절한 관계대명사를 이용하여 빈칸에 알맞은 말을 쓰시오.

sticking _____ to one of the phones

_____ _____ _____ _____

07 적절한 관계대명사를 이용하여 밑줄 친ⓕ를 설명하는 문장을 완성하시오.

many people _____ used the phone with _____.

08 글의 내용에 맞게 다음 대화의 빈칸에 알맞은 말을 쓰시오.

A: What did a man _____ to one of the pay phones?

B: He _____ _____ to one of them. I think he wanted people _____ _____ the phone to call _____ they loved.

09 글의 내용에 맞게 다음 빈칸에 알맞은 말을 쓰시오.

The man stuck coins to one of the phones as well as _____ _____ _____ _____.

[10~18] 다음 글을 읽고 물음에 답하시오.

The Red Arrow Man

A few years ago, the maps at bus stops in Seoul were very confusing. ⓐThey didn't have enough information. People had to ask others to explain the maps. "Where is this bus stop on the map? Does this bus go to Gwanghwamun?" Many people often took the wrong bus and wasted their time.

One day, a young man decided to solve this problem. He bought lots of red arrow stickers. Every day he rode his bicycle around the city and stuck the stickers on the bus maps. ⓑNobody asked him to do this. He just wanted to help others. Thanks to his effort, people could understand the maps easily and save time.

10 밑줄 친 ⓐ가 가리키는 것을 위 글에서 찾아 쓰시오.

➡ _____

11 다음은 밑줄 친 ⓑ와 같은 의미의 문장이다. 적절한 관계대명사를 이용하여 빈칸에 알맞은 말을 쓰시오.

There was no one _____ _____
_____ _____ _____ _____.

12 Why did people have to ask others to explain the maps at bus stops in Seoul?

➡ It was because _____

_____

13 글의 내용에 맞게 다음 물음에 완전한 문장의 영어로 답하시오.

Q: What did the young man stick on the bus maps?

➡ _____

14 주어진 단어를 이용하여 다음 우리말을 영어로 쓰시오.

그의 노력은 사람들이 지도를 쉽게 이해하는 것을 가능하게 했다. (enable)

➡ _____

_____

15 글의 내용에 맞게 다음 빈칸에 알맞은 말을 쓰시오.

The color of the stickers _____ the young man bought _____ _____.

16 다음은 위 글을 요약한 것이다. 빈칸에 알맞은 말을 쓰시오.

The bus maps in Seoul were very _____. So, a young man stuck red arrow stickers on _____. Thanks to him, people didn't have to _____ their time.

17 주어진 단어를 이용하여 다음 우리말을 영어로 쓰시오.

나는 버스 정류장의 지도들이 충분한 정보를 가지길 원했다. (want)

➡ _____

_____

18 Write the reason why the man stuck red arrow stickers on bus maps every day. Use the phrase 'it's because'.

➡ _____

해석

A: 나는 과학을 잘 못해. 어떻게 해야 할까?

B: 내가 도와줄게. 더 쉬운 책으로 시작하는 게 어때?

A: 응, 한번 시도 해볼게. 조언 고마워.

B: 괜찮아. 네가 좋아하니 기뻐.

Real Life Communication B

A: I'm not good at science. What can I do?
be good at: ~을 잘하다

B: Let me help you. Why don't you start with easier books?
~하는 게 어때?(= How about ~?= Let's~)

A: Okay, I'll give it a try. Thanks for the tip.
한번 해 보다

B: No problem. I'm glad you like it.

구문해설 • try: 시도 • tip: 조언

Let's Write

Be a Mentor!

My name is Semi and I'm in the second grade. I want to help my mentee with
2학년에   to부정사를 목적어로 취하는 동사

her homework. I can meet my mentee after school. I'll ask my mentee to be on
ask+목적어+to부정사: 목적어가 V하도록 요청하다

time. I think a good mentor can be a good friend. So I want to become a good
think의 목적어가 되는 명사절   그래서

friend whom my mentee can trust.
목적격 관계대명사로 생략 가능

구문해설 • grade: 점수, 학년 • mentor: 멘토(경험 없는 사람에게 오랜 기간에 걸쳐 조언과 도움을 베풀어 주는 선배)
• mentee: 멘티(멘토로부터 상담이나 조언을 받는 사람) • after school: 방과 후에
• be on time: 시간을 지키다

멘토가 되세요!

제 이름은 세미이고 저는 2학년입니다. 저는 제 멘티의 숙제를 돕고 싶습니다. 저는 방과 후에 제 멘티를 만날 수 있습니다. 저는 제 멘티에게 시간을 지키라고 요청할 것입니다. 저는 좋은 멘토는 좋은 친구가 될 수 있다고 생각합니다. 그래서 저는 제 멘티가 믿을 수 있는 좋은 친구가 되고 싶습니다.

Culture & Life

Do you see toys inside the bars of soap? Children in South Africa wash their
toys를 수식하는 형용사구

hands more often to get the toys. Washing your hands can prevent many health
to부정사의 부사적 용법 중 '목적'   동명사(주어)

problems. Thanks to this idea, fewer children are getting sick.
~ 덕분에   few의 비교급

구문해설 • bar: 바, 막대 • inside: ~ 안에 • South Africa: 남아프리카 • get: 얻다 • prevent: 예방하다
• get sick: 병에 걸리다

비누들 안에 들어 있는 장난감이 보이나요? 남아프리카의 어린이들은 장난감을 갖기 위해 더 자주 손을 씻습니다. 손을 씻는 것은 많은 건강 문제를 막을 수 있습니다. 이 아이디어 덕분에, 병에 걸리는 어린이들이 줄어들고 있습니다.

영역별 핵심문제

01 다음 영영풀이가 가리키는 것을 고르시오.

> a device or room that is used to keep things cold

① toaster ② refrigerator
③ closet ④ stove
⑤ blender

02 다음 중 밑줄 친 부분의 뜻풀이가 바르지 <u>않은</u> 것은?

① They <u>plan</u> to go abroad after graduating from high school. ~할 계획이다
② You need much <u>effort</u> to finish the project. 여유
③ Each student found out a different <u>solution</u> to the problem. 해결책
④ Where should we put our <u>trash</u>? 쓰레기
⑤ I put my jeans in the <u>basket</u>. 바구니

03 다음 우리말에 맞게 빈칸에 알맞은 말을 쓰시오.

(1) 너의 시간을 낭비하지 마라.
➡ Don't _____ _____ _____ .
(2) 너는 그 문제를 네 스스로 해결해야 한다.
➡ You should solve the problem _____ _____ _____ .
(3) 그는 컴퓨터 게임을 멈추고 나를 바라보았다.
➡ He _____ _____ computer games and looked at me.

04 다음 짝지어진 단어의 관계가 같도록 빈칸에 알맞은 말을 쓰시오.

> teacher : student = mentor : _____

05 다음 문장의 빈칸에 들어갈 말을 보기에서 골라 쓰시오.

> ┤ 보기 ├
> the other day / come up with / on your own

(1) We can _____ _____ _____ creative ideas.
(2) _____ _____ _____ , I came across my English teacher on the street.
(3) I can't believe you made it _____ _____ _____ .

06 다음 주어진 문장의 밑줄 친 rest와 <u>다른</u> 의미로 쓰인 것은?

> • The riders can take a <u>rest</u> at the parking lot.

① It is important for me to have an hour for <u>rest</u> during work.
② We needed a <u>rest</u> for a while because we didn't stop working.
③ You look so tired. Get some <u>rest</u>.
④ You'd better stop singing for a while and try to <u>rest</u>.
⑤ The <u>rest</u> of students spent time reading the books in the library.

[07~09] 다음 대화를 읽고 물음에 답하시오.

> Tom: Hojun and I planned to give out free stickers today, but I think he forgot.
> Sora: Really? (A)<u>Let me help you then.</u> Why are you going to give out stickers?
> Tom: It's part of our volunteer club activity.
> Sora: I see. What does this sticker mean?
> Tom: It means that when we smile at each other, the world will become a better place.
> Sora: That's a wonderful idea.

07 위 대화의 밑줄 친 (A)와 바꾸어 쓸 수 있는 것은?

① Can you help me then?
② Let me give you a hand then.
③ I need your help then.
④ Would you help me then?
⑤ I wonder if you can help me then.

08 위 대화에서 다음 영영풀이가 뜻하는 말을 찾아 쓰시오.

> a person who does a job without being paid for it

➡ _____

09 위 대화의 내용과 일치하지 <u>않는</u> 것은?

① Hojun과 Tom은 함께 봉사활동을 할 계획이었다.
② Sora가 Hojun 대신 Tom을 도와 줄 것이다.
③ Tom은 무료 스티커를 나누어 줄 계획이다.
④ 스티커는 우리가 서로 웃을 때 세상은 더 좋은 곳이 될 것이라는 것을 의미한다.
⑤ Sora는 Tom과 같은 봉사 동아리에서 활동하고 있다.

[10~12] 다음 대화를 읽고 물음에 답하시오.

> Mike: Jimin, what are all these things in the box?
> Jimin: (A) I'm going to give her my old books today.
> Mike: (B) Do you teach her every weekend?
> Jimin: (C) Yes. I feel ⓐ<u>happy</u> when I teach her.
> Mike: (D) You are a good mentor. Oh, the box looks heavy. Let me help you.
> Jimin: (E) Thanks.

10 위 대화의 (A)~(E) 중 주어진 문장이 들어가기에 적절한 곳은?

> They're for my mentee at the children's center.

① (A) ② (B) ③ (C) ④ (D) ⑤ (E)

11 위 대화의 밑줄 친 ⓐ와 바꾸어 쓸 수 <u>없는</u> 것은? (2개)

① delighted   ② pleased
③ joyful   ④ amazing
⑤ discouraged

12 위 대화의 내용과 일치하지 <u>않는</u> 것은?

① Jimin teaches her mentee at the children's center.
② Jimin is going to give her old books to her mentee.
③ Jimin meets her mentee every weekend.
④ Mike is going to give his hand to Jimin.
⑤ Mike is going to read some books at the children's center.

[13~15] 다음 대화를 읽고 물음에 답하시오.

> **Alex:** Mom, this is for you. I made it with plastic bags. ⓐ
> **Mom:** That's very cute, Alex. ⓑ
> **Alex:** You talked about it when we were having dinner the other day. ⓒ
> **Mom:** How nice! I really like this basket. It has many different colors. ⓓ
> **Alex:** I'm glad you like it. ⓔ

13 위 대화의 ⓐ~ⓔ 중 주어진 문장이 들어가기에 적절한 곳은?

> How did you know that I needed a new basket?

① ⓐ   ② ⓑ   ③ ⓒ   ④ ⓓ   ⑤ ⓔ

14 What did Alex make for her mom?

➡ _____

15 When did Alex's mom talk about a new basket?

➡ _____
_____

16 다음 대화가 자연스럽게 이어지도록 순서대로 배열하시오.

> (A) I'm glad you like it.
> (B) That's a great story.
> (C) Sure. Why is he special, Yujin?
> (D) I read a story about a special boy in India. Do you want to hear about it?
> (E) Many children in his town couldn't go to school and had to work. So he taught them in his house every day.

➡ _____

17 다음 빈칸에 들어갈 말로 가장 적절한 것은?

> The man warned us _____ the house. Because the roof of the house leaks.

① buy   ② not buying
③ buying   ④ not to buy
⑤ not to buying

18 다음 빈칸에 알맞은 말을 쓰시오.

> Korea is one of the countries ⓐ_____ lacks water. So teachers advise us ⓑ_____ water when we take a shower. Because saving water is the most important thing that we can do now.

➡ ⓐ _____ ⓑ _____

19 다음 대화의 빈칸에 들어갈 말이 바르게 짝지어진 것은?

> **A:** I want you _____ me what Katie's favorite flower is.
> **B:** Tulips are the flowers _____ Katie likes most.

① tell – whose   ② telling – which
③ to tell – that   ④ to tell – what
⑤ telling – what

20 다음 중 빈칸에 공통으로 들어갈 말로 가장 적절한 것은?

> • The novel _____ she wrote ten years ago is going to be published again.
> • Ann, _____ hat do you like better, this or that?

① which   ② that   ③ who
④ whose   ⑤ whom

21 다음 중 어법상 바르지 <u>않은</u> 것은?

① The poor management caused the disease to spread fast.

② Slow music helps us to stay calm and think carefully.

③ The teacher ordered us not to make any troubles.

④ I would like you accept my apology.

⑤ Don't let her stay alone in the park at night.

22 다음 우리말을 영어로 옮길 때 빈칸에 알맞은 말을 쓰시오.

• 그녀에게 이 편지를 복사하라고 요청해 주겠니?

= Can you _____ _____ _____ _____ this letter?

23 다음 중 어법상 바르지 <u>않은</u> 것은?

The bananas ①which my friend ② wanted ③me ④to taste yesterday ⑤ was very sweet.

24 밑줄 친 부분 중 생략할 수 <u>없는</u> 것은?

① He is the boy <u>that</u> my mom always compares with me.

② The tree <u>that</u> you planted grows well.

③ Did you think about the suggestion <u>that</u> I made?

④ I want to become a good friend <u>that</u> my friends can trust.

⑤ There are kids <u>that</u> have been left alone all day.

25 다음 빈칸에 적절하지 <u>않은</u> 것은?

My mentor _____ me to do my best.

① persuaded ② wanted

③ advised ④ told

⑤ said

Reading

[26~29] 다음 글을 읽고 물음에 답하시오.

Here ①<u>are</u> two stories which I read yesterday. Do you want to hear about them?

Call Someone You Love
New York had many pay phones on its streets. However, (A)[everybody / nobody] really used ②<u>them</u>. One day, a man (B)[came up with / came down with] an idea. He ③<u>stuck</u> coins to one of the phones. He also put up a sign that said, "Call Someone You Love." Soon, many people were ④<u>used</u> the phone. When they were talking to someone ⓐ _____, they didn't stop ⑤<u>smiling</u>. His idea became a big success. During the day, all the coins (C)[appeared / disappeared]. The man was very happy because his small idea gave happiness to many people.

26 알맞은 관계대명사를 이용하여 빈칸 ⓐ에 들어갈 말을 세 단어로 쓰시오.

➡ _____

27 (A)~(C)에서 글의 흐름상 적절한 것끼리 바르게 짝지은 것은?

① everybody – came up with – appeared

② nobody – came up with – disappeared

③ everybody – came down with – appeared

④ nobody – came down with – disappeared

⑤ everybody – came up with – disappeared

28 ①~⑤ 중 어법상 틀린 것을 찾아 바르게 고치시오.

➡ _____

29 다음 중 글을 읽고 답할 수 없는 것은?

① What idea did a man come up with?
② Where were the pay phones in New York?
③ When did people start to use the pay phone?
④ What did people keep doing while using the pay phone?
⑤ How many phone calls did people make?

[30~34] 다음 글을 읽고 물음에 답하시오.

The Red Arrow Man

A few years ago, the maps at bus stops in Seoul were very confusing. They didn't have enough information. People had to ask others (A)_____ the maps. "Where is this bus stop on the map? Does this bus go to Gwanghwamun?" Many people often ⓐtook the wrong bus and wasted their time.

One day, a young man decided (B)_____ this problem. ① Every day he rode his bicycle around the city and stuck the stickers on the bus maps. ② Nobody asked him (C)_____ this. ③ He just wanted to help others. ④ Thanks to his effort, people could understand the maps easily and save time. ⑤

30 주어진 단어를 문맥과 어법에 맞게 빈칸 (A)~(C)에 쓰시오.

(solve / explain / do)

➡ (A) _____ (B) _____ (C) _____

31 ①~⑤ 중 다음 문장이 들어가기에 가장 적절한 곳은?

He bought lots of red arrow stickers.

①   ②   ③   ④   ⑤

32 다음 중 밑줄 친 ⓐ와 의미가 같은 것은?

① Do you take sugar in your coffee?
② I will take the black jacket.
③ Katherine forgot to take her purse with her.
④ What are you going to take to get there?
⑤ Can you take my hand for a moment?

33 다음 중 위 글의 내용과 일치하지 않는 것은?

① The maps at bus stops in Seoul made people confused a few years ago.
② There wasn't enough information on the maps.
③ People in Seoul took the wrong bus all the time.
④ The young man stuck stickers on his own.
⑤ The man thought that his effort would help other people.

34 위 글의 내용에 맞게 다음 물음에 완전한 문장의 영어로 답하시오.

Q: What happened to people because of the bus maps?

➡ _____
_____

[01~03] 다음 대화를 읽고 물음에 답하시오.

Tom: Hojun and I planned to give out ⓐfree stickers today, but I think he forgot.

Sora: (A) Why are you going to give out stickers?

Tom: (B) It's part of our volunteer club activity.

Sora: (C) I see. What does this sticker mean?

Tom: (D) It means that when we smile at each other, the world will become a better place.

Sora: (E) That's a wonderful idea.

출제율 90%

01 위 대화의 (A)~(E) 중 주어진 문장이 들어가기에 적절한 곳은?

> Really? Let me help you then.

① (A) ② (B) ③ (C) ④ (D) ⑤ (E)

출제율 95%

02 위 대화의 밑줄 친 ⓐfree와 같은 의미로 쓰인 것은?

① They are fighting for free speech.
② Jane felt free like a bird.
③ I usually listen to music in my free time.
④ Please feel free to contact me.
⑤ We don't have to pay for the drinks because they're all free.

출제율 90%

03 위 대화를 읽고 대답할 수 없는 것은?

① What did Hojun and Tom plan to do today?
② Why did Tom want to give out stickers?
③ What did the stickers mean?
④ Which club did Tom belong to?
⑤ Why didn't Hojun appear to do his volunteer club activity?

[04~05] 다음 대화를 읽고 물음에 답하시오.

Alex: Mom, this is for you. I made it with plastic bags.

Mom: That's very cute, Alex. How did you know that I needed a new basket?

Alex: You talked about it when we were having dinner the other day.

Mom: (A)How nice! I really like this basket. It has many different colors.

Alex: (B)엄마가 좋아하시니 저도 기뻐요. (glad)

출제율 95%

04 위 대화의 밑줄 친 (A)와 바꾸어 쓸 수 있는 것을 모두 고르시오.

① How nice the basket is!
② How much is it?
③ What do you think about it?
④ How is the basket?
⑤ What a nice basket!

출제율 90%

05 위 대화의 밑줄 친 우리말 (B)를 주어진 단어를 사용하여 영작하시오.

➡ _____

[06~07] 다음 대화를 읽고 물음에 답하시오.

Yujin: I read a story about a special boy in India. Do you want to hear about it?

Jack: Sure. Why is he special, Yujin?

Yujin: Many children in his town couldn't go to school and had to work. So he taught them in his house every day.

Jack: (A)_____

Yujin: I'm glad you like it.

06 위 대화의 빈칸 (A)에 들어갈 말로 <u>어색한</u> 것은?

① It's so touching.

② What a beautiful story!

③ How wonderful it is!

④ That's a great story.

⑤ I'm sorry to hear that.

07 위 대화의 내용과 일치하도록 빈칸을 완성하시오.

> Q: Why was the boy in India special?
> A: Because he taught (A)_____
> _____ who (B)_____
> _____ in his house
> every day.

[08~10] 다음 대화를 읽고 물음에 답하시오.

> Emily: Welcome back, Brian. Are you feeling ⓐbetter?
> Brian: Yes, thanks. I tried to study on my own in the hospital, but it was hard.
> Emily: Let me help you. (A)<u>Why don't you join my study group?</u> (how)
> Brian: Did you start a study group? That's ⓑwonderful.
> Emily: Thanks. I think that we can learn ⓒbetter when we teach each other.
> Brian: I ⓓdisagree. I'll try hard to be a good member. Thanks for helping me.
> Emily: You're welcome. I'm ⓔglad you like my idea.

08 위 대화의 밑줄 친 (A)와 바꾸어 쓸 수 있는 말을 주어진 단어를 사용하여 쓰시오.

➡ _____

09 위 대화의 밑줄 친 ⓐ~ⓔ 중 대화의 흐름상 <u>어색한</u> 말을 찾아 바르게 고치시오.

➡ _____

10 위 대화의 내용과 일치하지 <u>않는</u> 것은?

① Brian은 몸이 좋지 않았었다.

② Emily는 스터디 모임을 시작했다.

③ Emily는 서로 가르쳐 주면 더 잘 배울 수 있을 것이라고 생각한다.

④ Emily는 Brain에게 스터디 모임에 함께 할 것을 제안하였다.

⑤ Brain은 Emily와 함께 병원에서 공부하였다.

11 다음 빈칸에 들어갈 말이 바르게 짝지어진 것은?

> • The thing _____ Ann asked me _____ is preparing for the party.

① which – do ② that – doing

③ what – to do ④ which – to do

⑤ that – did

12 다음 우리말을 영어로 옮길 때 빈칸에 들어갈 말로 가장 적절한 것은?

> 내가 답변해 주기를 원하는 질문이 뭐니?
> What is the question _____?

① that you want to ask

② which you want me to answer

③ that you want to answer

④ which I want to answer

⑤ that I want you to answer

13 다음 중 어법상 바르지 <u>않은</u> 것은?

① I want you to consider the option.

② The cup that is on the table is mine.

③ Men who work hard is diligent.

④ Molly will ask you to help her.

⑤ Don't tell me to join the club.

14 주어진 단어를 활용하여 다음 우리말을 영어로 쓰시오.
[출제율 85%]

> 내가 사고 싶은 차는 미니밴(minivan)이야.
> (that)

➡ _____

15 다음 두 문장을 하나의 문장으로 쓰시오.
[출제율 90%]

(1) He gave some candies to the little kids. He saw them.

➡ _____

(2) There was a festival. Many people took part in the festival.

➡ _____

(3) The dish was not that expensive. You broke it.

➡ _____

16 다음 상황을 읽고 빈칸에 알맞은 말을 쓰시오.
[출제율 95%]

> I felt a little cold. When I looked around, I found that the window was open. Jimmy sat next to the window. So I asked Jimmy _____ _____ _____ _____.

17 다음 중 보기의 밑줄 친 that과 쓰임이 같은 것은?
[출제율 100%]

> ┌ 보기 ┐
> The fact that you lied to me never changes.

① Jack is the man that saved my life.
② The train that you took is slow.
③ I heard the news that you won the game.
④ The pen that you bought is here.
⑤ Always cook the foods that you eat.

[18~21] 다음 글을 읽고 물음에 답하시오.

> Here are two stories which I read yesterday. Do you want to hear about them?
>
> Call Someone You Love
> New York had many pay phones on its streets. However, nobody really used them. One day, a man came up with an idea. He stuck coins to one of the phones. He also put up a sign ⓐ_____ said, "Call Someone You Love." Soon, many people were using the phone. When they were talking to someone whom they loved, they didn't stop smiling. His idea became a big success. During the day, all the coins disappeared. The man was very happy because his small idea gave happiness to many people.

18 빈칸 ⓐ에 알맞은 말을 모두 쓰시오.
[출제율 90%]

➡ _____

19 다음 중 글의 내용과 일치하는 것의 개수는?
[출제율 95%]

> ⓐ There are many public telephones in New York.
> ⓑ People in New York enjoy using a public phone.
> ⓒ It is difficult to know who stuck the coins to the phone.
> ⓓ People used all the coins during the day.
> ⓔ The man thought his idea failed in the end.

① 1개   ② 2개   ③ 3개
④ 4개   ⑤ 5개

20 다음 중 위 글에 이어질 내용으로 가장 적절한 것은?

① what I did yesterday

② another story I wrote

③ another interesting story I heard

④ the other story I read

⑤ other people I called

21 글의 내용에 맞게 빈칸에 알맞은 말을 쓰시오.

> His small idea gave happiness to many people, so _____.

22 주어진 문장과 자연스러운 연결이 되도록 (A)~(D)를 바르게 나열하시오.

> A few years ago, the maps at bus stops in Seoul were very confusing.

(A) "Where is this bus stop on the map? Does this bus go to Gwanghwamun?" Many people often took the wrong bus and wasted their time.

(B) Every day he rode his bicycle around the city and stuck the stickers on the bus maps. Nobody asked him to do this. He just wanted to help others.

(C) One day, a young man decided to solve this problem. He bought lots of red arrow stickers.

(D) They didn't have enough information. People had to ask others to explain the maps.

➡ _____

[23~25] 다음 글을 읽고 물음에 답하시오.

The Red Arrow Man

A few years ago, the maps at bus stops in Seoul were very confusing. They didn't have enough information. People had to ask others to explain the maps. "Where is this bus stop on the map? Does this bus go to Gwanghwamun?" Many people often took the wrong bus and wasted their time.

One day, a young man decided to solve this problem. He bought lots of red arrow stickers. Every day he rode his bicycle around the city and stuck the stickers on the bus maps. Nobody asked him to ⓐdo this. He just wanted to help others. Thanks to his effort, people could understand the maps easily and save time.

23 위 글의 밑줄 친 ⓐdo this가 가리키는 것을 우리말로 간단히 쓰시오.

➡ _____

24 다음 중 위 글의 내용과 일치하지 않는 것은?

① The maps at bus stops in Seoul were not easy to understand.

② The stickers that the man bought were arrow shapes.

③ The young man had his bike.

④ What the man wanted was to help other people.

⑤ The man stuck the stickers every weekend.

25 What happened after the young man's effort? Answer in English with a full sentence.

➡ _____

_____

[01~03] 다음 대화를 읽고 물음에 답하시오.

> Mike: Jimin, what are all these things in the box?
>
> Jimin: They're for my mentee at the children's center. I'm going to give her my old books today.
>
> Mike: Do you teach her every weekend?
>
> Jimin: Yes. I feel happy when I teach her.
>
> Mike: You are a good mentor. Oh, the box looks heavy. Let me help you.
>
> Jimin: Thanks.

01 What is Jimin going to give to her mentee today?

➡ _____

02 How does Jimin feel when she teaches her mentee?

➡ _____

03 What is Mike going to do to help Jimin?

➡ _____

04 다음 빈칸에 알맞은 말을 쓰시오.

> The dentist told me _____ _____ my mouth. But I was so scared that I couldn't open it.

05 주어진 단어를 활용하여 다음 우리말을 영어로 쓰시오.

> 너는 우리가 도서관에서 대출한 그 책을 가지고 있니?
> (have / which / check out / from)

➡ _____

_____

06 주어진 단어를 활용하여 다음 문장과 같은 의미의 문장을 쓰시오.

> My mom let me stay out late.
> (allow)

➡ _____

07 다음 상황을 읽고 주어진 단어를 활용하여 빈칸을 알맞게 채우시오.

> Paul: Jimmy, would you get in line, please? We are all waiting in line here.

> ask

➡ Paul _____.

08 적절한 관계대명사를 이용하여 다음 우리말을 영어로 쓰시오.

> 네가 읽고 있는 책은 흥미롭니?

➡ _____

09 다음 우리말에 맞도록 빈칸에 알맞은 말을 쓰시오.

> 어제 네가 길에서 이야기하고 있었던 소년은 누구였니?
> Who was the boy _____ _____ _____ _____ on the street yesterday?

[10~12] 다음 글을 읽고 물음에 답하시오.

Call Someone You Love

New York had many pay phones on its streets. However, nobody really used them. One day, ⓐa man came up with an idea. He stuck coins ①to one of the ②phones. He also put up a sign that ③said, "Call Someone You Love." Soon, many people were using the phone. When they were talking to someone whom they loved, they didn't stop ④to smile. His idea became ⑤a big success. During the day, all the coins disappeared. The man was very happy because his small idea gave happiness to many people.

10 ①~⑤ 중 어법상 **틀린** 것을 골라 바르게 고치시오.

➡ _____

11 다음은 밑줄 친 ⓐ와의 대화이다. 빈칸에 알맞은 말을 쓰시오.

> A: What are you doing?
> B: I am _____ _____ to this pay phone.
> A: Why?
> B: It will enable people _____ _____ someone _____ _____. And people will have an interest in using pay phones.
> A: What a great idea!

12 글의 내용에 맞도록 다음 물음의 대답을 완성하시오.

> Q: Why was the man happy?
> A: It's because _____.

➡ _____

[13~14] 다음 글을 읽고 물음에 답하시오.

The Red Arrow Man

A few years ago, the maps at bus stops in Seoul were very confusing. They didn't have enough information. People had to ask others to explain the maps. "Where is this bus stop on the map? Does this bus go to Gwanghwamun?" Many people often took the wrong bus and wasted their time.

One day, a young man decided to solve this problem. He bought lots of red arrow stickers. Every day he rode his bicycle around the city and stuck the stickers on the bus maps. Nobody asked him to do this. He just wanted to help others. Thanks to his effort, people could understand the maps easily and save time.

13 다음 우리말에 맞게 빈칸에 알맞은 말을 쓰시오.

> 그가 그 문제를 해결하기 위하여 산 것들은 빨간 화살표 스티커였다.
> The things _____ _____ _____ _____ _____ were red arrow stickers.

14 What did people have to do to take the right bus in Seoul? Answer in English with a full sentence.

➡ _____

01 다음 대화의 내용과 일치하도록 Brian의 일기를 완성하시오.

> Emily: Welcome back, Brian. Are you feeling better?
> Brian: Yes, thanks. I tried to study on my own in the hospital, but it was hard.
> Emily: Let me help you. Why don't you join my study group?
> Brian: Did you start a study group? That's wonderful.
> Emily: Thanks. I think that we can learn better when we teach each other.
> Brian: I agree. I'll try hard to be a good member. Thanks for helping me.
> Emily: You're welcome. I'm glad you like my idea.

⬇

> Tue, May 28th, 2019
> I was happy to come back to school. Emily welcomed me very warmly. We talked about lots of things including study. While I was in the hospital, I tried to study (A)_____ but it was hard. When I talked about it to Emily, she gave me a hand. She suggested (B)_____. She started it because she thought that (C)_____. I agreed to her idea. I decided to (D)_____. I really appreciated her.

02 알맞은 관계대명사를 이용하여 다음 사물이나 직업을 설명하는 문장을 완성하시오.

> a painter / a purse / a baker / a chair

(1) _____

(2) _____

(3) _____

(4) _____

03 주어진 동사로 여러 가지 문장을 쓰시오.

> ask / encourage / force / enable / allow / tell

(1) _____

(2) _____

(3) _____

(4) _____

(5) _____

단원별 모의고사

01 다음 짝지어진 단어의 관계가 같도록 빈칸에 알맞은 말을 쓰시오.

> same : different = inside : _____

02 다음 영영풀이가 가리키는 것을 고르시오.

> a person who is advised and helped by more experienced person

① mentee
② teacher
③ mentor
④ professor
⑤ president

03 다음 우리말을 주어진 단어를 이용하여 영작하시오.

(1) 박쥐는 대개 낮 동안에 잠을 잔다. (mostly, during)

➡ _____

(2) 나는 나의 엄마에게 전화하기 위해 공중전화를 사용했다. (pay, call, mom)

➡ _____

(3) 그는 회의에서 좋은 아이디어를 생각해 냈다. (came, great)

➡ _____

[04~06] 다음 대화를 읽고 물음에 답하시오.

> Alex: Mom, this is for you. I made it with plastic bags.
> Mom: That's very cute, Alex. How did you know that I needed a new basket?
> Alex: You talked about it when we were having dinner the other day.
> Mom: (A)_____ nice! I really like this basket. It has many different colors.
> Alex: I'm glad you like it.

04 위 대화의 빈칸 (A)에 알맞은 것은?

① Why
② How
③ What
④ When
⑤ Where

05 위 대화를 통해 알 수 있는 엄마의 심경으로 적절한 것은?

① lonely
② happy
③ nervous
④ upset
⑤ dissatisfied

06 위 대화를 읽고 대답할 수 없는 것은?

① What did Alex make for his mom?
② What did Alex use to make his gift for his mom?
③ How did Alex know that his mother needed a new basket?
④ How did Alex feel when his mother liked his gift?
⑤ Where did Alex learn how to make a basket?

[07~09] 다음 대화를 읽고 물음에 답하시오.

> Emily: Welcome back, Brian. Are you feeling better?
> Brian: Yes, thanks. I tried to study (A)[of / on] my own in the hospital, but it was hard.
> Emily: Let me help you. Why don't you join my study group?
> Brian: Did you start a study group? That's wonderful.
> Emily: Thanks. I think (B)[which / that] we can learn better when we teach each other.

Brian: I agree. I'll try hard to be a good member. Thanks for helping me.

Emily: (D)_____ I'm glad you (C)[like / to like] my idea.

07 위 대화의 괄호 (A)~(C)에서 알맞은 말을 고르시오.

➡ (A)_____, (B)_____, (C)_____

08 위 대화의 빈칸 (D)에 들어가기에 <u>어색한</u> 것은?

① Don't mention it.
② It's my pleasure.
③ Not at all.
④ You're welcome.
⑤ Don't blame me.

09 위 대화를 읽고 대답할 수 <u>없는</u> 것은?

① What did Brian try to do in the hospital?
② What did Emily start?
③ What did Emily suggest to Brian?
④ What did Emily think about a study group?
⑤ What did Emily and Brain learn in a study group?

[10~11] 다음 대화를 읽고 물음에 답하시오.

Henry: Your bag looks heavy. Let me help you.

Sujin: Thanks. Where is the bus stop around here?

Henry: It's over there. I'll carry your bag to the bus stop for you.

Sujin: You're very kind.

Henry: No problem. I am going that way, too.

10 What was Sujin looking for?

➡ _____

11 How did Henry help Sujin?

➡ _____

12 다음 중 짝지어진 대화가 <u>어색한</u> 것은?

① A: I made this picture frame for you.
   B: Thanks. It's wonderful.
② A: Sounds great. I like your story.
   B: I'm glad you like it.
③ A: You're so kind to say like that.
   B: My pleasure.
④ A: I really appreciate your help.
   B: Don't mention it.
⑤ A: I enjoyed baking this cake for you.
   B: I'm sorry to hear that.

13 다음 중 빈칸에 공통으로 들어갈 말로 가장 적절한 것은?

• The dog _____ you take care of has a long tail.
• The children _____ she is looking at look excited.

① that   ② which   ③ whose
④ who   ⑤ what

14 다음 빈칸에 알맞은 말을 쓰시오.

I don't like to eat vegetables. But my mother wants me _____ _____ them.

15 다음 중 빈칸에 들어갈 말로 적절하지 <u>않은</u> 것은?

> I _____ you to answer the phone.

① would like   ② want
③ ask   ④ allow
⑤ make

16 주어진 어구를 활용하여 다음 우리말을 영어로 쓰시오.

> 나는 많은 사람들이 아주 좋아할 영화를 만들고 싶어.
> (a movie / will love)

➡ _____

17 주어진 어구를 바르게 배열하여 다음 우리말을 영어로 쓰시오. 필요하다면 단어를 추가하시오.

> 그 선생님은 우리에게 정각에 오라고 말씀하셨다.
> (on / the teacher / be / us / time / told)

➡ _____

[18~21] 다음 글을 읽고 물음에 답하시오.

Call Someone You Love
New York had many pay phones on its streets. However, nobody really used them. One day, a man came up with an idea. He stuck coins to one of the phones. He also put up a sign that said, "Call Someone You Love." Soon, many people were using the phone. When they were talking to someone whom they loved, they didn't stop (A)<u>smiling</u>. His idea became a big success. During the day, all the coins disappeared. The man was very happy (B) _____ his small idea gave happiness to many people.

18 밑줄 친 (A)와 쓰임이 <u>다른</u> 하나는?

① I am tired of <u>hearing</u> the noise.
② Do you mind <u>opening</u> the door?
③ Norman finished <u>reading</u> the paper.
④ What are they <u>doing</u> now?
⑤ The boys practiced <u>playing</u> soccer after school.

19 다음 중 빈칸 (B)에 들어갈 말로 적절한 것을 <u>모두</u> 고르면?

① though   ② until   ③ as
④ if   ⑤ because

20 다음 중 글의 내용과 일치하는 것은?

① Everybody used play phones in New York.
② A man stuck coins to a pay phone in New York.
③ A man talked with people about using pay phones.
④ People started to use the pay phone after having a conversation with the man.
⑤ Many coins were left at night.

21 주어진 어구를 바르게 배열하여 위 글을 요약하는 문장을 완성하시오.

> (thanks to / when / someone they loved / many people in New York / a man's idea / became happy / they called).

➡ _____
_____

[22~25] 다음 글을 읽고 물음에 답하시오.

The Red Arrow Man

A few years ago, the maps at bus stops in Seoul (A)[was / were] very confusing. They didn't have enough information. People had to ask others to explain the maps. "Where is this bus stop on the map? Does this bus go to Gwanghwamun?" Many people (B)[often took / took often] the wrong bus and wasted their time.

One day, a young man decided to solve this problem. He bought ⓐ_____ red arrow stickers. Every day he rode his bicycle around the city and stuck (C)[it / them] on the bus maps. Nobody asked him to do this. He just wanted to help others. Thanks to his effort, people could understand the maps easily and save time.

22 다음 중 빈칸 ⓐ에 들어갈 말로 적절하지 <u>않은</u> 것은?

① lots of
② many
③ a lot of
④ a number of
⑤ much

23 (A)~(C)에서 어법상 옳은 것끼리 바르게 짝지은 것은?

① was – often took – it
② were – often took – them
③ was – took often – it
④ were – took often – it
⑤ was – took often – them

24 다음 중 위 글을 읽고 답할 수 있는 것의 개수는?

ⓐ What was the matter with the maps at bus stops in Seoul?
ⓑ How many bus stops were there in Seoul a few years ago?
ⓒ What bus did people take to go to Gwanghwamun?
ⓓ What did the man do to solve the problem?
ⓔ Why did people often take the wrong bus?

① 1개
② 2개
③ 3개
④ 4개
⑤ 5개

25 위 글의 내용에 맞게 빈칸에 알맞은 말을 쓰시오.

The young man wanted to help _____ _____ _____ the maps easily.

INSIGHT
on the textbook
교과서 파헤치기

※ 다음 영어를 우리말로 쓰시오.

01 planet	_____	22 upset	_____
02 bite	_____	23 healthy	_____
03 truth	_____	24 decide	_____
04 soon	_____	25 smart	_____
05 clean	_____	26 personal	_____
06 dear	_____	27 hobby	_____
07 break	_____	28 print	_____
08 during	_____	29 traffic	_____
09 beef	_____	30 tip	_____
10 email	_____	31 fall	_____
11 toy	_____	32 space	_____
12 handle	_____	33 not ~ anymore	_____
13 jogging	_____	34 think of	_____
14 lie	_____	35 by the way	_____
15 nail	_____	36 these days	_____
16 false	_____	37 change into	_____
17 wish	_____	38 come true	_____
18 sure	_____	39 be into	_____
19 try	_____	40 do one's best	_____
20 vacation	_____	41 each other	_____
21 homeroom teacher	_____	42 on one's way home	_____
		43 be interested in	_____

※ 다음 우리말을 영어로 쓰시오.

01 곧

02 교통

03 조언, 정보

04 틀린, 거짓의

05 똑똑한, 명석한

06 봄

07 인쇄하다

08 미술 , 예술

09 건강한, 튼튼한

10 가을

11 우주

12 결정하다

13 종류

14 컵케이크

15 개인적인

16 잡다, 쥐다

17 주의, 조심

18 취미

19 화난, 속상한

20 재미있는, 익살맞은

21 야채

22 거짓말을 하다

23 행성

24 깨뜨리다, 부수다

25 물다; 물린 자국

26 사실, 진실

27 방학

28 소고기

29 틀린, 거짓의

30 손잡이

31 손톱

32 장난감

33 서로

34 집에 오는 길에

35 ~에 열중하다

36 변화를 이루다

37 실현되다

38 그건 그렇고, 그런데

39 더 이상 ~하지 않다

40 최선을 다하다

41 그 당시에

42 ~로 변하다

43 ~에 흥미가 있다

※ 다음 영영풀이에 알맞은 단어를 <보기>에서 골라 쓴 후, 우리말 뜻을 쓰시오.

1 _____ : meat from a cow: _____

2 _____ : all through a period of time: _____

3 _____ : a teacher in charge of a class: _____

4 _____ : to make a choice about something: _____

5 _____ : to send a message to someone by email: _____

6 _____ : to press down on or cut into someone or something with the teeth: _____

7 _____ : the hard covering at the end of a finger or toe: _____

8 _____ : a feeling of wanting to do or have something: _____

9 _____ : a part that is designed especially to be grasped by the hand: _____

10 _____ : belonging or relating to a particular person: _____

11 _____ : a large, round object in space that travels around a star: _____

12 _____ : an activity that a person does for pleasure when not working: _____

13 _____ : to do or use something in order to find out if you like it: _____

14 _____ : the methods and skills used for painting, sculpting, drawing, etc.:
_____

15 _____ : the movement of vehicles or pedestrians through an area or along a route:
_____

16 _____ : to produce letters, pictures, etc. on paper using a machine that puts ink
on the surface: _____

※ 다음 우리말과 일치하도록 빈칸에 알맞은 말을 쓰시오.

Listen & Speak 1 A

Brian: Julia, _____ was your _____ _____?

Julia: It was great. _____ _____ _____? I took *muay thai* lessons _____ _____ _____.

Brian: That's amazing. I didn't know that _____ _____ _____ _____ *muay thai*.

Julia: Yes. It was _____ _____.

Brian: Really? I _____ _____ _____ it.

Listen & Speak 1 B

Jimin: You _____ _____, Tim? Mr. Smith is my _____ _____ this year.

Tim: That's great, Jimin. _____ _____ _____ last year was _____ _____ _____ _____.

Jimin: Who's your homeroom teacher _____ _____?

Tim: It's Ms. Kim. She's a _____ _____.

Jimin: _____ _____ _____ _____?

Tim: She _____ _____.

Listen & Speak 2 A

Jane: Minsu, Sujin and I _____ _____ _____ _____ a club.

Minsu: Really? _____ _____ _____ _____ _____?

Jane: We want to _____ _____ _____ and _____. So, we're _____ of _____ a space science club.

Minsu: _____ good. _____ _____ are you _____ to meet?

Jane: Maybe _____ _____.

Minsu: I see. Where _____ you _____?

Jane: In Room 101. Minsu, do you _____ _____ _____ _____ _____?

Minsu: Yes, _____ _____ _____ space, _____.

Listen & Speak 2 B

Alex: Mom, I _____ *bulgogi* at school today. _____ _____ _____ _____ *bulgogi* _____ _____.

Mom: That _____ _____, Alex.

Alex: Do we have any vegetables _____ _____, Mom? _____ _____ _____?

Mom: We have some _____, but we _____ _____ beef. _____ _____ _____ _____ _____ _____ _____ _____.

Alex: Great.

Alex: 엄마, 오늘 학교에서 불고기를 만들었어요. 오늘 저녁으로 불고기를 요리할 생각이에요.
Mom 그거 멋지구나, Alex.
Alex: 집에 채소 있어요, 엄마? 소고기는요?
Mom 채소는 좀 있는데 소고기는 없어. 집에 오는 길에 좀 사올게.
Alex: 좋아요.

Real Life Communication A

Emily: You _____ _____, Junsu? _____ _____ _____ _____ a _____ _____.

Junsu: Really? Why did you _____ _____ _____ a painting class, Emily?

Emily: Because _____ _____ _____ _____ _____ _____ _____ _____ _____ _____.

Junsu: _____ you _____ _____ _____ an artist in the future?

Emily: I hope so. I'm _____ _____ _____ pictures.

Junsu: That's great. I hope your wish _____ _____.

Emily: Thanks. I'll _____ _____ _____.

Emily 준수야, 그거 아니? 나는 미술 수업을 들을 생각이야.
Junsu 정말? 왜 미술 수업을 들으려고 결심했니, Emily?
Emily 예술 고등학교에 가고 싶어서야.
Junsu 장래에 미술가가 될 생각이니?
Emily 그러고 싶어. 나는 그림 그리는 것에 흥미가 있어.
Junsu 그거 잘 됐다. 네 꿈이 이뤄지길 바라.
Emily 고마워. 최선을 다할 거야.

Real Life Communication B

Sue: You know what? Jenny's family is _____ _____ _____ to Japan.

Jack: Is that right? Jenny _____ _____ _____ _____ it.

Sue: She _____ _____ it just last week and she's very _____ now.

Jack: _____ _____ _____ _____ _____. I am _____ _____ _____ her so much.

Sue: Me, too. She said she would _____ _____ _____ _____ us.

Sue 있잖아, Jenny 가족이 일본으로 이민을 간대.
Jack 정말이야? Jenny가 그것에 관해 얘기하지 않았는데.
Sue Jenny도 지난주에야 알았어. 그래서 지금 매우 기분이 안 좋아.
Jack 나는 Jenny의 기분을 이해할 수 있어. Jenny가 정말 그리울 거야.
Sue 나도 그래. Jenny는 우리와 계속 연락할 거라고 했어.

※ 다음 우리말에 맞도록 대화를 영어로 쓰시오.

Listen & Speak 1 A

Brian: _____

Julia: _____

Brian: _____

Julia: _____

Brian: _____

Brian: Julia, 네 겨울 방학은 어땠니?
Julia: 좋았어. 그거 아니? 나는 방학 동안 무에타이 수업을 받았어.
Brian: 그거 멋지다. 나는 네가 무에타이에 관심이 있는지 몰랐어.
Julia: 응. 아주 재미있었어.
Brian: 그래? 나도 해 보고 싶다.

Listen & Speak 1 B

Jimin: _____

Tim: _____

Jimin: _____

Tim: _____

Jimin: _____

Tim: _____

Jimin: 그거 아니, Tim? Smith 선생님이 올해 우리 반 담임 선생님이야.
Tim: 그거 잘됐다, 지민아. 작년 Smith 선생님의 과학 수업은 아주 재미있었어.
Jimin: 올해 너희 반 담임 선생님은 누구니?
Tim: 김 선생님이야. 그녀는 새로 오신 선생님이야.
Jimin: 그분은 어떤 과목을 가르치시니?
Tim: 미술을 가르치셔.

Listen & Speak 2 A

Jane: _____

Minsu: _____

Jane: _____

_____

Minsu: _____

Jane: _____

Minsu: _____

Jane: _____

Minsu: _____

Jane: 민수야, 수진이와 나는 동아리를 만들 생각이야.
Minsu: 정말? 어떤 종류의 동아리야?
Jane: 우리는 별과 행성에 대해 배우고 싶어. 그래서 우주 과학 동아리를 만들 생각이야.
Minsu: 그거 멋지다. 얼마나 자주 모일 예정이니?
Jane: 아마도 일주일에 한 번쯤.
Minsu: 그렇구나. 어디에서 모일 거니?
Jane: 101호에서. 민수야, 우리 동아리에 가입할래?
Minsu: 응, 나도 우주에 관심 있어.

Listen & Speak 2 B

Alex: _____

_____

Mom: _____

Alex: _____

Mom: _____

_____

Alex: _____

Real Life Communication A

Emily: _____

Junsu: _____

Emily: _____

Junsu: _____

Emily: _____

Junsu: _____

Emily: _____

Real Life Communication B

Sue: _____

Jack: _____

Sue: _____

Jack: _____

Sue: _____

※ 다음 우리말과 일치하도록 빈칸에 알맞은 것을 골라 쓰시오.

1 My friend Eric and I _____ some interesting _____ _____ the vacation.

A. during   B. changes   C. made

2 We _____ each _____ and talked _____ our changes.

A. about   B. emailed   C. other

3 _____ _____,

A. Eric   B. dear

4 _____'s a beautiful _____ _____ Seoul.

A. in   B. spring   C. it

5 The _____ winter _____ was a great _____ _____ me.

A. for   B. vacation   C. time   D. last

6 I _____ two _____ changes _____ the vacation.

A. during   B. personal   C. made

7 _____ is _____ new _____.

A. hobby   B. my   C. one

8 It's _____ _____.

A. cupcakes   B. making

9 _____ my _____ cupcakes _____ a lot of fun.

A. is   B. own   C. making

10 The _____ _____ is _____ one of my bad _____.

A. habits   B. breaking   C. change   D. other

11 In the _____, I often _____ my _____.

A. nails   B. bit   C. past

12 Now I _____.

A. anymore   B. don't

13 I _____ great _____ the changes I _____.

A. made   B. about   C. feel

14 _____ you _____ to make some changes, I'm sure you will _____ great _____ me.

A. like   B. feel   C. try   D. if

15 I _____ to _____ _____ you soon.

A. from   B. hear   C. hope

16 _____ _____, Junho.

A. friend   B. your

---

1 내 친구 Eric과 나는 방학 동안 흥미로운 변화가 있었다.

2 우리는 서로에게 이메일을 보냈고 우리의 변화에 관해 이야기했다.

3 안녕 Eric.

4 서울은 아름다운 봄이야.

5 지난 겨울 방학은 나에게 멋진 시간이었어.

6 나는 방학 동안 두 가지 개인적인 변화가 있었어.

7 하나는 나의 새로운 취미야.

8 그것은 컵케이크를 만드는 거야.

9 나만의 컵케이크를 만드는 것은 정말 재미있어.

10 나머지 다른 변화는 나의 나쁜 습관 중 하나를 없애는 거야.

11 예전에 나는 종종 손톱을 물어뜯곤 했어.

12 이제 나는 더 이상 그러지 않아.

13 나는 내가 만든 변화가 정말 기분 좋아.

14 만약 네가 변화하려고 노력한다면, 너도 나처럼 기분이 좋을 거라고 확신해.

15 곧 소식 전해 줘.

16 너의 친구 준호가

17 _____ _____ ,

A. Junho   B. dear

18 _____ Sydney, _____ 's _____ in March.

A. fall   B. it   C. in

19 You _____ _____ your _____ in your email.

A. changes   B. about   C. talked

20 Now, it's _____ _____ _____ _____ my new changes.

A. about   B. to   C. talk   D. time

21 _____ _____ , I'm _____ 3D printing.

A. into   B. days   C. these

22 I _____ two _____ _____ a 3D printer.

A. with   B. things   C. printed

23 _____ is a model _____ my _____ car.

A. dream   B. of   C. one

24 If the _____ is _____ , it will _____ _____ a flying car.

A. into   B. change   C. heavy   D. traffic

25 The _____ is a _____ cup _____ my grandfather.

A. for   B. special   C. other

26 He can't _____ his cup well _____ he's _____ .

A. sick   B. because   C. hold

27 My special cup has three _____ , _____ it is easy _____ _____ .

A. hold   B. so   C. to   D. handles

28 _____ grandfather is very _____ .

A. happy   B. my

29 _____ the way, I want _____ _____ your cupcakes _____ day, Junho.

A. try   B. by   C. some   D. to

30 _____ _____ .

A. care   B. take

31 _____ _____ , Eric.

A. wishes   B. best

---

17 안녕 준호,

18 시드니에서는 3월이 가을이야.

19 너는 이메일에서 너에게 일어난 변화들을 말해 주었지.

20 이제 나의 새로운 변화를 말해 줄 차례야.

21 요즈음, 나는 3D 프린팅에 빠져 있어.

22 나는 3D 프린터로 2가지를 인쇄했어.

23 하나는 나의 꿈의 자동차의 모형이야.

24 교통이 혼잡할 때, 그것은 날 수 있는 차로 바뀌어.

25 나머지 다른 하나는 우리 할아버지를 위한 특수 컵이야.

26 할아버지는 편찮으셔서 컵을 잘 들지 못하셔.

27 나의 특수 컵은 손잡이가 3개 있어서 들기 쉬워.

28 할아버지는 아주 행복해 하셔.

29 그건 그렇고, 너의 컵케이크를 언젠가 먹어 보고 싶다, 준호야.

30 잘 지내.

31 행운을 빌어, Eric.

※ 다음 우리말과 일치하도록 빈칸에 알맞은 말을 쓰시오.

1 My friend Eric and I _____ _____ _____ _____ _____ _____ _____.

2 We _____ _____ _____ and _____ _____ _____ _____.

3 _____ Eric,

4 _____'s a _____ _____ _____ Seoul.

5 _____ _____ _____ _____ was a great _____ for me.

6 I _____ two _____ _____ _____ the vacation.

7 _____ is my _____ _____.

8 It's _____ _____.

9 _____ my _____ cupcakes _____ a _____ of fun.

10 _____ _____ _____ is _____ one of my bad _____.

11 In the _____, I _____ _____ _____ _____ _____.

12 Now I _____ _____.

13 I _____ _____ _____ the _____ I _____.

14 _____ you _____ _____ _____ some changes, I'm _____ you _____ _____ great _____ me.

15 I _____ _____ _____ _____ you soon.

16 _____ _____, Junho.

1 내 친구 Eric과 나는 방학 동안 흥미로운 변화가 있었다.

2 우리는 서로에게 이메일을 보냈고 우리의 변화에 관해 이야기했다.

3 안녕 Eric,

4 서울은 아름다운 봄이야.

5 지난 겨울 방학은 나에게 멋진 시간이었어.

6 나는 방학 동안 두 가지 개인적인 변화가 있었어.

7 하나는 나의 새로운 취미야.

8 그것은 컵케이크를 만드는 거야.

9 나만의 컵케이크를 만드는 것은 정말 재미있어.

10 나머지 다른 변화는 나의 나쁜 습관 중 하나를 없애는 거야.

11 예전에 나는 종종 손톱을 물어뜯곤 했어.

12 이제 나는 더 이상 그러지 않아.

13 나는 내가 만든 변화가 정말 기분 좋아.

14 만약 네가 변화하려고 노력한다면, 너도 나처럼 기분이 좋을 거라고 확신해.

15 곧 소식 전해 줘.

16 너의 친구 준호가.

17 _____ Junho,

18 _____ Sydney, _____'s fall _____ _____.

19 You _____ _____ your _____ in your email.

20 Now, it's _____ _____ _____ _____ my new changes.

21 _____ _____, I'm _____ _____ _____.

22 I _____ _____ _____ _____ a 3D printing.

23 _____ is a _____ _____ my _____ _____.

24 _____ the traffic _____ _____, it _____ _____ _____ _____ _____ _____.

25 _____ _____ is a _____ _____ _____ my grandfather.

26 He _____ _____ his cup _____ _____ he's _____.

27 My special cup has _____ _____, so it is _____ _____ _____.

28 _____ grandfather is very _____.

29 _____ _____ _____, I want _____ _____ your cupcakes _____ _____, Junho.

30 _____ _____.

31 _____ _____, Eric.

17 안녕 준호,

18 시드니에서는 3월이 가을이야.

19 너는 이메일에서 너에게 일어난 변화들을 말해 주었지.

20 이제 나의 새로운 변화를 말해 줄 차례야.

21 요즈음, 나는 3D 프린팅에 빠져 있어.

22 나는 3D 프린터로 2가지를 인쇄 했어.

23 하나는 나의 꿈의 자동차의 모형이야.

24 교통이 혼잡할 때, 그것은 날 수 있는 차로 바뀌어.

25 나머지 다른 하나는 우리 할아버지를 위한 특수 컵이야.

26 할아버지는 편찮으셔서 컵을 잘 들지 못하셔.

27 나의 특수 컵은 손잡이가 3개 있어서 들기 쉬워.

28 할아버지는 아주 행복해 하셔.

29 그건 그렇고, 너의 컵케이크를 언젠가 먹어 보고 싶다, 준호야.

30 잘 지내.

31 행운을 빌어, Eric.

Step3

※ 다음 문장을 우리말로 쓰시오.

1 My friend Eric and I made some interesting changes during the vacation.
➡ _____

2 We emailed each other and talked about our changes.
➡ _____

3 Dear Eric,
➡ _____

4 It's a beautiful spring in Seoul.
➡ _____

5 The last winter vacation was a great time for me.
➡ _____

6 I made two personal changes during the vacation.
➡ _____

7 One is my new hobby.
➡ _____

8 It's making cupcakes.
➡ _____

9 Making my own cupcakes is a lot of fun.
➡ _____

10 The other change is breaking one of my bad habits.
➡ _____

11 In the past, I often bit my nails.
➡ _____

12 Now I don't anymore.
➡ _____

13 I feel great about the changes I made.
➡ _____

14 If you try to make some changes, I'm sure you'll feel great like me.
➡ _____

15 I hope to hear from you soon.
➡ _____

16 Your friend, Junho.
➡ _____

17 Dear Junho,

➡ _____

18 In Sydney, it's fall in March.

➡ _____

19 You talked about your changes in your email.

➡ _____

20 Now, it's time to talk about my new changes.

➡ _____

21 These days, I'm into 3D printing.

➡ _____

22 I printed two things with a 3D printer.

➡ _____

23 One is a model of my dream car.

➡ _____

24 If the traffic is heavy, it will change into a flying car.

➡ _____

25 The other is a special cup for my grandfather.

➡ _____

26 He can't hold his cup well because he's sick.

➡ _____

27 My special cup has three handles, so it is easy to hold.

➡ _____

28 My grandfather is very happy.

➡ _____

29 By the way, I want to try your cupcakes some day, Junho.

➡ _____

30 Take care.

➡ _____

31 Best wishes, Eric.

➡ _____

※ 다음 괄호 안의 단어들을 우리말에 맞도록 바르게 배열하시오.

1 (friend / my / Eric / and / made / I / interesting / some / changes / vacation. / the / during)
➡ _____

2 (each / we / other / emailed / and / about / talked / changes. / our)
➡ _____

3 (Eric, / Dear)
➡ _____

4 (a / it's / spring / beautiful / Seoul. / in)
➡ _____

5 (last / the / winter / was / vacation / great / a / time / me. / for)
➡ _____

6 (made / I / personal / two / changes / vacation. / the / during)
➡ _____

7 (is / one / new / hobby. / my)
➡ _____

8 (cupcakes. / making / it's)
➡ _____

9 (my / making / own / cupcakes / a / is / lot / fun. / of)
➡ _____

10 (other / the / change / is / breaking / of / one / habits. / bad / my)
➡ _____

11 (past, / the / in / I / bit / often / nails. / my)
➡ _____

12 (I / now / anymore. / don't)
➡ _____

13 (feel / I / great / about / changes / the / made. / I)
➡ _____

14 (you / if / to / try / some / make / changes, / I'm / feel / you'll / sure / me. / like / great)
➡ _____

15 (hope / I / hear / to / soon. / from / you)
➡ _____

16 (Junho. / friend, / your)
➡ _____

1 내 친구 Eric과 나는 방학 동안 흥미로운 변화가 있었다.

2 우리는 서로에게 이메일을 보냈고 우리의 변화에 관해 이야기했다.

3 안녕 Eric.

4 서울은 아름다운 봄이야.

5 지난 겨울 방학은 나에게 멋진 시간이었어.

6 나는 방학 동안 두 가지 개인적인 변화가 있었어.

7 하나는 나의 새로운 취미야.

8 그것은 컵케이크를 만드는 거야.

9 나만의 컵케이크를 만드는 것은 정말 재미있어.

10 나머지 다른 변화는 나의 나쁜 습관 중 하나를 없애는 거야.

11 예전에 나는 종종 손톱을 물어뜯곤 했어.

12 이제 나는 더 이상 그러지 않아.

13 나는 내가 만든 변화가 정말 기분 좋아.

14 만약 네가 변화하려고 노력한다면, 너도 나처럼 기분이 좋을 거라고 확신해.

15 곧 소식 전해 줘.

16 너의 친구 준호가.

17 (Junho, / dear,)

➡ _____

18 (Sydney, / in / fall / it's / March. / in)

➡ _____

19 (talked / you / about / changes / your / email. / in / your)

➡ _____

20 (now, / time / it's / talk / to / about / changes. / new / my)

➡ _____

21 (days, / these / into / I'm / printing. / 3D)

➡ _____

22 (printed / I / things / two / with / printer. / 3D / a)

➡ _____

23 (is / one / model / a / of / car. / dream / my)

➡ _____

24 (the / if / traffic / heavy, / is / will / it / change / into / car. / flying / a)

➡ _____

25 (other / the / is / specail / a / cup / for / grandfather. / my)

➡ _____

26 (can't / he / hold / cup / his / well / he's / sick. / because)

➡ _____

27 (my / cup / special / has / handles, / three / so / is / it / hold. / to / easy)

➡ _____

28 (grandfather / my / is / happy. / very)

➡ _____

29 (the / by / way, / I / to / want / your / try / cupcakes / some / Junho. / day,)

➡ _____

30 (care. / take)

➡ _____

31 (wishes, / Eric / best)

➡ _____

17 안녕 준호.

18 시드니에서는 3월이 가을이야.

19 너는 이메일에서 너에게 일어난 변화들을 말해 주었지.

20 이제 나의 새로운 변화를 말해 줄 차례야.

21 요즈음, 나는 3D 프린팅에 빠져 있어.

22 나는 3D 프린터로 2가지를 인쇄 했어.

23 하나는 나의 꿈의 자동차의 모형이야.

24 교통이 혼잡할 때, 그것은 날 수 있는 차로 바뀌어.

25 나머지 다른 하나는 우리 할아 버지를 위한 특수 컵이야.

26 할아버지는 편찮으셔서 컵을 잘 들지 못하셔.

27 나의 특수 컵은 손잡이가 3개 있 어서 들기 쉬워.

28 할아버지는 아주 행복해 하셔.

29 그건 그렇고, 너의 컵케이크를 언젠가 먹어 보고 싶다. 준호야.

30 잘 지내.

31 행운을 빌어. Eric.

※ 다음 우리말을 영어로 쓰시오.

1 내 친구 Eric과 나는 방학 동안 흥미로운 변화가 있었다.

➡ _____

2 우리는 서로에게 이메일을 보냈고 우리의 변화에 관해 이야기했다.

➡ _____

3 안녕 Eric,

➡ _____

4 서울은 아름다운 봄이야.

➡ _____

5 지난 겨울 방학은 나에게 멋진 시간이었어.

➡ _____

6 나는 방학 동안 두 가지 개인적인 변화가 있었어.

➡ _____

7 하나는 나의 새로운 취미야.

➡ _____

8 그것은 컵케이크를 만드는 거야.

➡ _____

9 나만의 컵케이크를 만드는 것은 정말 재미있어.

➡ _____

10 나머지 다른 변화는 나의 나쁜 습관 중 하나를 없애는 거야.

➡ _____

11 예전에 나는 종종 손톱을 물어뜯곤 했어.

➡ _____

12 이제 나는 더 이상 그러지 않아.

➡ _____

13 나는 내가 만든 변화가 정말 기분 좋아.

➡ _____

14 만약 네가 변화하려고 노력한다면, 너도 나처럼 기분이 좋을 거라고 확신해.

➡ _____

15 곧 소식 전해 줘.

➡ _____

16 너의 친구 준호가.

➡ _____

17 안녕 준호,

➡ _____

18 시드니에서는 3월이 가을이야.

➡ _____

19 너는 이메일에서 너에게 일어난 변화들을 말해 주었지.

➡ _____

20 이제 나의 새로운 변화를 말해 줄 차례야.

➡ _____

21 요즈음, 나는 3D 프린팅에 빠져 있어.

➡ _____

22 나는 3D 프린터로 2가지를 인쇄했어.

➡ _____

23 하나는 나의 꿈의 자동차의 모형이야.

➡ _____

24 교통이 혼잡할 때, 그것은 날 수 있는 차로 바뀌어.

➡ _____

25 나머지 다른 하나는 우리 할아버지를 위한 특수 컵이야.

➡ _____

26 할아버지는 편찮으셔서 컵을 잘 들지 못하셔.

➡ _____

27 나의 특수 컵은 손잡이가 3개 있어서 들기 쉬워.

➡ _____

28 할아버지는 아주 행복해 하셔.

➡ _____

29 그건 그렇고, 너의 컵케이크를 언젠가 먹어 보고 싶다, 준호야.

➡ _____

30 잘 지내.

➡ _____

31 행운을 빌어, Eric.

➡ _____

※ 다음 우리말과 일치하도록 빈칸에 알맞은 말을 쓰시오.

Real Life Communication - Step 2

1. A: You know _____? I'm _____ _____ _____ a diary in English.

2. B: _____ did you _____ _____ _____ that?

3. A: It's _____ I want to _____ _____ _____ English writing.

4. B: That's _____.

1. A: 그거 아니? 나는 영어로 일기를 쓸 생각이야.
2. B: 왜 그런 결심을 했어?
3. A: 왜냐하면 영어 쓰기를 잘하고 싶기 때문이야.
4. B: 멋지다.

My Writing Portfolio

1. _____ me,

2. You are very _____ and _____.

3. _____, you still want to make two changes, _____ _____?

4. _____ is to have more good friends. _____ _____ is to _____ _____.

5. _____ _____ my tips for your _____.

6. If you are _____ _____ _____ and eat more vegetables, you'll _____ _____ _____.

7. _____, Me

1. 나에게,
2. 너는 매우 영리하고 재미있어.
3. 하지만 너는 두 가지 변화를 이루고 싶어 해, 그렇지 않니?
4. 하나는 더 많은 좋은 친구를 사귀는 거야. 다른 하나는 더 건강해지는 거야.
5. 여기 너의 소망을 위한 조언이 있어.
6. 다른 사람들에게 더 친절하게 하고 더 많은 채소를 먹는다면, 너는 이러한 변화들을 이룰 수 있을 거야.
7. 사랑하는, 내가

Words in Action B

1. Bobo is _____ _____ _____.

2. She has _____ _____.

3. _____ is black. _____ _____ is white.

4. She has _____ _____.

5. _____ is a ball. _____ _____ is a plastic duck.

6. She has _____ _____.

7. One is _____ TV. The other is _____ on my chair.

1. 보보는 내 애완견이다.
2. 그녀는 동생이 둘 있다.
3. 하나는 검정색이다. 다른 하나는 하얀색이다.
4. 그녀는 장난감이 두 개 있다.
5. 하나는 공이다. 다른 하나는 플라스틱 오리이다.
6. 그녀는 두 가지 습관이 있다.
7. 하나는 TV를 보는 것이다. 다른 하나는 내 의자 위에서 자는 것이다.

※ 다음 우리말을 영어로 쓰시오.

Real Life Communication - Step 2

1. A: 그거 아니? 나는 영어로 일기를 쓸 생각이야.
   ➡ _____

2. B: 왜 그런 결심을 했어?
   ➡ _____

3. A: 왜냐하면 영어 쓰기를 잘하고 싶기 때문이야.
   ➡ _____

4. B: 멋지다.
   ➡ _____

My Writing Portfolio

1. 나에게,
   ➡ _____

2. 너는 매우 영리하고 재미있어.
   ➡ _____

3. 하지만 너는 두 가지 변화를 이루고 싶어 해, 그렇지 않니?
   ➡ _____

4. 하나는 더 많은 좋은 친구를 사귀는 거야. 다른 하나는 더 건강해지는 거야.
   ➡ _____

5. 여기 너의 소망을 위한 조언이 있어.
   ➡ _____

6. 다른 사람들에게 더 친절하게 하고 더 많은 채소를 먹는다면, 너는 이러한 변화들을 이룰 수 있을 거야.
   ➡ _____

7. 사랑하는, 내가
   ➡ _____

Words in Action B

1. 보보는 내 애완견이다.
   ➡ _____

2. 그녀는 동생이 둘 있다.
   ➡ _____

3. 하나는 검정색이다. 다른 하나는 하얀색이다.
   ➡ _____

4. 그녀는 장난감이 두 개 있다.
   ➡ _____

5. 하나는 공이다. 다른 하나는 플라스틱 오리이다.
   ➡ _____

6. 그녀는 두 가지 습관이 있다.
   ➡ _____

7. 하나는 TV를 보는 것이다. 다른 하나는 내 의자 위에서 자는 것이다.
   ➡ _____

※ 다음 영어를 우리말로 쓰시오.

01 shake	_____	22 wet	_____
02 solve	_____	23 protect	_____
03 empty	_____	24 escape	_____
04 fall	_____	25 serious	_____
05 follow	_____	26 worry	_____
06 strange	_____	27 avoid	_____
07 space	_____	28 sore	_____
08 hurt	_____	29 dangerous	_____
09 floor	_____	30 slippery	_____
10 injury	_____	31 earthquake	_____
11 pole	_____	32 forget	_____
12 knife	_____	33 disaster	_____
13 low	_____	34 survive	_____
14 medicine	_____	35 get out of	_____
15 safety	_____	36 take cover	_____
16 amazing	_____	37 a little	_____
17 break	_____	38 stay away from	_____
18 scary	_____	39 be worried about	_____
19 decide	_____	40 hold on to	_____
20 slip	_____	41 keep ~ in mind	_____
21 strike	_____	42 feel better	_____
		43 take a rest	_____

※ 다음 우리말을 영어로 쓰시오.

01 씌우다, 덮다 _____

02 닦다 _____

03 탈출하다 _____

04 심각한 _____

05 재난, 재해 _____

06 잊어버리다 _____

07 바닥, 마루 _____

08 아픈 _____

09 방지하다, 막다, 피하다 _____

10 계단 _____

11 ~까지 _____

12 걱정, 근심; 걱정하다 _____

13 살아남다, 생존하다 _____

14 준비하다, 대비하다 _____

15 승강기 _____

16 미끄러운 _____

17 위험한 _____

18 보호하다 _____

19 상황 _____

20 지진 _____

21 목구멍 _____

22 (방송) 프로그램 _____

23 안전 _____

24 비어 있는, 빈 _____

25 미끄러지다 _____

26 깨다, 부수다, 부서지다 _____

27 상처, 부상 _____

28 해결하다 _____

29 젖은 _____

30 이상한, 낯선 _____

31 규칙, 법칙 _____

32 공간 _____

33 흔들림, 떨림; 흔들다 _____

34 약 _____

35 휴식을 취하다 _____

36 ~에 대해 걱정하다 _____

37 (기분이) 나아지다 _____

38 ~을 꼭 잡다 _____

39 ~에서 떨어져 있다 _____

40 ~을 기억하다 _____

41 하나씩, 차례차례 _____

42 ~하는 게 어때? _____

43 (~에서) 나가다, 떠나다 _____

※ 다음 영영풀이에 알맞은 단어를 <보기>에서 골라 쓴 후, 우리말 뜻을 쓰시오.

1 _____ : to find a way to deal with and end a problem: _____

2 _____ : to keep someone or something from being harmed, lost, etc.: _____

3 _____ : to be unable to think of or remember something: _____

4 _____ : the state of not being dangerous or harmful: _____

5 _____ : to clean or dry something by using a towel, your hand, etc.: _____

6 _____ : not having any people, not occupied; containing nothing: _____

7 _____ : to come or go down suddenly from a standing position: _____

8 _____ : short, quick movement back and forth or up and down: _____

9 _____ : a long, thin stick made of wood or metal, used to hold something up:
   _____

10 _____ : a shaking of a part of the Earth's surface that often causes great damage:
   _____

11 _____ : to do what instructions or orders say you should do, to move behind
   someone or something and go where they go: _____

12 _____ : to stay away from; to prevent the occurrence of something bad, unpleasant,
   etc.: _____

13 _____ : to cause pain or injury to yourself, someone else, or a part of your body:
   _____

14 _____ : harm or damage; an act or event that causes someone or something to no
   longer be fully healthy or in good condition: _____

15 _____ : something such as a flood, tornado, fire, plane crash, etc. that happens
   suddenly and causes much suffering or loss to many people: _____

16 _____ : to separate something into parts or pieces often in a sudden and forceful
   or violent way, to cause to separate into two or more pieces: _____

보기			
pole	shake	injury	break
safety	wipe	solve	empty
avoid	disaster	follow	hurt
fall	forget	protect	earthquake

※ 다음 우리말과 일치하도록 빈칸에 알맞은 말을 쓰시오.

해석

Listen & Speak 1 A

Tom: Yujin, what's _____?

Yujin: _____ my leg. It _____ _____ _____.

Tom: _____ _____ _____ _____ _____ a doctor?

Yujin: I'm _____ _____ _____ after school today.

Tom: I hope _____ _____ _____ soon.

Yujin: I _____ _____, _____.

Listen & Speak 1 B

Brian: What _____ you _____?

Jane: It's a _____ _____ _____.

Brian: _____ _____. _____ _____ _____ _____ _____ these days.

Jane: _____, _____. This program has some _____ _____.

Brian: Really? What _____ it _____?

Jane: When things _____ _____ _____, you need to _____ _____ under a table.

Brian: Oh, I _____ _____ that.

Listen & Speak 2 A

Jack: Dad, I'm _____ _____ _____ _____ basketball with Minu.

Dad: Did you _____ _____ _____ _____ _____?

Jack: No, _____. Can I do it _____?

Dad: No. _____ _____ _____ _____ _____ _____.

Jack: Okay. I'll _____ my room and then _____ _____.

Dad: Good. _____ to be home _____ _____ _____.

Jack: Okay.

Listen & Speak 2 B

Emily: _____ _____ is the movie?

Tom: It starts at 4:30.

Emily: Oh, no. We only have 20 minutes _____. _____ _____!

Tom: No! _____ _____ _____ _____ _____ _____ _____.

　　You _____ _____ _____ _____ _____.

Emily: You're _____. We can be _____ _____ _____.

Tom: Yes. _____ _____ _____ _____.

Emily: 영화는 몇 시에 하니?

Tom: 4시 30분에 시작해.

Emily: 이런. 우리 20분밖에 남지 않았어. 뛰자!

Tom: 안 돼! 넘어져서 다칠 수 있어. 계단에서는 걸어가야 해.

Emily: 네 말이 맞아. 우리 좀 늦을 수도 있겠어.

Tom: 그래. 후회하는 것보다 안전한 게 낫지.

Real Life Communication

Brian: There was _____ _____ _____ at the _____ _____ yesterday.

Mina: Yes, I _____ _____ it. _____ _____ _____ _____ _____ _____.

Brian: _____ _____. Everybody was okay. They all _____ the _____ _____.

Mina: Really? _____ are the rules?

Brian: You need to _____ your nose and mouth _____ _____ _____ _____. Then _____ _____ and _____.

Mina: Oh, I _____ _____ that.

Brian: You should _____ _____ _____ _____. It might be _____ _____ _____.

Brian: 어제 시립 도서관에 큰 불이 났어.

Mina: 응, 그것에 대해 들었어. 거기 있었던 사람들이 걱정 됐어.

Brian: 걱정하지 마. 모두들 무사했어. 사람들이 모두 안전 규칙을 따랐대.

Mina: 정말? 그게 뭔데?

Brian: 젖은 수건으로 코와 입을 가려야 해. 그 다음, 몸을 낮게 유지하고 탈출하는 거야.

Mina: 아, 그건 몰랐어.

Brian: 넌 그것을 명심해야 해. 언젠가 도움이 될 수도 있어.

Let's Check

Sujin: It's _____. I'm _____ _____ _____ _____ in the afternoon.

Mom: It is going to rain _____ _____ today. _____ _____ _____ _____.

Sujin: You're right, Mom. I'll _____ my friend and _____ _____ _____.

Sujin: 비가 와요. 오후에 있을 소풍이 걱정 돼요.

Mom: 오늘 오후 늦게까지 비가 올 거야. 다른 날 소풍 가는 것이 좋을 것 같구나.

Sujin: 맞아요, 엄마. 친구에게 전화해서 다른 날을 정해야겠어요.

※ 다음 우리말에 맞도록 대화를 영어로 쓰시오.

Listen & Speak 1 A

Tom: _____

Yujin: _____

Tom: _____

Yujin: _____

Tom: _____

Yujin: _____

Tom: 유진아, 무슨 일이야?
Yujin: 내 다리가 걱정돼서. 많이 아프거든.
Tom: 병원에 가보는 게 어때?
Yujin: 오늘 방과 후에 갈 거야.
Tom: 곧 괜찮아지기를 바라.
Yujin: 나도 그러길 바라.

Listen & Speak 1 B

Brian: _____

Jane: _____

Brian: _____

Jane: _____

Brian: _____

Jane: _____

Brian: _____

Brian: 무엇을 시청하고 있니?
Jane: 지진에 관한 프로그램이야.
Brian: 그거 재미있겠다. 나는 요즘 지진이 걱정돼.
Jane: 나도 그래. 이 프로그램에는 도움이 되는 몇 가지 조언이 있어.
Brian: 그래? 뭐라고 하는데?
Jane: 물건들이 흔들리기 시작하면 탁자 아래에 숨어야 해.
Brian: 아, 그건 몰랐어.

Listen & Speak 2 A

Jack: _____

Dad: _____

Jack: _____

Dad: _____

Jack: _____

Dad: _____

Jack: _____

Jack: 아빠, 저 민우와 농구하러 나갈 거예요.
Dad: 네 방 청소는 끝냈니?
Jack: 아니요, 아직 안했어요. 나중에 해도 돼요?
Dad: 아니. 너는 네 방을 먼저 청소해야 해.
Jack: 알았어요. 방을 청소하고 농구할게요.
Dad: 착하구나. 6시까지 집에 오는 것 잊지 마라.
Jack: 알겠어요.

Listen & Speak 2 B

Emily: _____

Tom: _____

Emily: _____

Tom: _____

Emily: _____

Tom: _____

Emily: 영화는 몇 시에 하니?
Tom: 4시 30분에 시작해.
Emily: 이런. 우리 20분밖에 남지 않았어. 뛰자!
Tom: 안 돼! 넘어져서 다칠 수 있어. 계단에서는 걸어가야 해.
Emily: 네 말이 맞아. 우리 좀 늦을 수도 있겠어.
Tom: 그래. 후회하는 것보다 안전한 게 낫지.

Real Life Communication

Brian: _____

Mina: _____

Brian: _____

Mina: _____

Brian: _____

_____

Mina: _____

Brian: _____

Brian: 어제 시립 도서관에 큰 불이 났어.
Mina: 응, 그것에 대해 들었어. 거기 있었던 사람들이 걱정 됐어.
Brian: 걱정하지 마. 모두들 무사했어. 사람들이 모두 안전 규칙을 따랐대.
Mina: 정말? 그게 뭔데?
Brian: 젖은 수건으로 코와 입을 가려야 해. 그 다음, 몸을 낮게 유지하고 탈출하는 거야.
Mina: 아, 그건 몰랐어.
Brian: 넌 그것을 명심해야 해. 언젠가 도움이 될 수도 있어.

Let's Check

Sujin: _____

Mom: _____

Sujin: _____

Sujin: 비가 와요. 오후에 있을 소풍이 걱정 돼요.
Mom: 오늘 오후 늦게까지 비가 올 거야. 다른 날 소풍 가는 것이 좋을 것 같구나.
Sujin: 맞아요, 엄마. 친구에게 전화해서 다른 날을 정해야겠어요.

※ 다음 우리말과 일치하도록 빈칸에 알맞은 것을 골라 쓰시오.

1 Do you know _____ _____ do _____ an earthquake _____?

A. strikes   B. when   C. to   D. what

2 _____ this quiz and think about _____ to be safe _____ this kind of natural _____.

A. disaster   B. during   C. how   D. take

3 When _____ start to _____, run _____ quickly. (o / x)

A. outside   B. shake   C. things

4 _____ _____ from windows. (o / x)

A. away   B. stay

5 _____ the stairs to get _____ _____ buildings. (o / x)

A. of   B. out   C. use

6 When you are _____, _____ on to a _____ or a tree. (o / x)

A. pole   B. hold   C. outside

7 _____ did you do _____ the quiz?

A. on   B. how

8 Can you _____ an earthquake _____?

A. safely   B. survive

9 _____ are some _____ tips _____ can be _____ in an earthquake.

A. helpful   B. which   C. safety   D. here

10 Let's _____ them one _____ one and learn _____ to do.

A. what   B. by   C. check

11 Don't _____ outside _____ things are _____.

A. shaking   B. when   C. run

12 _____ a table or a desk and _____ _____ under it.

A. cover   B. take   C. find

13 You can _____ _____ to the legs _____ _____ yourself.

A. protect   B. to   C. on   D. hold

14 Also, _____ _____ _____ windows.

A. from   B. away   C. stay

1 지진이 발생할 때 해야 할 일을 알고 있습니까?

2 이 퀴즈를 풀며 이러한 종류의 자연 재해가 발생하는 동안 어떻게 해야 안전할 수 있는지를 생각해 보세요.

3 물건들이 흔들리기 시작하면, 빨리 밖으로 뛰어나가세요.

4 창문으로부터 멀리 떨어지세요.

5 건물에서 나갈 때는 계단을 이용하세요.

6 밖에 나가서는 기둥이나 나무를 붙들고 있으세요.

7 퀴즈가 어떠셨나요?

8 당신은 지진에서 안전하게 살아남을 수 있나요?

9 여기에 지진 발생 시 도움이 될 수 있는 안전 지침이 있습니다.

10 하나하나 확인하면서 무엇을 해야 하는지를 배워 봅시다.

11 물건들이 흔들리기 시작할 때 밖으로 뛰어나가지 마세요.

12 탁자나 책상을 찾아서 그 밑에 숨으세요.

13 자신을 보호하기 위해 탁자나 책상 다리를 붙들고 있으세요.

14 또한, 창문으로부터 멀리 떨어지세요.

15 They can _____ during an _____ and _____ you.
A. hurt   B. earthquake   C. break

16 You can _____ _____ when the _____ _____.
A. stops   B. shaking   C. outside   D. go

17 To _____ _____ of buildings, _____ _____ the elevator.
A. use   B. don't   C. out   D. get

18 _____ the _____.
A. stairs   B. take

19 It's _____ _____.
A. safer   B. much

20 _____ you are outside, _____ an _____ space that is _____ from buildings.
A. far   B. empty   C. find   D. once

21 There _____ be people who want to _____ on to a _____ or a tree, _____ think again.
A. but   B. pole   C. hold   D. may

22 That's a bad idea _____ it can _____ _____ you.
A. on   B. fall   C. because

23 Earthquakes _____ _____ _____.
A. anytime   B. strike   C. can

24 They can be _____ _____ for _____.
A. everyone   B. experiences   C. scary

25 So learn _____ to be _____ in an _____.
A. earthquake   B. safe   C. how

26 You can _____ _____ and _____ yourself.
A. protect   B. injuries   C. avoid

27 _____ these _____ and be _____!
A. safe   B. tips   C. follow

15 지진이 일어나는 동안 창문들이 깨져 다칠 수 있으니까요.

16 흔들림이 멈추었을 때 밖으로 나가도 됩니다.

17 건물에서 나가기 위해 엘리베이터를 이용하지 마세요.

18 계단을 이용하세요.

19 그것이 훨씬 더 안전합니다.

20 일단 밖으로 나가면, 건물로부터 멀리 떨어진 공터를 찾으세요.

21 기둥이나 나무를 꼭 잡고 있으려는 사람들이 있을 수 있지만, 다시 생각해 보세요.

22 그것이 당신 위로 넘어질 수 있으므로 그것은 좋지 않은 생각입니다.

23 지진은 언제든지 발생할 수 있습니다.

24 지진은 모두에게 무서운 경험일 것입니다.

25 따라서 지진이 날 때 안전을 지키는 법을 배우세요.

26 부상을 방지하고 자신을 보호할 수 있습니다.

27 이 지침을 따르고 안전을 지키세요!

※ 다음 우리말과 일치하도록 빈칸에 알맞은 말을 쓰시오.

1 Do you know _____ _____ _____ when an _____ _____?

2 _____ this quiz and think about _____ _____ _____ safe _____ this kind of _____ _____.

3 When things start _____ _____, run outside _____. (o / x)

4 _____ _____ _____ windows. (o / x)

5 _____ the stairs _____ _____ _____ _____ _____ buildings. (o / x)

6 _____ you are _____, _____ _____ _____ a pole or a tree. (o / x)

7 _____ did you do _____ _____ _____?

8 Can you _____ _____ _____ _____?

9 _____ _____ some safety tips _____ can be _____ _____ _____ _____.

10 _____ check _____ _____ _____ _____ and learn _____ _____ _____.

11 _____ run outside _____ _____ _____ _____ _____.

12 _____ a table or a desk and _____ _____ _____ it.

13 You can _____ on to the legs _____ _____ _____.

14 Also, _____ _____ _____ _____.

1 지진이 발생할 때 해야 할 일을 알고 있습니까?

2 이 퀴즈를 풀며 이러한 종류의 자연 재해가 발생하는 동안 어떻게 해야 안전할 수 있는지를 생각해 보세요.

3 물건들이 흔들리기 시작하면, 빨리 밖으로 뛰어나가세요.

4 창문으로부터 멀리 떨어지세요.

5 건물에서 나갈 때는 계단을 이용하세요.

6 밖에 나가서는 기둥이나 나무를 붙들고 있으세요.

7 퀴즈가 어떠셨나요?

8 당신은 지진에서 안전하게 살아남을 수 있나요?

9 여기에 지진 발생 시 도움이 될 수 있는 안전 지침이 있습니다.

10 하나하나 확인하면서 무엇을 해야 하는지를 배워 봅시다.

11 물건들이 흔들리기 시작할 때 밖으로 뛰어나가지 마세요.

12 탁자나 책상을 찾아서 그 밑에 숨으세요.

13 자신을 보호하기 위해 탁자나 책상 다리를 붙들고 있으세요.

14 또한, 창문으로부터 멀리 떨어지세요.

15 _____ can _____ _____ an earthquake and hurt you.

16 You can _____ _____ when _____ _____ _____.

17 _____ _____ _____ _____ buildings, _____ _____

the elevator.

18 _____ the _____.

19 It's _____ _____.

20 _____ you are outside, _____ _____ _____ _____ _____

that _____ _____ _____ buildings.

21 There may be people _____ _____ _____ _____

_____ _____ a pole or a tree, _____ _____ again.

22 That's a bad idea _____ _____ can _____ _____ you.

23 _____ can _____ _____ _____.

24 They can be _____ _____ _____ _____ _____.

25 So learn _____ _____ _____ _____ _____ in an earthquake.

26 You _____ _____ _____ and _____ _____.

27 _____ _____ _____ and _____ safe!

15 지진이 일어나는 동안 창문들이 깨져 다칠 수 있으니까요.

16 흔들림이 멈추었을 때 밖으로 나가도 됩니다.

17 건물에서 나가기 위해 엘리베이터를 이용하지 마세요.

18 계단을 이용하세요.

19 그것이 훨씬 더 안전합니다.

20 일단 밖으로 나가면, 건물로부터 멀리 떨어진 공터를 찾으세요.

21 기둥이나 나무를 꼭 잡고 있으려는 사람들이 있을 수 있지만, 다시 생각해 보세요.

22 그것이 당신 위로 넘어질 수 있으므로 그것은 좋지 않은 생각입니다.

23 지진은 언제든지 발생할 수 있습니다.

24 지진은 모두에게 무서운 경험일 것입니다.

25 따라서 지진이 날 때 안전을 지키는 법을 배우세요.

26 부상을 방지하고 자신을 보호할 수 있습니다.

27 이 지침을 따르고 안전을 지키세요!

※ 다음 문장을 우리말로 쓰시오.

1 ▶ Do you know what to do when an earthquake strikes?

➡ _____

2 ▶ Take this quiz and think about how to be safe during this kind of natural disaster.

➡ _____

3 ▶ When things start to shake, run outside quickly.

➡ _____

4 ▶ Stay away from windows.

➡ _____

5 ▶ Use the stairs to get out of buildings.

➡ _____

6 ▶ When you are outside, hold on to a pole or a tree.

➡ _____

7 ▶ How did you do on the quiz?

➡ _____

8 ▶ Can you survive an earthquake safely?

➡ _____

9 ▶ Here are some safety tips which can be helpful in an earthquake.

➡ _____

10 ▶ Let's check them one by one and learn what to do.

➡ _____

11 ▶ Don't run outside when things are shaking.

➡ _____

12 ▶ Find a table or a desk and take cover under it.

➡ _____

13 ▶ You can hold on to the legs to protect yourself.

➡ _____

14 ▶ Also, stay away from windows.

➡ _____

15 They can break during an earthquake and hurt you.

➡ _____

16 You can go outside when the shaking stops.

➡ _____

17 To get out of buildings, don't use the elevator.

➡ _____

18 Take the stairs.

➡ _____

19 It's much safer.

➡ _____

20 Once you are outside, find an empty space that is far from buildings.

➡ _____

21 There may be people who want to hold on to a pole or a tree, but think again.

➡ _____

22 That's a bad idea because it can fall on you.

➡ _____

23 Earthquakes can strike anytime.

➡ _____

24 They can be scary experiences for everyone.

➡ _____

25 So learn how to be safe in an earthquake.

➡ _____

26 You can avoid injuries and protect yourself.

➡ _____

27 Follow these tips and be safe!

➡ _____

※ 다음 괄호 안의 단어들을 우리말에 맞도록 바르게 배열하시오.

1 (know / you / do / what / do / to / when / strikes? / earthquake / an)
➡ _____

2 (this / take / quiz / and / about / think / to / how / be / safe / this / during / kind / disaster. / natural / of)
➡ _____

3 (things / when / to / start / shake, / quickly. / outside / run)
➡ _____

4 (away / stay / windows. / from)
➡ _____

5 (the / use / to / stairs / get / of / out / buildings. / of)
➡ _____

6 (you / when / outside, / are / on / hold / to / pole / a / tree. / a / or)
➡ _____

7 (did / how / do / you / quiz? / on / the)
➡ _____

8 (survive / you / can / an / safely? / earthquake)
➡ _____

9 (are / here / safety / some / tips / which / be / can / in / earthquake. / an / helpful)
➡ _____

10 (check / let's / them / by / one / and / one / learn / do. / to / what)
➡ _____

11 (run / outside / don't / when / shaking. / are / things)
➡ _____

12 (a / find / table / or / desk / a / and / cover / take / it. / under)
➡ _____

13 (can / you / hold / to / on / the / to / legs / yourself. / protect)
➡ _____

14 (stay / also, / windows. / from / away)
➡ _____

1 지진이 발생할 때 해야 할 일을 알고 있습니까?

2 이 퀴즈를 풀며 이러한 종류의 자연 재해가 발생하는 동안 어떻게 해야 안전할 수 있는지를 생각해 보세요.

3 물건들이 흔들리기 시작하면, 빨리 밖으로 뛰어나가세요.

4 창문으로부터 멀리 떨어지세요.

5 건물에서 나갈 때는 계단을 이용하세요.

6 밖에 나가서는 기둥이나 나무를 붙들고 있으세요.

7 퀴즈가 어떠셨나요?

8 당신은 지진에서 안전하게 살아남을 수 있나요?

9 여기에 지진 발생 시 도움이 될 수 있는 안전 지침이 있습니다.

10 하나하나 확인하면서 무엇을 해야 하는지를 배워 봅시다.

11 물건들이 흔들리기 시작할 때 밖으로 뛰어나가지 마세요.

12 탁자나 책상을 찾아서 그 밑에 숨으세요.

13 자신을 보호하기 위해 탁자나 책상 다리를 붙들고 있으세요.

14 또한, 창문으로부터 멀리 떨어지세요.

15 (can / they / break / during / earthquake / and / an / you. / hurt)

➡ _____

16 (go / can / you / outside / when / stops. / shaking / the)

➡ _____

17 (get / to / out / buildings, / of / don't / elevator. / the / use)

➡ _____

18 (stairs. / the / take)

➡ _____

19 (much / it's / safer.)

➡ _____

20 (are / you / once / outside, / an / find / space / empty / that / from / buildings. / far / is)

➡ _____

21 (may / there / be / people / who / to / want / hold / on / to / or / pole / a / tree, / a / again. / but / think)

➡ _____

➡ _____

22 (a / idea / that's / bad / because / can / it / fall / you. / on)

➡ _____

23 (can / earthquakes / anytime. / strike)

➡ _____

24 (can / they / scary / be / everyone. / for / experiences)

➡ _____

25 (learn / so / to / how / safe / be / earthquake. / an / in)

➡ _____

26 (can / you / avoid / injuries / yourself. / and / protect)

➡ _____

27 (these / follow / and / tips / safe! / be)

➡ _____

15 지진이 일어나는 동안 창문들이 깨져 다칠 수 있으니까요.

16 흔들림이 멈추었을 때 밖으로 나가도 됩니다.

17 건물에서 나가기 위해 엘리베이터를 이용하지 마세요.

18 계단을 이용하세요.

19 그것이 훨씬 더 안전합니다.

20 일단 밖으로 나가면, 건물로부터 멀리 떨어진 공터를 찾으세요.

21 기둥이나 나무를 꼭 잡고 있으려는 사람들이 있을 수 있지만, 다시 생각해 보세요.

22 그것이 당신 위로 넘어질 수 있으므로 그것은 좋지 않은 생각입니다.

23 지진은 언제든지 발생할 수 있습니다.

24 지진은 모두에게 무서운 경험일 것입니다.

25 따라서 지진이 날 때 안전을 지키는 법을 배우세요.

26 부상을 방지하고 자신을 보호할 수 있습니다.

27 이 지침을 따르고 안전을 지키세요!

※ 다음 우리말을 영어로 쓰시오.

1 지진이 발생할 때 해야 할 일을 알고 있습니까?

➡ _____

2 이 퀴즈를 풀며 이러한 종류의 자연 재해가 발생하는 동안 어떻게 해야 안전할 수 있는지를 생각해 보세요.

➡ _____

3 물건들이 흔들리기 시작하면, 빨리 밖으로 뛰어나가세요.

➡ _____

4 창문으로부터 멀리 떨어지세요.

➡ _____

5 건물에서 나갈 때는 계단을 이용하세요.

➡ _____

6 밖에 나가서는 기둥이나 나무를 붙들고 있으세요.

➡ _____

7 퀴즈가 어떠셨나요?

➡ _____

8 당신은 지진에서 안전하게 살아남을 수 있나요?

➡ _____

9 여기에 지진 발생 시 도움이 될 수 있는 안전 지침이 있습니다.

➡ _____

10 하나하나 확인하면서 무엇을 해야 하는지를 배워 봅시다.

➡ _____

11 물건이 흔들리기 시작할 때 밖으로 뛰어나가지 마세요.

➡ _____

12 탁자나 책상을 찾아서 그 밑에 숨으세요.

➡ _____

13 자신을 보호하기 위해 탁자나 책상 다리를 붙들고 있으세요.

➡ _____

14 또한, 창문으로부터 멀리 떨어지세요.

➡ _____

15 지진이 일어나는 동안 창문들이 깨져 다칠 수 있으니까요.

➡ _____

16 흔들림이 멈추었을 때 밖으로 나가도 됩니다.

➡ _____

17 건물에서 나가기 위해 엘리베이터를 이용하지 마세요.

➡ _____

18 계단을 이용하세요.

➡ _____

19 그것이 훨씬 더 안전합니다.

➡ _____

20 일단 밖으로 나가면, 건물로부터 멀리 떨어진 공터를 찾으세요.

➡ _____

21 기둥이나 나무를 꼭 잡고 있으려는 사람들이 있을 수 있지만, 다시 생각해 보세요.

➡ _____

22 그것이 당신 위로 넘어질 수 있으므로 그것은 좋지 않은 생각입니다.

➡ _____

23 지진은 언제든지 발생할 수 있습니다.

➡ _____

24 지진은 모두에게 무서운 경험일 것입니다.

➡ _____

25 따라서 지진이 날 때 안전을 지키는 법을 배우세요.

➡ _____

26 부상을 방지하고 자신을 보호할 수 있습니다.

➡ _____

27 이 지침을 따르고 안전을 지키세요!

➡ _____

구석구석 지문 Test

※ 다음 우리말과 일치하도록 빈칸에 알맞은 말을 쓰시오.

Real Life Communication B

1. A: I _____ _____ your accident. I _____ _____ _____ you.

2. B: Thanks. I _____ my hand, but it's _____ _____. I'll be okay.

3. A: Good. You _____ _____ your hands _____ you _____ the door.

4. B: You're _____. I _____.

Culture & Life

1. _____ an earthquake _____ in Italy in 2016, people found Georgia _____ _____ Leo, a dog.

2. Leo _____ the eight-year-old girl 16 hours _____ _____ _____ _____.

Culture & Life Project

1. _____ _____ the items for _____ _____ _____.

2. We _____ _____ _____ and water.

3. We _____ them _____ _____.

4. We also _____ some _____ that might be helpful _____ _____.

5. We _____ medicine _____ the bag, _____.

6. We might _____ it for _____.

1. A: 네 사고에 대해 들었어. 나는 너를 걱정했어.
2. B: 고마워. 손을 다쳤지만 심각하지 않아. 괜찮을 거야.
3. A: 다행이야. 문을 닫을 때 손을 조심해야 해.
4. B: 맞아. 그럴게.

1. 2016년 이탈리아에 지진이 발생했을 때, 사람들은 Leo라는 개 덕분에 Georgia를 발견했다.
2. Leo는 지진 발생 후 16시간이 지나 이 8살짜리 소녀를 발견했다.

1. 여기 우리의 생존 가방에 들어갈 물품이 있습니다.
2. 우리는 약간의 음식과 물을 챙겼습니다.
3. 우리는 생존하기 위해서 그것들이 필요합니다.
4. 우리는 또한 재난 발생 시 유용할 수 있는 성냥을 챙겼습니다.
5. 가방에 약품도 넣었습니다.
6. 부상당했을 때 필요할 수 있습니다.

Step2

※ 다음 우리말을 영어로 쓰시오.

Real Life Communication B

1. A: 네 사고에 대해 들었어. 나는 너를 걱정했어.
   ➡ _____

2. B: 고마워. 손을 다쳤지만 심각하지 않아. 괜찮을 거야.
   ➡ _____

3. A: 다행이야. 문을 닫을 때 손을 조심해야 해.
   ➡ _____

4. B: 맞아. 그럴게.
   ➡ _____

Culture & Life

1. 2016년 이탈리아에 지진이 발생했을 때, 사람들은 Leo라는 개 덕분에 Georgia를 발견했다.
   ➡ _____

2. Leo는 지진 발생 후 16시간이 지나 이 8살짜리 소녀를 발견했다.
   ➡ _____

Culture & Life Project

1. 여기 우리의 생존 가방에 들어갈 물품이 있습니다.
   ➡ _____

2. 우리는 약간의 음식과 물을 챙겼습니다.
   ➡ _____

3. 우리는 생존하기 위해서 그것들이 필요합니다.
   ➡ _____

4. 우리는 또한 재난 발생 시 유용할 수 있는 성냥을 챙겼습니다.
   ➡ _____

5. 가방에 약품도 넣었습니다.
   ➡ _____

6. 부상당했을 때 필요할 수 있습니다.
   ➡ _____

※ 다음 영어를 우리말로 쓰시오.

01 rest	_____	22 trash _____
02 avoid	_____	23 secret _____
03 pay phone	_____	24 disappear _____
04 activity	_____	25 different _____
05 arrow	_____	26 frame _____
06 danger	_____	27 outside _____
07 say	_____	28 children's center _____
08 effort	_____	29 coin _____
09 success	_____	30 solve _____
10 possible	_____	31 map _____
11 volunteer club	_____	32 free _____
12 plan	_____	33 plastic bag _____
13 solution	_____	34 sign _____
14 mentee	_____	35 come up with _____
15 wonderful	_____	36 during the day _____
16 street	_____	37 on one's own _____
17 explain	_____	38 give it a try _____
18 confusing	_____	39 put up _____
19 refrigerator	_____	40 stop -ing _____
20 need	_____	41 thanks to _____
21 forget	_____	42 have to _____
		43 one day _____

※ 다음 우리말을 영어로 쓰시오.

01	딱지, 스티커	
02	바구니	
03	동전	
04	표지판	
05	혼란스러운	
06	비밀; 비밀의	
07	해결하다	
08	몇몇의	
09	버스 정류장	
10	아동 센터	
11	사라지다	
12	틀, 테	
13	무료의	
14	비누	
15	기쁜	
16	듣다	
17	지도	
18	다른	
19	멘토	
20	바깥의, 외부의	
21	비닐봉지	

22	쓰레기	
23	냉장고	
24	설명하다	
25	노력	
26	결심하다	
27	피하다	
28	쓰레기	
29	위험	
30	쉬다, 휴식하다	
31	성공	
32	공중전화	
33	해결책	
34	잊어버리다	
35	며칠 전에, 지난번	
36	~을 나누어 주다	
37	(생각을) 찾아내다, 제시하다	
38	낮 동안	
39	~하는 것을 멈추다	
40	자기 스스로	
41	설치하다, 세우다	
42	~ 덕분에	
43	시도하다, 한번 해 보다	

※ 다음 영영풀이에 알맞은 단어를 <보기>에서 골라 쓴 후, 우리말 뜻을 쓰시오.

1 _____ : not many, but some: _____

2 _____ : difficult to understand: _____

3 _____ : to begin doing or using something: _____

4 _____ : to stop being visible: _____

5 _____ : not costing any money: _____

6 _____ : kept hidden from others: _____

7 _____ : something that is done as work for a particular purpose: _____

8 _____ : to be aware of sounds with your ears: _____

9 _____ : the correct or desired result of an attempt: _____

10 _____ : a device or room that is used to keep things cold: _____

11 _____ : a mark that is shaped like an arrow and that is used to show direction:
_____

12 _____ : a person who is advised and helped by more experienced person:
_____

13 _____ : a piece of paper, wood, etc., with words or pictures on it that gives information
about something: _____

14 _____ : to stop working or doing an activity for a time and sit down or lie down
to relax: _____

15 _____ : a drawing or plan of the earth's surface or past of it, showing countries,
towns, rivers, etc.: _____

16 _____ : someone who teaches or gives help and advice to a less experienced and
often younger person: _____

보기			
start	activity	mentor	few
map	confusing	sign	refrigerator
hear	free	arrow	mentee
disappear	secret	rest	success

※ 다음 우리말과 일치하도록 빈칸에 알맞은 말을 쓰시오.

Listen & Speak 1 A

Tom: Hojun and I _____ _____ _____ _____ free stickers today, but I _____ he _____.

Sora: Really? _____ _____ _____ _____ _____ _____. Why are you _____ to _____ _____ stickers?

Tom: It's _____ of our _____ _____ _____.

Sora: I see. What does this sticker _____?

Tom: _____ _____ _____ when we _____ _____ _____, the world will _____ _____ _____ _____ _____.

Sora: That's a _____ _____.

Tom: 호준이와 나는 오늘 무료 스티커를 나눠주기로 계획했는데 호준이가 잊어버린 것 같아.
Sora: 그래? 그럼 내가 도와줄게. 너희는 스티커를 왜 나눠주려고 하니?
Tom: 그건 우리 자원봉사 동아리 활동의 일부야.
Sora: 그렇구나. 이 스티커는 무엇을 의미하니?
Tom: 그건 우리가 서로에게 미소 지을 때, 세상이 더 좋은 곳이 될 거라는 의미야.
Sora: 그거 멋진 아이디어구나.

Listen & Speak 1 B

Mike: Jimin, what are all these things _____ _____ _____?

Jimin: They're for _____ _____ at the children's center. I'm _____ _____ her my old books today.

Mike: _____ _____ _____ _____ _____ _____ _____?

Jimin: Yes. I _____ _____ when I _____ her.

Mike: _____ _____ _____ _____ _____ _____. Oh, the box _____ _____. _____ me _____ you.

Jimin: Thanks.

Mike: 지민아, 상자에 들어 있는 이게 전부 뭐니?
Jimin: 그건 아동 센터에 있는 내 멘티를 위한 거야. 오늘 내가 보던 책들을 줄 거야.
Mike: 너는 그녀를 주말마다 가르치니?
Jimin: 응. 나는 그녀를 가르칠 때 행복해.
Mike: 넌 좋은 멘토구나. 아, 상자 무거워 보인다. 내가 도와줄게.
Jimin: 고마워.

Listen & Speak 2 A

Alex: Mom, _____ _____ _____ _____ _____ _____. I _____ it _____ plastic bags.

Mom: That's very cute, Alex. _____ _____ _____ _____ _____ I _____ a new basket?

Alex: You _____ _____ it when we were having dinner _____ _____ _____.

Mom: _____ _____! I really like this basket. It has _____ _____ _____.

Alex: _____ _____ _____ _____ _____ _____ _____.

Alex: 엄마, 이거 선물이에요. 제가 비닐봉지로 만들었어요.
Mom: 그것 참 예쁘구나, Alex. 내가 새로운 바구니가 필요한 걸 어떻게 알았니?
Alex: 엄마가 지난번에 저녁 먹을 때 말씀하셨어요.
Mom: 아주 멋지구나! 이 바구니가 아주 좋은 걸. 색깔이 아주 다양하구나.
Alex: 엄마가 좋아하시니 저도 기뻐요.

Listen & Speak 2 B

Yujin: _____ _____ _____ _____ _____ _____
_____ _____ _____ _____ . Do you want to _____
_____ it?

Jack: Sure. _____ _____ _____ _____, Yujin?

Yujin: Many children in his town _____ _____ to school and
_____ _____ _____ . So he _____ them in his house
_____ _____ .

Jack: That's a _____ _____ .

Yujin: _____ _____ _____ _____ _____ .

Real Life Communication

Emily: Welcome back, Brian. _____ _____ _____ _____ ?

Brian: Yes, thanks. I _____ _____ study _____ _____
_____ in the hospital, _____ it was hard.

Emily: _____ _____ _____ _____ . Why don't you _____
_____ _____ _____ ?

Brian: Did you start a _____ _____ ? That's wonderful.

Emily: Thanks. I think that _____ _____ _____ _____
_____ _____ _____ _____ .

Brian: I agree. I'll _____ _____ to be a good member. _____
_____ _____ _____ .

Emily: You're _____ . I'm _____ you _____ my idea.

Let's Check 1

Henry: Your bag _____ . _____ _____
_____ .

Sujin: Thanks. _____ _____ _____ _____ _____
_____ _____ ?

Henry: It's _____ _____ . I'll _____ your bag to the bus stop for
you.

Sujin: You're _____ _____ .

Henry: _____ _____ . I am _____ that way, _____ .

Yujin: 내가 인도의 특별한 소년에 대한 이야기를 읽었어. 들어 볼래?
Jack: 그래. 왜 그가 특별하다는 거니, 유진아?
Yujin: 그 소년의 마을에 있는 많은 아이들이 학교에 갈 수 없었고 일을 해야만 했어. 그래서 그가 매일 자신의 집에서 아이들을 가르쳤다는 거야.
Jack: 그거 멋진 이야기구나.
Yujin: 네가 좋아하니 나도 기뻐.

Emily: 돌아온 걸 환영해, Brian. 좀 나아졌니?
Brian: 응, 고마워. 나는 병원에서 혼자 공부하려고 했는데, 어려웠어.
Emily: 내가 도와줄게. 우리 스터디 모임에 함께 하는 게 어때?
Brian: 스터디 모임을 시작했니? 그거 멋지다.
Emily: 고마워. 나는 우리가 서로를 가르쳐주면 더 잘 배울 수 있을 거라고 생각해.
Brian: 맞아. 나는 좋은 구성원이 되려고 열심히 노력할게. 도와줘서 고마워.
Emily: 천만에. 내 아이디어를 좋아해 줘서 나도 기뻐.

Henry: 가방이 무거워 보이네요. 제가 도와 드릴게요.
Sujin: 고마워요. 이 근처에 버스 정류장이 어디 있나요?
Henry: 저쪽에 있어요. 버스 정류장까지 가방을 들어 드릴게요.
Sujin: 정말 친절하군요.
Henry: 별말씀을요. 저도 그쪽으로 가는 길인 걸요.

※ 다음 우리말에 맞도록 대화를 영어로 쓰시오.

해석

Listen & Speak 1 A

Tom: _____

Sora: _____

Tom: _____

Sora: _____

Tom: _____

_____

Sora: _____

Listen & Speak 1 B

Mike: _____

Jimin: _____

_____

Mike: _____

Jimin: _____

Mike: _____

Jimin: _____

Listen & Speak 2 A

Alex: _____

Mom: _____

Alex: _____

Mom: _____

Alex: _____

Listen & Speak 2 B

Yujin: _____

Jack: _____

Yujin: _____
_____

Jack: _____

Yujin: _____

Yujin: 내가 인도의 특별한 소년에 대한 이야기를 읽었어. 들어 볼래?

Jack: 그래. 왜 그가 특별하다는 거니, 유진아?

Yujin: 그 소년의 마을에 있는 많은 아이들이 학교에 갈 수 없었고 일을 해야만 했어. 그래서 그가 매일 자신의 집에서 아이들을 가르쳤다는 거야.

Jack: 그거 멋진 이야기구나.

Yujin: 네가 좋아하니 나도 기뻐.

Real Life Communication

Emily: _____

Brian: _____

Emily: _____

Brian: _____

Emily: _____

Brian: _____

Emily: _____

Emily: 돌아온 걸 환영해, Brian. 좀 나아졌니?

Brian: 응, 고마워. 나는 병원에서 혼자 공부하려고 했는데, 어려웠어.

Emily: 내가 도와줄게. 우리 스터디 모임에 함께 하는 게 어때?

Brian: 스터디 모임을 시작했니? 그거 멋지다.

Emily: 고마워. 나는 우리가 서로를 가르쳐주면 더 잘 배울 수 있을 거라고 생각해.

Brian: 맞아. 나는 좋은 구성원이 되려고 열심히 노력할게. 도와줘서 고마워.

Emily: 천만에. 내 아이디어를 좋아해줘서 나도 기뻐.

Let's Check 1

Henry: _____

Sujin: _____

Henry: _____

Sujin: _____

Henry: _____

Henry: 가방이 무거워 보이네요. 제가 도와 드릴게요.

Sujin: 고마워요. 이 근처에 버스 정류장이 어디 있나요?

Henry: 저쪽에 있어요. 버스 정류장까지 가방을 들어 드릴게요.

Sujin: 정말 친절하군요.

Henry: 별말씀요. 저도 그쪽으로 가는 길인 걸요.

※ 다음 우리말과 일치하도록 빈칸에 알맞은 것을 골라 쓰시오.

1 Here _____ two stories _____ I _____ yesterday.
A. read   B. which   C. are

2 Do you _____ to _____ _____ them?
A. about   B. hear   C. want

3 _____ Someone _____ _____.
A. Love   B. You   C. Call

4 New York _____ many _____ phones _____ its _____.
A. streets   B. on   C. pay   D. had

5 _____, _____ really _____ them.
A. used   B. nobody   C. however

6 _____ day, a man came _____ _____ an idea.
A. with   B. up   C. one

7 He _____ coins _____ one _____ the phones.
A. of   B. to   C. stuck

8 He also _____ _____ a sign _____ said, "Call Someone You Love."
A. that   B. up   C. put

9 Soon, _____ people _____ _____ the phone.
A. using   B. were   C. many

10 _____ they were _____ to someone _____ they loved, they didn't stop _____.
A. smiling   B. whom   C. talking   D. when

11 _____ idea _____ a big _____.
A. success   B. became   C. his

12 _____ the day, _____ the coins _____.
A. disappeared   B. all   C. during

13 The man was very happy _____ his small idea _____ _____ to many people.
A. happiness   B. gave   C. because

---

1 여기 내가 어제 읽은 이야기가 두 개 있어.

2 들어볼래?

3 당신이 사랑하는 누군가에게 전화하세요.

4 뉴욕에는 길거리에 공중전화가 많이 있었다.

5 그러나 아무도 그것들을 실제로 사용하지는 않았다.

6 어느 날. 한 남자에게 좋은 아이디어가 떠올랐다.

7 그는 공중전화 하나에 동전들을 붙였다.

8 그는 또한 "당신이 사랑하는 사람에게 전화하세요."라고 쓰인 표지판을 설치했다.

9 곧. 많은 사람들이 그 전화기를 사용하고 있었다.

10 그들이 사랑하는 누군가에게 전화하고 있을 때. 그들은 미소 짓기를 멈추지 않았다.

11 그의 아이디어는 커다란 성공이었다.

12 낮 동안. 모든 동전이 사라졌다.

13 그 남자는 자신의 작은 아이디어가 많은 사람에게 행복을 가져다 주었기 때문에 매우 행복했다.

14 The Red _____ _____

    A. Man   B. Arrow

15 A _____ years _____, the maps at bus stops in Seoul _____ very _____.

    A. confusing   B. were   C. ago   D. few

16 They _____ have _____ _____.

    A. information   B. enough   C. didn't

17 People _____ to ask _____ to _____ the maps.

    A. explain   B. others   C. had

18 "_____ is this bus stop _____ the map? Does this bus _____ _____ Gwanghwamun?"

    A. to   B. go   C. on   D. where

19 Many people _____ _____ the wrong bus and _____ their time.

    A. wasted   B. took   C. often

20 _____ day, a young man _____ _____ _____ this problem.

    A. solve   B. to   C. decided   D. one

21 He _____ _____ of red _____ stickers.

    A. arrow   B. lots   C. bought

22 Every day he _____ his bicycle _____ the city and _____ the stickers _____ the bus maps.

    A. on   B. stuck   C. around   D. rode

23 Nobody _____ him _____ _____ this.

    A. do   B. to   C. asked

24 He _____ wanted to _____ _____.

    A. others   B. help   C. just

25 _____ to his effort, people _____ understand the maps _____ and _____ time.

    A. save   B. easily   C. could   D. thanks

14 빨간 화살표 청년

15 몇 년 전에, 서울의 버스 정류장의 지도는 매우 혼란스러웠다.

16 지도에는 충분한 정보가 없었다.

17 사람들은 다른 사람들에게 지도를 설명해 달라고 요청해야 했다.

18 "이 버스 정류장은 지도의 어디에 있는 건가요? 이 버스가 광화문으로 가나요?"

19 많은 사람이 종종 버스를 잘못 타서 시간을 낭비하곤 했다.

20 어느 날, 한 젊은 청년이 이 문제를 해결해 보기로 했다.

21 그는 빨간 화살표 스티커를 많이 샀다.

22 매일 그는 자전거를 타고 서울 시내를 돌아다니며 버스 지도에 스티커를 붙였다.

23 아무도 그 청년에게 이 일을 하라고 요청하지 않았다.

24 그는 단지 다른 사람들을 돕고 싶었다.

25 그의 노력 덕분에, 사람들은 지도를 쉽게 이해하고 시간을 절약할 수 있었다.

※ 다음 우리말과 일치하도록 빈칸에 알맞은 말을 쓰시오.

1 Here _____ two stories _____ I _____ yesterday.

2 Do you want _____ _____ _____ them?

3 _____ Someone _____ _____.

4 New York _____ many _____ _____ on its streets.

5 _____, _____ really _____ them.

6 One day, a man _____ _____ _____ an idea.

7 He _____ _____ _____ one of the phones.

8 He also _____ _____ a sign _____ _____, " _____ Someone You _____."

9 Soon, _____ people _____ _____ the phone.

10 _____ they _____ _____ to someone _____ _____ _____, they _____ _____ _____.

11 His idea _____ _____ _____ _____ _____.

12 _____ _____ _____, all the coins _____.

13 The man was very happy _____ his small idea _____ _____ _____ many people.

1 여기 내가 어제 읽은 이야기가 두 개 있어.

2 들어볼래?

3 당신이 사랑하는 누군가에게 전화하세요.

4 뉴욕에는 길거리에 공중전화가 많이 있었다.

5 그러나 아무도 그것들을 실제로 사용하지는 않았다.

6 어느 날, 한 남자에게 좋은 아이디어가 떠올랐다.

7 그는 공중전화 하나에 동전들을 붙였다.

8 그는 또한 "당신이 사랑하는 사람에게 전화하세요."라고 쓰인 표지판을 설치했다.

9 곧, 많은 사람들이 그 전화기를 사용하고 있었다.

10 그들이 사랑하는 누군가에게 전화하고 있을 때, 그들은 미소 짓기를 멈추지 않았다.

11 그의 아이디어는 커다란 성공이었다.

12 낮 동안, 모든 동전이 사라졌다.

13 그 남자는 자신의 작은 아이디어가 많은 사람에게 행복을 가져다주었기 때문에 매우 행복했다.

14 The _____ _____ _____

15 _____ _____ _____ _____, the maps at bus stops in Seoul _____ very _____.

16 They _____ _____ _____ _____.

17 People had to _____ _____ _____ _____ the maps.

18 "_____ is this bus stop _____ _____ _____? Does this bus _____ _____ Gwanghwamun?"

19 Many people _____ _____ _____ _____ _____ and _____ their time.

20 One day, a young man _____ _____ _____ this problem.

21 He bought _____ _____ _____ _____ _____ _____.

22 _____ _____ he _____ his bicycle _____ the city and _____ the stickers _____ the bus maps.

23 Nobody _____ _____ _____ _____ this.

24 He just _____ _____ _____ others.

25 _____ _____ _____ _____, people _____ _____ the maps _____ and _____ .

14	빨간 화살표 청년
15	몇 년 전에, 서울의 버스 정류장의 지도는 매우 혼란스러웠다.
16	지도에는 충분한 정보가 없었다.
17	사람들은 다른 사람들에게 지도를 설명해 달라고 요청해야 했다.
18	"이 버스 정류장은 지도의 어디에 있는 건가요? 이 버스가 광화문으로 가나요?"
19	많은 사람이 종종 버스를 잘못타서 시간을 낭비하곤 했다.
20	어느 날, 한 젊은 청년이 이 문제를 해결해 보기로 했다.
21	그는 빨간 화살표 스티커를 많이 샀다.
22	매일 그는 자전거를 타고 서울 시내를 돌아다니며 버스 지도에 스티커를 붙였다.
23	아무도 그 청년에게 이 일을 하라고 요청하지 않았다.
24	그는 단지 다른 사람들을 돕고 싶었다.
25	그의 노력 덕분에, 사람들은 지도를 쉽게 이해하고 시간을 절약할 수 있었다.

※ 다음 문장을 우리말로 쓰시오.

1 ▶ Here are two stories which I read yesterday.

➡ _____

2 ▶ Do you want to hear about them?

➡ _____

3 ▶ Call Someone You Love

➡ _____

4 ▶ New York had many pay phones on its streets.

➡ _____

5 ▶ However, nobody really used them.

➡ _____

6 ▶ One day, a man came up with an idea.

➡ _____

7 ▶ He stuck coins to one of the phones.

➡ _____

8 ▶ He also put up a sign that said, "Call Someone You Love."

➡ _____

9 ▶ Soon, many people were using the phone.

➡ _____

10 ▶ When they were talking to someone whom they loved, they didn't stop smiling.

➡ _____

11 ▶ His idea became a big success.

➡ _____

12 ▶ During the day, all the coins disappeared.

➡ _____

13 ▶ The man was very happy because his small idea gave happiness to many people.

➡ _____

14 ▶ The Red Arrow Man

➡ _____

15 ▶ A few years ago, the maps at bus stops in Seoul were very confusing.

➡ _____

16 ▶ They didn't have enough information.

➡ _____

17 ▶ People had to ask others to explain the maps.

➡ _____

18 ▶ "Where is this bus stop on the map? Does this bus go to Gwanghwamun?"

➡ _____

19 ▶ Many people often took the wrong bus and wasted their time.

➡ _____

20 ▶ One day, a young man decided to solve this problem.

➡ _____

21 ▶ He bought lots of red arrow stickers.

➡ _____

22 ▶ Every day he rode his bicycle around the city and stuck the stickers on the bus maps.

➡ _____

23 ▶ Nobody asked him to do this.

➡ _____

24 ▶ He just wanted to help others.

➡ _____

25 ▶ Thanks to his effort, people could understand the maps easily and save time.

➡ _____

※ 다음 괄호 안의 단어들을 우리말에 맞도록 바르게 배열하시오.

1 (are / here / stories / two / I / which / yesterday. / read)
➡ _____

2 (you / do / to / want / them? / about / hear)
➡ _____

3 (You / Call / Love / Someone)
➡ _____

4 (York / New / many / had / phones / pay / streets. / its / on)
➡ _____

5 (nobody / however, / used / them. / really)
➡ _____

6 (day, / one / man / a / up / came / idea. / with / an)
➡ _____

7 (stuck / he / to / coins / of / one / phones. / the)
➡ _____

8 (also / he / up / put / sign / a / said, / that / "Call / You / Love." / Someone)
➡ _____

9 (many / soon, / people / using / were / phone. / the)
➡ _____

10 (were / they / when / talking / someone / to / whom / loved, / they / smiling. / stop / didn't / they)
➡ _____
_____

11 (idea / his / became / success. / big / a)
➡ _____

12 (day, / the / during / the / all / disappeared. / coins)
➡ _____

13 (man / the / very / was / happy / because / small / his / idea / happiness / gave / people. / many / to)
➡ _____
_____

1 여기 내가 어제 읽은 이야기가 두 개 있어.

2 들어볼래?

3 당신이 사랑하는 누군가에게 전화하세요.

4 뉴욕에는 길거리에 공중전화가 많이 있었다.

5 그러나 아무도 그것들을 실제로 사용하지는 않았다.

6 어느 날, 한 남자에게 좋은 아이디어가 떠올랐다.

7 그는 공중전화 하나에 동전들을 붙였다.

8 그는 또한 "당신이 사랑하는 사람에게 전화하세요."라고 쓰인 표지판을 설치했다.

9 곧, 많은 사람들이 그 전화기를 사용하고 있었다.

10 그들이 사랑하는 누군가에게 전화하고 있을 때, 그들은 미소 짓기를 멈추지 않았다.

11 그의 아이디어는 커다란 성공이었다.

12 낮 동안, 모든 동전이 사라졌다.

13 그 남자는 자신의 작은 아이디어가 많은 사람에게 행복을 가져다주었기 때문에 매우 행복했다.

14 (Arrow / The / Man / Red)

➡ _____

16 (few / ago, / a / years / the / maps / bus / at / stops / Seoul / in / confusing. / very / was)

➡ _____

15 (didn't / they / have / information. / enough)

➡ _____

17 (had / people / ask / to / others / explain / to / maps. / the)

➡ _____

18 (is / "where / bus / this / stop / the / on / map? // this / go / does / bus / Gwanghwamun?" / to)

➡ _____

19 (people / many / took / often / wrong / the / bus / and / time / their / wasted)

➡ _____

20 (day, / one / young / a / man / to / decided / problem. / this / solve)

➡ _____

21 (bought / he / of / lots / red / stickers. / arrow)

➡ _____

22 (day / every / rode / he / bicycle / his / the / around / city / and / stuck / stickers / on / the / maps. / bus / the)

➡ _____

23 (asked / to / nobody / this. / do / him)

➡ _____

24 (just / wanted / he / others. / help / to)

➡ _____

25 (to / thanks / effort, / his / could / people / understand / maps / the / easily / time. / save / and)

➡ _____

14 빨간 화살표 청년

15 몇 년 전에, 서울의 버스 정류장의 지도는 매우 혼란스러웠다.

16 지도에는 충분한 정보가 없었다.

17 사람들은 다른 사람들에게 지도를 설명해 달라고 요청해야 했다.

18 "이 버스 정류장은 지도의 어디에 있는 건가요? 이 버스가 광화문으로 가나요?"

19 많은 사람이 종종 버스를 잘못 타서 시간을 낭비하곤 했다.

20 어느 날, 한 젊은 청년이 이 문제를 해결해 보기로 했다.

21 그는 빨간 화살표 스티커를 많이 샀다.

22 매일 그는 자전거를 타고 서울 시내를 돌아다니며 버스 지도에 스티커를 붙였다.

23 아무도 그 청년에게 이 일을 하라고 요청하지 않았다.

24 그는 단지 다른 사람들을 돕고 싶었다.

25 그의 노력 덕분에, 사람들은 지도를 쉽게 이해하고 시간을 절약할 수 있었다.

※ 다음 우리말을 영어로 쓰시오.

1 여기 내가 어제 읽은 이야기가 두 개 있어.

➡ _____

2 들어볼래?

➡ _____

3 당신이 사랑하는 누군가에게 전화하세요.

➡ _____

4 뉴욕에는 길거리에 공중전화가 많이 있었다.

➡ _____

5 그러나 아무도 그것들을 실제로 사용하지는 않았다.

➡ _____

6 어느 날, 한 남자에게 좋은 아이디어가 떠올랐다.

➡ _____

7 그는 공중전화 하나에 동전들을 붙였다.

➡ _____

8 그는 또한 "당신이 사랑하는 사람에게 전화하세요."라고 쓰인 표지판을 설치했다.

➡ _____

9 곧, 많은 사람들이 그 전화기를 사용하고 있었다.

➡ _____

10 그들이 사랑하는 누군가에게 전화하고 있을 때, 그들은 미소 짓기를 멈추지 않았다.

➡ _____

11 그의 아이디어는 커다란 성공이었다.

➡ _____

12 낮 동안, 모든 동전이 사라졌다.

➡ _____

13 그 남자는 자신의 작은 아이디어가 많은 사람에게 행복을 가져다 주었기 때문에 매우 행복했다.

➡ _____

14 빨간 화살표 청년

➡ _____

15 몇 년 전, 서울의 버스 정류장의 지도는 매우 혼란스러웠다.

➡ _____

16 지도에는 충분한 정보가 없었다.

➡ _____

17 사람들은 다른 사람들에게 지도를 설명해 달라고 요청해야 했다.

➡ _____

18 "이 버스 정류장은 지도의 어디에 있는 건가요? 이 버스가 광화문으로 가나요?"

➡ _____

19 많은 사람이 종종 버스를 잘못 타서 시간을 낭비하곤 했다.

➡ _____

20 어느 날, 한 젊은 청년이 이 문제를 해결해 보기로 했다.

➡ _____

21 그는 빨간 화살표 스티커를 많이 샀다.

➡ _____

22 매일 그는 자전거를 타고 서울 시내를 돌아다니며 버스 지도에 스티커를 붙였다.

➡ _____

23 아무도 그 청년에게 이 일을 하라고 요청하지 않았다.

➡ _____

24 그는 단지 다른 사람들을 돕고 싶었다.

➡ _____

25 그의 노력 덕분에, 사람들은 지도를 쉽게 이해하고 시간을 절약할 수 있었다.

➡ _____

※ 다음 우리말과 일치하도록 빈칸에 알맞은 말을 쓰시오.

Real Life Communication B

1. A: I'm _____ _____ _____ science. _____ can I do?
2. B: _____ _____ _____ you. _____ _____ you start with easier books?
3. A: Okay, I'll _____ _____ _____ _____. Thanks for the tip.
4. B: No _____. I'm _____ you like it.

1. A: 나는 과학을 잘 못해. 어떻게 해야 할까?
2. B: 내가 도와줄게. 좀 더 쉬운 책으로 시작하는 게 어때?
3. A: 응, 한번 시도해 볼게. 조언 고마워.
4. B: 괜찮아. 네가 좋아하니 기뻐.

Let's Write

1. _____ a Mentor!
2. My name is Semi and I'm _____ _____ _____ _____.
3. I _____ _____ _____ my mentee _____ her homework.
4. I _____ _____ my mentee _____ _____.
5. I'll _____ my mentee _____ _____ on time.
6. I _____ a good mentor _____ _____ a good friend.
7. So I want to become a good friend _____ _____ _____ _____ _____.

1. 멘토가 되세요!
2. 제 이름은 세미이고 저는 2학년입니다.
3. 저는 제 멘티의 숙제를 돕고 싶습니다.
4. 저는 방과 후에 제 멘티를 만날 수 있습니다.
5. 저는 제 멘티에게 시간을 지키라고 요청할 것입니다.
6. 저는 좋은 멘토는 좋은 친구가 될 수 있다고 생각합니다.
7. 그래서 저는 제 멘티가 믿을 수 있는 좋은 친구가 되고 싶습니다.

Culture & Life

1. Do you _____ toys _____ the bars of soap?
2. Children in South Africa _____ _____ _____ more often _____ _____ the toys.
3. _____ your hands _____ _____ many health problems.
4. _____ _____ this idea, _____ children are _____ _____.

1. 비누 안에 들어 있는 장난감이 보이나요?
2. 남아프리카의 어린이들은 장난감을 갖기 위해 더 자주 손을 씻습니다.
3. 손을 씻는 것은 많은 건강 문제를 막을 수 있습니다.
4. 이 아이디어 덕분에, 아픈 어린이들이 줄어들고 있습니다.

구석구석 지문 Test

※ 다음 우리말을 영어로 쓰시오.

Real Life Communication B

1. A: 나는 과학을 잘 못해. 어떻게 해야 할까?
➡ _____

2. B: 내가 도와줄게. 좀 더 쉬운 책으로 시작하는 게 어때?
➡ _____

3. A: 응, 한번 시도해 볼게. 조언 고마워.
➡ _____

4. B: 괜찮아. 네가 좋아하니 기뻐.
➡ _____

Let's Write

1. 멘토가 되세요!
➡ _____

2. 제 이름은 세미이고 저는 2학년입니다.
➡ _____

3. 저는 제 멘티의 숙제를 돕고 싶습니다.
➡ _____

4. 저는 방과 후에 제 멘티를 만날 수 있습니다.
➡ _____

5. 저는 제 멘티에게 시간을 지키라고 요청할 것입니다.
➡ _____

6. 저는 좋은 멘토는 좋은 친구가 될 수 있다고 생각합니다.
➡ _____

7. 그래서 저는 제 멘티가 믿을 수 있는 좋은 친구가 되고 싶습니다.
➡ _____

Culture & Life

1. 비누 안에 들어 있는 장난감이 보이나요?
➡ _____

2. 남아프리카의 어린이들은 장난감을 갖기 위해 더 자주 손을 씻습니다.
➡ _____

3. 손을 씻는 것은 많은 건강 문제를 막을 수 있습니다.
➡ _____

4. 이 아이디어 덕분에, 아픈 어린이들이 줄어들고 있습니다.
➡ _____

MEMO

1학기

정답 및 해설

지학 | 민찬규

중 2

New Beginnings

시험대비 실력평가   p.08

01 private   02 ②   03 ⑤   04 ④

05 (1) am interested in   (2) is into   (3) heard from

    (4) make changes   06 ④

01 주어진 관계는 반의어를 나타낸다. public: 공공의, private: 사적인

02 planet: 행성, space: 우주

03 주어진 문장과 ⑤번에서 handle은 '손잡이'를 가리키지만 나머지 문장에서는 '다루다'를 의미한다.

04 nail은 '못' 또는 '손톱'을 뜻한다.

05 be interested in: ~에 관심이 있다, be into:~에 열중하다, hear from: ~로부터 소식을 듣다, make changes: 변화를 이루다

06 각각의 문장에서 tip은 '끝', '사례금', '정보'를 가리킨다. on the tip of one's tongue: 말이 (기억은 나지 않고) 혀끝에서 뱅뱅 도는

서술형 시험대비   p.09

01 false

02 homeroom teacher

03 planet

04 (1) Would you buy milk for me on your way home?

   (2) It's time to use a new program to make changes.

   (3) He doesn't take the computer class anymore.

05 (1) break my bad habit

   (2) By the way

   (3) comes true

   (4) It's time to

06 (1) bite   (2) kind   (3) wish   (4) handles

07 (A) from, (B) By, (C) into

01 주어진 단어는 반의어 관계를 가리킨다. true: 사실인, 참인, false: 거짓의

02 학급을 담당하는 교사를 가리키는 말은 homeroom teacher(담임 선생님)이다.

03 별 주위를 도는 우주의 크고 둥근 물체를 가리키는 말은

---

planet(행성)이다.

05 break one's bad habit: 나쁜 습관을 그만 두다 by the way: 그건 그렇고, 그런데 come true: 이루어지다, 실현되다 It's time to ~: ~할 시간이다

06 bite: 물다, kind: 종류, wish: 바라다, handle: 손잡이

07 hear from: ~로부터 소식을 듣다. by the way: 그건 그렇고, 그런데, change into: ~로 변하다

교과서 Conversation

핵심 Check   p.10~11

1 You know what   2 Guess what

3 (A) Look! (B) promise

4 (B) I'm going [planning] to

5 (A) I'm going to (B) decide

6 (A) I'm thinking of cooking

교과서 대화문 익히기

Check(√) True or False   p.12

(1) T   (2) F   (3) T   (4) F

교과서 확인학습   p.14~15

Listen & Talk 1 A

You konw what / you were interested in

Listen & Talk 1 B

homeroom teacher / fun / What does she teach / art

Listen & Speak 2 A

are thinking of starting / What kind of club / stars, planets / once a week / I'm interested in

Listen & Speak 2 B

I'm thinking of cooking / What about beef / I'll buy some for you on my way home

Real Life Communication A

I'm thinking of taking, painting class / decide / I want to go to an art high school / artist / comes true / do my best

Real Life Communication B

move / upset / I can understand her feelings / keep in touch with

01 You know what　　　02 (B) → (C) → (D) → (A)

03 Who's[Who is] your homeroom teacher this year?

04 ⑤

02 (B) 사실 확인 → (C) 구체적인 사실 설명 → (D) 반응 및 그리움 표현 → (A) 동의 표현

04 Jimin과 Tim은 각자 다른 반으로 다른 담임 선생님에 대해 이야기하고 있다.

시험대비 실력평가　　　　　　　p.17~18

01 ④　　　　02 ③　　　　03 (E) → (B) → (A) → (D) → (C)　　04 ①　　　05 ④　　　06 keep in touch with　　07 ③　　08 ⓔ in → on　09 ⑤

10 How often are you going to meet?

11 They want to learn about stars and planets.

12 He is interested in space.

01 (A) 방학이 어떠하였는지를 묻고 있으므로 how, (B) amazing: 놀라운, 굉장한, amazed: 놀란, (C) be interested in: ~에 관심이 있다

02 ③ Brian은 Julia가 무에타이에 관심이 있는지 몰랐다.

03 (E) Emily의 계획에 대한 이유 질문 → (B) 이유 대답 → (A) 장래 희망 질문 → (D) 대답 및 관심사 표현 → (C) 반응 및 소망이 이루어지기를 기원

04 주어진 문장은 대화를 시작하기 전에 상대방의 주의를 끄는 말로 (A)에 들어가는 것이 알맞다. concert hall: 콘서트 홀, 연주회장

05 Ms. Kim은 새로 오신 선생님으로 작년에 수업이 어떠했는지 알 수 없다.

06 keep in touch with: ~와 연락하다

07 pleased: 기쁜, nervous: 긴장한, frustrated: 불안스러워하는, lonely: 외로운, excited: 흥분한

08 on one's way home: 집에 오는 길에

09 대화를 통해 Alex의 엄마가 지금 어디에 있는지 알 수 없다.

11 Sujin과 Jane은 우주 과학 동아리에서 별과 행성에 대해 배우고 싶어 한다.

12 민수는 우주에 관심이 있다

01 *muay thai*

02 She took *muay thai* lessons during the winter vacation.

03 She was interested in *muay thai*.

04 (E) → (D) → (C) → (B) → (A)

05 I'm thinking of learning yoga.

06 (A) stars and planets (B) once a week (C) Room 101

02 Julia는 겨울 방학 동안 무에타이 수업을 들었다.

03 Julia는 무에타이에 관심을 갖고 있다.

04 (E) 반응 및 Mr. Smith 선생님의 수업에 대한 설명 → (D) 상대방의 담임 선생님이 누구인지 질문 → (C) 대답 → (B) 무슨 과목 선생님인지 질문 → (A) 대답

06 오늘 Jane은 내게 새로운 동아리를 시작하는 것에 대해 이야기를 했다. Sujin과 그녀는 별과 행성에 관심이 있어서 우주과학 동아리를 만들고 싶어 했다. 그들은 일주일에 한 번 Room 101에서 만날 계획이었다. 이것은 좋은 생각이었다. 그래서 나는 동아리에 가입하기로 결심했다. 나는 우주에 대해 배우는 것을 매우 기대하고 있다.

교과서
Grammar

핵심 Check　　　　　　　　　p.20~21

1 (1) One, the other　(2) One, Another, The others

 (3) Some books, other books[others]

2 (1) arrive, we will　(2) Unless, will be　(3) if

시험대비 기본평가　　　　　　　p.22

01 (1) will tell → tell　(2) Another → Other

 (3) practices → will practice　(4) other → the other

02 (1) rains　(2) One, the other　(3) Unless　(4) another, the others

03 (1) Some flowers are white, and others are yellow.

 (2) If you want this magazine, I will lend it to you.

 (3) You have two watches. One is here. Where is the other?

 (4) If you win, we will be happy.

01 (1) 조건의 부사절에서 현재형으로 미래를 나타낼 수 있다. (2) 복수 명사를 수식해야 하므로 other를 쓰는 것이 옳다. (3) If가 명사절을 이끌 경우 내용과 시제를 맞추어 준다. (4) 둘 중 남은 하나는 the other이다.

02 (1) 조건의 부사절에서 현재형으로 미래를 나타낼 수 있다. (2) 둘 중 하나는 one, 나머지 하나는 the other이다. (3) 일찍 일어나지 않으면 늦을 것이라는 의미가 자연스럽다. (4) 5개 중에서 제일 처음 가리키는 것은 one, 남은 것 중 다른 하나를 가리

킬 때는 another, 나머지 전체를 가리키는 말은 the others이다.

03 (1) 불특정 복수명사를 지칭할 때 some, 또 다른 것들을 묶어서 말할 때 others (2), (4) 조건의 부사절에서 현재형으로 미래를 나타낼 수 있다. (3) 둘 중 하나는 one, 남은 하나를 지칭할 때 the other

01 ①, ④   02 ⑤   03 ④   04 One, another, the other   05 ⑤   06 ④
07 ③   08 If you have time, will you do me a favor?   09 ③   10 Do you know if there is another one?   11 ③   12 ④
13 One, Another, The other   14 ⑤   15 ③
16 ⓐ: One ⓑ: Another ⓒ: Another ⓓ: Another ⓔ: The other   17 If she invites you, will you go to the party?   18 ③   19 Unless   20 ⑤
21 ③   22 ②   23 ⑤   24 Some people like blue and others like green.

01 '빈칸이 이끄는 절은 현재시제이지만 주절은 미래이므로, 빈칸에는 시간이나 조건의 부사절이 들어가야 한다. 따라서 ①, ④번이 옳다.

02 둘 중 다른 하나를 가리키는 대명사는 the other이다.

03 조건의 부사절에서 현재시제로 미래를 나타낼 수 있다.

04 셋 중 가장 처음에 언급하는 것은 one, 또 다른 하나를 가리킬 때에는 another, 남은 하나는 the other를 써서 표현한다.

05 둘 중 하나를 one으로 지칭하면, 남은 하나는 the other이며, 조건의 부사절에서 현재시제로 미래를 표현할 수 있다.

06 other people을 대신하는 말이 들어가야 하므로 others라고 쓰는 것이 옳다.

07 ③번은 '~인지 아닌지'로 해석되는 명사절을 이끄는 접속사 if이다. 나머지는 모두 조건절을 이끄는 if이다.

08 do ~ favor: ~의 부탁을 들어주다

09 ① other cars라고 쓰는 것이 옳다. ② unless는 부정어가 있는 문장을 이끌지 않는다. not을 빼는 것이 옳다. ④ the other necklaces이므로 the others라고 쓰는 것이 옳다. ⑤ 이번 주말에 노트북을 살 것인지 궁금하다는 의미이다. 명사절을 이끄는 접속사 if이므로 will buy가 옳다.

10 if는 명사절을 이끌고 있다. 또 다른 복사기를 의미하므로 another를 쓰는 것이 옳다.

11 조건절과 명사절을 모두 이끌 수 있는 것은 if이다.

12 둘 중 하나는 one, 다른 하나는 the other로 지칭한다.

13 셋 중 가장 먼저 지칭하는 것을 one, 남은 것 중 또 다른 하나를

another, 그리고 남은 마지막 하나는 the other로 지칭한다.

14 다른 하나를 사고 싶다는 것이므로 another가 옳다.

15 ① 조건의 부사절에서 현재시제로 미래를 나타내는 것이 옳다. ② other people 혹은 others라고 써야 한다. ④ 문맥상 Unless라고 쓰는 것이 옳다. ⑤ '또 다른 하나'를 가리키는 것이므로 another를 써야 한다.

16 첫 번째로 지칭하는 것을 one으로 하고 남은 하나씩의 손가락은 another로 지칭하고 마지막 손가락은 남은 하나이므로 the other를 쓴다.

17 조건의 부사절에서 현재시제가 미래시제를 대신한다. 따라서 If절은 현재시제를 쓴다.

18 손은 두 개이므로 '다른 손'은 the other로 지칭한다.

19 if … not은 unless와 같다.

20 동전은 두 개의 면을 가지고 있으므로, '다른 쪽 면'은 the other를 쓴다. 조건절의 시제가 현재라 할지라도 미래를 나타내고 있으므로, 주절에서는 의미에 맞게 미래시제를 쓴다.

21 Jenny의 자매 둘 중 한 명이 다른 한 명보다 더 크다는 의미이다. 둘 중 하나는 one, 남은 하나는 the other로 지칭한다. ②번에서 She를 Jenny로 생각한다면 others가 아니라 the others가 되어야 한다.

22 스타에게 사랑을 표현하는 여러 가지 방법 중에 어떤 학생들은 콘서트에서 소리를 지르고 또 어떤 학생들은 몇 시간을 기다리기도 한다는 의미이다. 따라서 불특정 복수명사를 지칭하는 some과 남은 몇몇을 무리지어 지칭하는 others를 쓴다.

23 둘 중에서 나머지 다른 하나는 the other로 지칭한다.

24 불특정 복수명사는 some, 다른 무리의 복수명사는 others로 지칭한다. other people을 줄여 others로 쓸 수 있다.

01 if I find it, I will tell you.

02 The other

03 Unless it rains

04 If I don't feel well tomorrow, I will stay at home. Unless I feel well tomorrow, I will stay at home.

05 I can speak two languages. One is Korean and the other is English.

06 comes, will go

07 If you see Jerry, you will like him.

08 One, another, the other

09 (1) Some, others
(2) One, The other
(3) three, One, Another, The other
(4) One, The others
(5) other

(6) another

(7) some, others

10 If you don't wear a helmet, you will be hurt.

If you cheat on the test, you will get caught.

If you have a car, will you take me to the airport?

11 the other chairs[the others]

12 ⓐit rains ⓑwill use ⓒ the other

13 There were two cookies in the cookie jar.

14 One, the other

01 시간·조건의 부사절에서 현재시제가 미래를 대신한다는 것에 유의하여 빈칸을 채운다. lip balm: 입술 크림

02 나머지 모든 아이들은 갈색 머리라는 의미이므로 남은 전체를 지칭하는 the other를 쓴다.

03 If ~ not은 Unless와 같다.

04 Unless는 If ~ not과 같다.

05 둘 중 하나가 one이면 다른 하나는 the other로 지칭한다.

06 조건의 부사절에서 현재시제로 미래를 나타낼 수 있다.

07 조건의 부사절에서 현재시제로 미래시제를 나타낼 수 있다.

08 세 가지 중 처음 가리키는 것이 one, 다른 하나는 another, 남아 있는 하나는 the other로 지칭한다.

09 불특정 복수명사를 some으로 지칭하며 다른 것을 묶어서 지칭할 때엔 other를 쓰고 'other+복수명사'를 묶어서 others로 표현한다. 둘 중 하나가 one이면 다른 하나는 the other이고 여러 개 중 하나를 one이라고 하고 나머지 전체를 가리킬 때에는 'the other+복수명사'를 쓰거나 줄여서 'the others'로 쓴다. another는 남은 것 중 또 다른 하나를 가리킬 때 사용한다.

10 Unless you wear a helmet을 써도 좋다. cheat: 부정행위를 하다 get caught: 들키다

11 나머지 전체를 지칭하는 것은 'the other+복수명사'이고, 'the other+복수명사'는 the others로 쓸 수 있다.

12 조건의 부사절에서 현재시제가 미래시제를 대신하므로 if절은 현재시제를, 주절은 내용에 맞게 미래시제를 써야 한다. 우산이 두 개 있으므로 다른 하나를 지칭할 때에는 the other를 쓴다.

13 지칭하는 대명사가 one과 the other이므로 쿠키가 두 개 있었다는 것을 알 수 있다.

14 둘 중 하나는 one, 다른 하나는 the other이다.

교과서
Reading

확인문제 p.28

1 F 2 T 3 T 4 F

확인문제 p.29

1 T 2 T 3 F 4 T 5 F 6 F

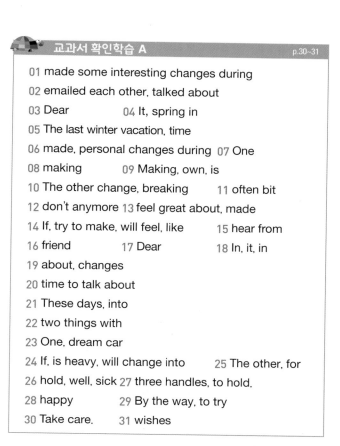

교과서 확인학습 A p.30~31

01 made some interesting changes during

02 emailed each other, talked about

03 Dear   04 It, spring in

05 The last winter vacation, time

06 made, personal changes during 07 One

08 making   09 Making, own, is

10 The other change, breaking   11 often bit

12 don't anymore 13 feel great about, made

14 If, try to make, will feel, like   15 hear from

16 friend   17 Dear   18 In, it, in

19 about, changes

20 time to talk about

21 These days, into

22 two things with

23 One, dream car

24 If, is heavy, will change into   25 The other, for

26 hold, well, sick 27 three handles, to hold.

28 happy   29 By the way, to try

30 Take care.   31 wishes

교과서 p.32~33

1 My friend Eric and I made some interesting changes during the vacation.

2 We emailed each other and talked about our changes.

3 Dear Eric,

4 It's a beautiful spring in Seoul.

5 The last winter vacation was a great time for me.

6 I made two personal changes during the vacation.

7 One is my new hobby.

8 It's making cupcakes.

9 Making my own cupcakes is a lot of fun.

10 The other change is breaking one of my bad habits.

11 In the past, I often bit my nails.

12 Now I don't anymore.

13 I feel great about the changes I made.

14 If you try to make some changes, I'm sure you'll feel great like me.

15 I hope to hear from you soon.

16 Your friend, Junho.

17 Dear Junho,

18 In Sydney, it's fall in March.

19 You talked about your changes in your email.

20 Now, it's time to talk about my new changes.

21 These days, I'm into 3D printing.

22 I printed two things with a 3D printer.

23 One is a model of my dream car.

24 If the traffic is heavy, it will change into a flying car.

25 The other is a special cup for my grandfather.

26 He can't hold his cup well because he's sick.

27 My special cup has three handles, so it is easy to hold.

28 My grandfather is very happy.

29 By the way, I want to try your cupcakes some day, Junho.

30 Take care.

31 Best wishes, Eric

시험대비 실력평가
p.34~37

01 The other 02 ⑤   03 the changes (that[which]) I made   04 ④   05 ④
06 ④   07 ③   08 ③   09 (A) flying, (B)to try   10 my special cup
11 ③   12 ⑤   13 ②   14 my grandfather, three handles, cup   15 ③
16 ③   17 breaking one of my bad habits
18 ④   19 (1) nail   (2) past   20 I feel great.   21 ②   22 ④   23 It has three handles.   24 ⑤   25 He wanted to help him because he couldn't hold his cup well.   26 ⑤   27 ⑤

01 두 개의 변화가 있었다고 하였고, 앞서 한 가지 변화에 관해 이야기하였으므로 나머지 하나는 The other로 받아준다.

02 hear from: ~로부터 연락을 받다 ① be thinking of ~ing: ~할 생각이다 ② on one's way home: 집에 오는 길에 ③ be interested in: ~에 흥미가 있다 ④ listen to: ~을 듣다 ⑤ come from: ~ 출신이다

03 앞서 언급한 두 가지 변화이므로 정관사 the를 써야 한다. 목적격 관계대명사 that이나 which는 생략할 수 있다.

04 밑줄 친 (A)는 날짜, 거리, 시간, 명암 등을 말할 때 쓰이는 비인칭 주어이며 해석되지 않는다. 따라서 ⓐ, ⓑ, ⓔ가 옳다. ⓒ:

인칭대명사 it(그것) ⓓ: 가주어 It

05 (B) 두 개의 변화 중 하나를 지칭할 때 one, (C) 동명사구 주어는 단수 취급, (D) '습관들 중 하나'이므로 habits가 옳다.

06 글쓴이와 Eric은 이메일을 주고받았다고 하였다. 따라서 ④번은 옳지 않다.

07 be into: ~에 열중하다 change into: ~로 변하다

08 편찮으시기 때문에 컵을 잘 들 수 없다고 말하는 것이 가장 적절하다.

09 (A) '날 수 있는 차'라는 의미이므로 flying, (B) want는 to부정사를 목적어로 취하는 동사이다.

10 자신이 만든 특수 컵을 가리키는 말이다.

11 by the way: 그건 그렇고, 그런데

12 Eric은 준호의 컵케이크를 언젠가 먹어 보고 싶다고 하였다. 따라서 ⑤번은 일치하지 않는다.

13 편지의 서두에서 준호가 변화에 관하여 이야기했다고 하였다. 따라서 ②번이 가장 적절하다.

14 이 컵은 아주 특별해. 나는 그것을 나의 할아버지를 위해 만들었어. 그것은 세 개의 손잡이를 가지고 있어서 이 컵을 드는 것은 쉬워.

15 새로운 취미에 대하여 언급한 후, 그것은 컵케이크를 만드는 것이라고 말하고 컵케이를 만드는 것은 정말 재미있다고 말하는 것이 적절하다.

16 ⓐ 흥미를 유발하는 변화이므로 interesting, ⓑ talk about: ~에 관하여 이야기하다

17 be동사의 보어 자리이므로 break를 동명사로 변형하여 써서 문장을 만든다.

18 준호가 손톱을 왜 많이 물어뜯었는지는 알 수 없다.

19 (1) 손가락 끝을 덮고 있는 딱딱한 층은 손톱이다. (2) 현재 이전의 시간은 '과거'이다.

20 준호가 만들어낸 변화에 대해 기분이 어떤지 묻고 있다.

21 주어진 문장은 목적어로 쓰인 명사적 용법의 to부정사이다. ①, ③ 감정의 원인을 나타내는 부사적 용법, ② 동사의 목적어로 쓰인 명사적 용법, ④, ⑤ 앞에 나오는 명사를 수식하는 형용사로 사용된 to부정사

22 (A) it's time to V: V할 때이다 (B) change into: ~으로 변하다 (C) '들기 쉬운'이라는 의미로 to부정사가 부사로 쓰여 형용사 easy를 수식하고 있다.

23 세 개의 손잡이를 가지고 있다고 하였다.

24 be into: ~에 열중하다 be crazy about: ~에 푹 빠지다

25 Eric이 할아버지를 위해 특수 컵을 만든 이유는 할아버지가 컵을 잘 들지 못하셨기 때문에 그를 돕기 위해 만든 것이다.

26 할아버지가 행복해 하신다고 하였으므로 ⑤번은 일치하지 않는다.

27 (C) 두 가지 변화 중 첫 번째 변화를 소개 → (B) 남은 다른 하나의 변화를 소개하며 기분이 좋았음을 말함 → (A) 변화하려고 노력한다면 자신처럼 기분이 좋을 것이라고 말함.

01 We emailed each other.

02 ⓐOne ⓑThe other

03 Now I don't bite my nails anymore.

04 He lives in Seoul.

05 bad habit, break

06 making my own cupcakes, another

07 If you break one of your bad habits, you will feel great.

08 Because he made two personal changes during the vacation.

09 If you hold this cup, you will know it is easy to hold.

10 He wrote the letter in Sydney in March.

11 will be → is / 조건의 부사절에서 현재시제로 미래를 나타내기 때문이다.

12 am satisfied with, happy

13 The other is a special cup for my grandfather.

14 He is into 3D printing these days.

15 Because my special cup has three handles, it is easy to hold.

16 They talk about their new changes.

17 Junho can make cupcakes.

01 email은 명사와 동사로 모두 쓰일 수 있다. each other: 서로

02 둘 중 하나는 one, 남은 하나는 the other로 지칭한다.

03 더 이상 손톱을 깨물지 않는다는 의미이다. 동사 bite의 과거형은 bit이다.

04 준호는 서울에서 살고 있다.

05 Jenny: Junho야, 없애고 싶은 나쁜 습관이 있니? Junho: 예전에 있었지. 하지만 그걸 없앴어.

06 준호의 새로운 취미는 컵케이크를 만드는 것이라고 하였다. 또다른 취미를 묻고 있으므로 another를 쓰는 것이 옳다.

07 조건의 부사절에서 현재시제로 미래를 나타내는 것에 유의하여 문장을 만든다. break a bad habit: 나쁜 습관을 그만두다

08 지난 겨울 방학이 준호에게 멋진 시간이었던 이유는 준호가 개인적인 변화를 만들었기 때문이다.

09 조건의 부사절에서 현재시제로 미래를 나타낼 수 있으며, hold, easy to hold 모두 위 글에서 찾을 수 있는 표현들이다.

10 부사(구)는 일반적으로 '장소-방법-시간' 순서로 쓴다. 편지의 내용으로 보아 Eric은 시드니에서 3월에 편지를 썼다.

12 be satisfied with: ~에 만족하다

13 나머지 다른 하나라고 하였으므로 정관사 the를 추가하여 문장을 만든다.

14 질문: Eric은 요즈음 무엇에 열중하고 있나요?

15 '특수 컵이 세 개의 손잡이를 가지고 있기 때문에 들기 편하다'는

문장으로 쓰면 된다.

17 Eric은 준호의 컵케이크를 먹어 보고 싶다고 하였다. 따라서 준호는 컵케이크를 만들 수 있다고 볼 수 있다.

01 (1) is into　(2) on my way home　(3) hear from

02 ①

03 (1) I decided to break my bad habit.
(2) I'll do my best to pass the test.
(3) He is into playing golf.

04 ③　　05 ①　　06 ⑤　　07 You know what?　　08 ⓑ for → during

09 ⑤　　10 (D) → (A) → (C) → (B)　　11 planet

12 ③　　13 ③　　14 It was a lot of fun.

15 They are going to learn art.　　16 ③

17 ⑤

18 ④　　19 I have three foreign friends. One is from Japan, and the others (are) from France.

20 ②　　21 ④　　22 Unless you do your best, you will not achieve anything.　　23 ⑤

24 If you don't wear warm clothes, you will catch a cold. / Unless you wear warm clothes, you will catch a cold.　　25 ④

26 If you go jogging every day, you will get healthier.

27 ②　　28 ③　　29 If you try to make some changes　　30 ④　　31 ⑤

32 handle　　33 Sydney, in 3D printing

34 Because it has three handles.

02 false: 거짓의

03 break one's bad habit: 나쁜 습관을 그만두다, do one's best: 최선을 다하다, be into: ~에 열중하다

04 bite는 '물다' 또는 '한 입, (물린) 상처'를 뜻한다. grab a bite: (간단히) 먹다 itch: 가려움 itchy: 가려운

05 주어진 문장과 ①번은 '종류'를 의미하며 나머지는 모두 '친절한'을 뜻한다.

06 ⑤번을 제외한 나머지는 모두 계획에 대해 이야기하고 있다.

08 for+일정한 기간, during+특정한 기간

09 Brian이 겨울 방학 동안에 어떤 수업을 들었는지는 알 수 없다.

10 (D) 저녁식사 계획 설명 → (A) 반응 → (C) 필요한 재료가 있는지 질문 → (B) 대답

11 별 주위를 도는 우주의 크고 둥근 물체를 가리키는 말은 planet(행성)이다.

12 be into: ~에 열중하다

13 ③ Jane과 Sujin은 일주일에 한 번 만나려고 한다.

14 작년에 Smith 선생님의 수업은 재미있었다.

7

15 새로 온 선생님은 미술 선생님이시다.

16 이탈리아는 또 다른 인기 있는 관광지이므로 **another**가 옳다.

17 현재시제로 미래를 표현하는 조건의 부사절이므로 **comes**를 쓰는 것이 옳다.

18 'other+복수명사'는 others로 쓸 수 있다.

19 셋 중 나머지 둘은 같은 곳에서 왔으므로 the others로 쓸 수 있다. the others are from France라고 해도 좋다.

20 ⓐ, ⓑ, ⓓ는 부사절을 이끄는 if로 '만약 ~라면'이라고 해석하고, ⓒ, ⓔ는 명사절을 이끄는 접속사 if이다.

21 'all comics'로 보아 나머지 모든 책을 가리키는 대명사가 나오는 것이 옳다. 따라서 the others라고 써야 한다.

22 Unless는 If ~ not과 같다. 조건의 부사절이므로 현재시제로 미래를 나타낼 수 있으며 주절의 시제는 내용과 일치시킨다.

23 둘 중 하나는 one, 남은 하나는 the other로 지칭한다. 딸이 둘이라고 하였으므로 the others가 아닌 the other가 옳다.

24 조건의 부사절에서는 현재시제로 미래를 나타내는 것에 유의한다. If ~ not은 Unless와 같다.

25 셋 중 하나는 one, 다른 하나는 **another**, 남은 하나는 the other로 지칭한다.

26 go Ving: V하러 가다

27 during은 '~ 동안'이라는 뜻으로 뒤에는 보통 숫자를 포함하지 않은 특정한 기간이 온다. ②번을 제외한 모든 곳에는 for가 들어간다.

28 one과 the other를 써서 변화를 설명하고 있으므로 '두 개의 변화'라고 보는 것이 옳다. 따라서 ③번이다. a couple of는 '둘의'라는 의미 외에도 '몇 개의'의 의미도 갖는다.

29 try to: ~하려고 노력하다

30 과거에 손톱을 물어뜯었다는 의미이다. 따라서 과거형 bit으로 쓰는 것이 옳다. ③은 The other change를 줄여서 쓴 말이다.

31 Eric의 할아버지가 왜 편찮으신지는 글을 읽고 답할 수 없다.

32 특히 손으로 쥘 수 있도록 만들어진 부분이 '손잡이(handle)'이다.

33 Eric은 시드니에 산다. 그는 3D 프린팅에 흥미가 있다.

34 Eric의 특수 컵이 들기에 쉬운 이유는 손잡이가 세 개 있어서이다.

단원별 예상문제
p.46~49

01 I met Mike on my way to the library.

02 ⑤   03 I hope your wish comes true.

04 She wants to be an artist in the future.

05 She is planning to take a painting class.

06 I'm thinking of keeping a diary in English.

07 ①   08 ②   09 ③

10 (D) → (E) → (C) → (B) → (A)   11 ③

12 ②   13 ⑤   14 lend me, will pay

15 One is blue. → Another is hot pink. → The other is yellow.

16 ③   17 ③   18 ⓑ making(또는 to make), ⓒ Making(또는 To make) ⓓ breaking(또는 to break)   19 ④번 am not → don't   20 ③

21 ③   22 ④   23 He printed a model of his dream car and a special cup for his grandfather.

24 He wants to try Junho's cupcakes some day.

25 ⑤

02 Alex와 엄마가 함께 부엌에서 이야기를 하고 있다는 설명은 대화의 내용과 일치하지 않는다.

04 Emily는 미래에 미술가가 되기를 원한다.

05 Emily는 예술 고등학교에 진학하기 위해 미술 수업을 들을 계획이다.

07 decide는 '결심하다'라는 뜻으로 determine과 바꾸어 쓸 수 있다. refuse: 거절하다, postpone: 미루다, delay: 미루다, bite: 물다

08 (A)의 '나도 그래.'와 바꾸어 쓸 수 있는 말은 'So am I.'이다

09 Jenny는 일본으로 이민을 가는 가게 되어서 지금 기분이 안 좋다.

10 (D) 방학이 어떠하였는지 질문→ (E) 대답 및 방학 동안에 한 일에 대한 구체적 설명 → (C) 놀라움 표현 → (B) 즐거웠음을 표현 → (A) 반응

11 다른 하나를 보여 달라는 의미이므로 another가 옳다.

12 책 읽기를 좋아한다면 언제든 빌릴 수 있는 책이 많이 있을 것이라는 의미로 조건절에서 현재가 미래를 대신하도록 문장을 쓸 수 있다. 따라서 ②번이 가장 적절하다.

13 첫 번째 문장은 다섯 명의 친구 중 둘을 제외한 나머지 모두가 오지 않았다는 것이므로 The others, 두 번째 문장은 어떤 학생들은 국어를 공부하고 다른 학생들은 영어를 공부한다는 말이므로 others를 쓴다.

14 be short of: ~이 부족하다 pay ~ back: (빌린 돈을) ~에게 갚다, ~에게 돌려주다

15 셋 중 하나는 one, 다른 하나는 another, 남은 하나는 the other로 지칭한다.

16 둘 중 남은 하나는 the other로 지칭하며, 조건의 부사절에서 현재시제로 미래를 표현한다. 단, 주절은 의미에 맞게 시제를 일치시킨다.

17 each other: 서로 ① 같은 스카프의 다른 색깔을 원하는 것이므로 another ② 둘 중 하나는 one, 남은 하나는 the other ③ 불특정 복수명사는 some, 다른 무리를 묶어서 other+복수명사 ④ 세 개의 인형 중 하나는 새 것이지만 나머지 둘은 낡았다는 의미이므로 the others, ⑤ 동사가 바로 따라오고 있으므로

other people을 대명사로 한 others

18 동사를 주어나 보어 자리에서 쓰기 위해서는 동명사나 to부정사 형태로 만들어 주어야 한다.

19 'I don't bite my nails anymore.'를 줄인 말이 들어간다. 따라서 don't라고 쓰는 것이 옳다.

20 편지 서두에 아름다운 봄이라고 하였다. used to: (과거에) ~하곤 했다

21 the other thing을 의미하는 대명사이므로 The other라고 쓰는 것이 옳다.

22 (A) 내용상 차가 '많을 때' 날 수 있는 차로 바뀐다고 말한 것이고, (B) 손잡이가 세 개 있어서 쥐기 쉬운 특수한 컵이라고 보는 것이 옳으며 (C) 편찮으시기 때문에 컵을 잘 들지 못한다고 하는 것이 적절하다.

23 Eric이 3D 프린터로 프린트한 것은 모형 드림 자동차와 할아버지를 위한 특수 컵이다.

24 Eric은 준호의 컵케이크를 먹어 보고 싶다고 하였다.

25 ⑤ Eric이 언제 준호의 컵케이크를 먹을지는 언급되지 않았다.

01 I'm thinking of cooking bulgogi for dinner.?
02 He needs some vegetables and beef.
03 She is going to buy some beef on her way home.
04 One is making food, and the other is washing the dishes.
05 If you need it, you can have it.
   If you want her to help you, she will help you.
   If your alarm clock is out of order, I will buy you a new one.
06 If you don't listen carefully, you won't know what to do.
   Unless you listen carefully, you won't know what to do.
07 One, The others
08 finish, will you do, will clean, finish
09 personal
10 He feels great about them.
11 making, One, the other, breaking
12 If the traffic is heavy, it will change into a flying car.
13 It looks special.

02 Alex는 불고기를 요리하기 위해 야채와 소고기가 필요하다.
03 Alex의 엄마는 집에 오는 길에 소고기를 살 것이다.
04 두 사람이라고 하였으므로 한 사람은 one, 다른 한 사람은 the other로 지칭한다.

05 네가 그것을 필요로 한다면, 그걸 가져도 좋아. / 네가 그녀가 널 돕길 원하면, 그녀가 도와 줄 거야. / 너의 알람 시계가 고장 났다면, 내가 하나 사줄게.

06 '주의 깊게 들어라. 그렇지 않으면 너는 무엇을 해야 할지 모를 것이다.'라는 의미이다. If와 Unless를 이용하여 문장을 만든다.

07 두 번째 빈칸 뒤의 동사가 복수동사인 것으로 보아 나머지 고양이 두 마리의 눈 색깔을 지칭하는 것을 알 수 있다. 따라서 The others를 쓴다. The other cats를 써도 무방하다.

08 조건의 부사절에서 현재시제로 미래를 나타낸다.

09 person의 형용사형 personal로 고친다.

10 the changes를 대명사 them으로 받아준다.

11 spend+시간+Ving: V하느라 시간을 보내다

12 교통이 혼잡하다는 표현은 'heavy'를 쓰고, 반면에 한산하다고 표현할 때에는 'light'를 쓴다.

13 Eric은 특수한 컵을 만들었다고 하였으므로 '특별해 보인다.'고 답하면 된다.

|모범답안|

01 (A) Jenny was going to move to Japan
   (B) Jenny was very upset
   (C) keep in touch

02 (1) There are two books on the table. One is a novel. The other is a textbook.
   (2) There are two cups. One is blue. The other is white.
   (3) There are two flowers in a vase. One is a tulip. The other is a rose.
   (4) There are two machines in the kitchen. One is a coffee machine. The other is a blender.
   (5) There are two teachers in the classroom. One teaches math. The other teaches English.

03 (1) If it is sunny tomorrow, I will go on a picnic
   (2) If it is windy tomorrow, I'll wear my coat.
   (3) If it is rainy tomorrow, I will stay at home and watch a movie.
   (4) If it is hot tomorrow, I will have lots of ice cream.

01 오늘 나는 Jenny가 일본으로 이사를 갈 것이라고 들었다. 나는 Jenny가 이에 대해 전혀 이야기를 하지 않았었기 때문에 너무 놀랐다. Sue는 Jenny가 매우 기분이 좋지 않다고 이야기 했다 왜냐하면 그녀의 가족이 지난주에야 이것에 대해 그녀에게 이야기했기 때문이다. 나는 그녀의 기분을 이해했다. 어쨌든 나는 그녀를 매우 그리워 할 것이고 그녀와 연락할 것이다.

01 false 　02 ② 　03 (1) truth 　(2) nail 　(3) personal

04 (1) come true 　(2) take, class 　(3) not, anymore 　(4) break a bad habit 　05 ② 　06 artist

07 I'm thinking of taking a painting class[an art class]. 　08 ④

09 I'm interested in space, too.

10 They are going to meet once a week.

11 ④ 　12 ⑤ 　13 ② 　14 ③

15 Kevin is different from the other boys.

16 If you take a taxi, it will take only 10 minutes.

17 ② 　18 ③ 　19 ⑤

20 The other change 　21 the changes he made

22 ⓐ: to talk ⓑ: flying 　23 ⑤ 　24 ②

25 ③

01 주어진 관계는 반의어를 나타낸다. false: 거짓의, true: 사실인

02 특히 손으로 쥐어지도록 고안된 부분을 가리키는 말은 handle(손잡이)이다.

05 (A) You know what?: 너 그거 아니?, (B) because of+명사(구), because+주어+동사, (D) be interested in: ~에 관심이 있다

06 그림이나 회화 같은 예술 작품을 만들어내는 사람을 가리키는 말은 artist(예술가)이다.

07 think of: ~할 생각이다

09 be interested in: ~에 관심이 있다

10 동아리 회원들은 일주일에 한 번 만날 예정이다.

11 주어진 문장은 '그녀의 기분을 이해할 수 있다.'는 의미이므로 Jenny의 기분을 설명하는 문장 다음에 이어질 말로 적절하므로 (D)가 알맞다.

12 대화를 통해 왜 Jenny의 가족이 이사하려고 하는지는 알 수 없다.

13 ② Unless는 부정어를 이끌 수 없다.

14 둘 중에서 남은 하나는 the other를 쓴다.

15 나머지 전체를 지칭하는 것은 the other+복수명사이다.

16 take a taxi: 택시를 타다

17 드레스를 두 벌 샀다고 하였으므로 파란색 드레스는 the other로 지칭하는 것이 옳다.

18 밑줄 친 ⓐ는 동명사로, 보어 역할을 하고 있다. 동명사는 명사로 쓰여 주어, 보어, 동사나 전치사의 목적어 역할을 한다. ③번은 '~하는 중'이라는 의미의 현재분사이다.

19 준호가 Eric에 대해 어떻게 느끼는지는 글을 읽고 답할 수 없다.

20 앞서 언급한 두 가지 변화 중 남은 한 가지 변화를 뜻하므로 The other change라고 쓴다.

21 이메일에서, 준호는 자신이 만든 변화들에 관하여 주로 이야기하고 있다.

22 ⓐ it's time toV: ~할 때이다 ⓑ '날 수 있는 자동차'라는 의미이므로 flying이 옳다.

23 빈칸에는 이유를 나타내는 because가 들어간다. ① while: 반면에 ② although: 비록 ~일지라도 ③ if: ~인지 아닌지 ④ unless: ~하지 않으면 ⑤ because: ~이기 때문에

24 '먹어 보고 싶다'는 의미로 쓰였으므로 ②번이 가장 적절하다.

25 ⓑ, ⓒ, ⓔ가 글의 내용과 일치한다.

Lesson 2

Better Safe Than Sorry

시험대비 실력평가   p.60

01 empty   02 (1) Keep in mind   (2) one by one   (3)
a little   (4) Stay away from   03 ③
04 (1) escape   (2) follow   (3) slip   (4) shake
05 ②, ③   06 ②   07 ③
08 (1) more   (2) often   (3) slowly

01 주어진 단어의 관계는 반의어 관계이다. empty: 비어 있는,
full: 가득 찬

02 keep in mind: ~을 기억하다, one by one: 하나씩, a little:
약간, stay away from: ~에서 떨어져 있다

03 ③ serious: 심각한

04 slip: 미끄러지다, shake: 흔들다, 흔들리다, escape: 탈출하
다, follow: 따르다

05 주어진 문장에서 pole은 '막대기, 기둥'을 나타낸다. 이와 같은
의미로 쓰인 것은 ②, ③번이다. ①, ④번은 '극, 극지방'을 의미
하며 ⑤ magnetic pole은 '자극'을 뜻한다.

06 갑자기 일어나 많은 사람들에게 많은 고통이나 손실을 야기하는
홍수, 토네이도, 화재, 비행기 사고 등과 같은 것을 가리키는 말
은 disaster(재난)이다.

서술형 시험대비   p.61

01 safe
02 (1) I'm worried about the English exam.
   (2) You should walk on the stairs.
   (3) Watch your head when you get out of the car.
      (When you get out of the car, watch your
      head.)
   (4) You should watch your hand when you close
      the door.
      (When you close the door, you should watch
      your hand.)
03 (A) about, (B) until, (C) another
04 (A) in (B) from (C) by
05 (1) feel better   (2) took cover   (3) earthquake,
   natural disaster
06 (1) Stay away from   (2) Hold on to   (3) get out
   of   (4) take cover

01 주어진 단어의 관계는 반의어 관계이다. safe: 안전한,
dangerous: 위험한

03 (A) be worried about: ~에 대해 걱정하다, (B) until: ~까지,
(C) another: 또 다른, one day: 언젠가

04 keep ~ in mind: ~을 기억하다, stay away from ~: ~에서
떨어져 있다, one by one: 하나씩

05 feel better: 기분이 나아지다, take cover: 숨다, natural
disaster: 자연 재해

06 stay away from: ~에서 떨어져 있다, hold on to: ~을 꼭 잡
다, get out of: ~에서 나가다, 떠나다, take cover: 숨다

[교과서] Conversation

핵심 Check   p.62~63

1 (A) I'm worried about
2 (A) Don't be anxious
3 (A) I'm concerned about
4 (B) You should
5 (B) Why don't you
6 (B) I think we need to

교과서 대화문 익히기

Check(√) True or False   p.64

(1) T   (2) T   (3) T   (4) F

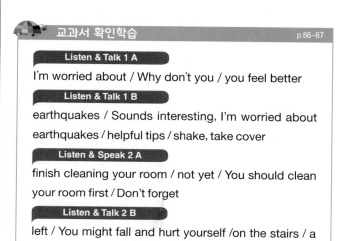

교과서 확인학습   p.66~67

Listen & Talk 1 A
I'm worried about / Why don't you / you feel better

Listen & Talk 1 B
earthquakes / Sounds interesting, I'm worried about
earthquakes / helpful tips / shake, take cover

Listen & Speak 2 A
finish cleaning your room / not yet / You should clean
your room first / Don't forget

Listen & Talk 2 B
left / You might fall and hurt yourself / on the stairs / a

little late / Better safe than sorry

Real Life Communication

a big fire / I was worried about the people there / safety / cover / with a wet towel, stay low, escape / keep that in mind

Let's Check

our picnic / until late afternoon / You should go another day / choose another day

시험대비 기본평가
p.68

01 ③, ⑤　　　　02 (E) → (C) → (B) → (D) → (A)　　03 fall
04 Better safe than sorry.

01 'I'm worried about ~'은 '~을 걱정하다'는 표현으로 'I'm anxious about ~' 또는 'I'm concerned about ~'으로 바꾸어 쓸 수 있다.

02 (E) 걱정 표현 → (C) 제안 → (B) 제안에 대한 대답 → (D) 희망 표현 → (A) 동의

03 서 있는 자세에서 갑자기 밑으로 가는 것을 가리키는 말은 fall(넘어지다)이다.

시험대비 실력평가
p.69~70

01 ⑤　　　　02 ⑤　　　　03 ③　　　　04 ①
05 you need to take cover under a table　　06 ⑤
07 He is going to play basketball with Minu.
08 He told Jack to clean his room first.
09 He should return home by six o'clock.　10 ②
11 ⑤　　　　12 (A) was (B) to cover (C) stay
13 ⑤

01 ⑤번을 제외한 나머지는 모두 '무슨 일이야?'라는 뜻이다.

02 ⑤번을 제외한 나머지는 모두 제안을 나타낸다.

03 Yujin은 다친 다리를 걱정하고 있으므로 anxious(걱정스러운)가 적절하다.

04 상대방의 'I'm worried about ~'에 대한 동의 표현으로 'So am I.'로 바꿀 수 있다.

07 Jack은 민우와 농구를 할 것이다.

08 아빠는 Jack에게 외출하기 전에 방청소를 먼저 하라고 말했다.

09 Jack은 6시까지 귀가해야 한다.

10 후회하는 것보다 안전한 것이 낫다는 ②번이 적절하다.

11 Tom은 안전한 것을 더 우선시 하였다.

12 (A) Everybody는 단수 취급하므로 was, (B) need to: ~할 필요가 있다. (C) 명령문은 동사로 시작하므로 stay

13 화재 시 몸을 낮게 유지해야 한다.

서술형 시험대비
p.71

01 (C) → (A) → (B) → (E) → (D)
02 Why don't you walk on the stairs?
03 Because Emily might fall and hurt herself.
04 There was a big fire at the city library yesterday.
05 Because they all followed the safety rules.
06 화재 시 젖은 수건으로 코와 입을 가리고 몸을 낮게 유지하여 탈출해야 한다는 것
07 You should watch your hands when you close the door.
(When you close the door, you should watch your hands.)

01 (C) 방청소를 끝냈는지 질문 → (A) 대답 및 요청 → (B) 거절 및 충고 → (E) 반응 및 약속 → (D) 칭찬 및 상기시키기

02 'You should ~'는 충고하는 표현으로 'Why don't you ~'와 바꾸어 쓸 수 있다.

03 Emily가 계단에서 넘어지거나 다칠 수 있기 때문이다.

04 어제 시립 도서관에서 큰 불이 났다.

05 큰불에도 모든 사람들이 다치지 않은 이유는 그들 모두가 안전 규칙을 따랐기 때문이다.

교과서
Grammar

핵심 Check
p.72~73

1 (1) how to drive / how I should drive
　(2) when to leave / we should leave
　(3) who(m) to trust / who(m) I should trust
2 (1) who　(2) whose sister

시험대비 기본평가
p.74

01 (1) when quit → when to quit
　(2) and which → which　(3) to going → to go
　(4) who → which[that]
02 (1) how to read　(2) are　(3) whose
　(4) who(m) to ask
03 (1) I will let you know when to come.
　(2) Is there anything that you want to have?
　(3) I don't know how to use the machine.
　(4) I read a book which a famous writer wrote.

01 (1) '의문사+to부정사' 형태를 쓰는 것이 옳다. (2) and를 없애야 한다. (3) '의문사+to부정사' 형태이므로 'to+동사원형'이 옳다. (4) 관계대명사 who는 선행사가 사람일 때 쓴다.

02 (1) '의문사+to부정사' 형태를 쓰는 것이 옳다. (2) 선행사가 the boys이므로 복수 동사를 쓴다. (3) '개의 꼬리'를 의미하므로 소유격 관계대명사를 쓴다. (4) '누구에게 물어봐야 할지'라는 의미가 되어야 하므로 '의문사+to부정사'를 쓴다.

03 (1) '언제 오실지'이므로 when to come을 쓴다. (2) '묻고 싶은 것'이므로 관계사절이 anything을 수식하도록 문장을 쓴다. (3) '그 기계를 사용하는 방법'이므로 how to use the machine을 쓴다. (4) '어느 유명한 작가가 쓴 책'이므로 관계사절이 a book을 수식하도록 단어를 나열한다. 작가가 이미 책을 쓴 것이므로 write를 과거형으로 변형하여 쓰는 것에 유의한다.

시험대비 실력평가   p.75~77

01 ③   02 ③   03 ④
04 The man who is cleaning the house lives here.
05 ②   06 ①, ④, ⑤   07 ④.
08 Let me know where to get off.   09 ④
10 ⑤   11 ④   12 which[that] is on the desk   13 ③   14 ④   15 ④
16 I don't know what to order.   17 ⑤
18 ②   19 ②   20 who[that] asked me, where to go   21 ③   22 where to meet   23 ④, ⑤   24 what, should do

01 '어느 것'이라고 하였으므로 which를 쓰는 것이 옳다.

02 ①, ④, ⑤번에는 관계대명사 who가 들어가며 ②번에는 '의문사+to부정사' 형태로 의문사 who가 들어간다. ③번은 소유격 관계대명사 whose의 자리이다.

03 '어디서'와 '시작하다'를 이용하여 where to start를 쓰면 된다.

04 '그 집을 청소하는 그 남자는 여기에 산다.'라는 문장으로 이어주면 된다.

05 '의문사+to부정사'는 '의문사+주어+should~'와 같다. 따라서 ②번이 옳다.

06 빈칸은 목적격 관계대명사 whom의 자리이다. whom을 대신하여 who, that을 쓸 수 있다.

07 위 문장은 '언제 시작할지' 혹은 '어떻게 시작할지'라는 의미가 될 수 있고, 아래 문장은 주격 관계대명사 자리이므로 ④번이 옳다.

08 해석: 어디에서 내릴지 알려주세요.

09 '어느 것을 살지'라는 의미에 부합하며, 사물을 선행사로 받아주는 관계대명사는 which이다.

10 모두 명사절을 이끄는 접속사 that이지만 ⑤번은 관계대명사

that이다.

11 ⓐ '의문사+to부정사' 형태이어야 하므로 how to make, ⓓ the key that was on the sofa라고 쓰는 것이 옳다.

12 the pen은 사물이고, 두 번째 문장에서 the pen을 가리키는 대명사 it이 주어 역할을 하므로 주격 관계대명사 which나 that을 써서 문장을 만든다.

13 주어가 the man이므로 tells가 옳다.

14 ① when to ask 혹은 when they should ask라고 쓰는 것이 옳다. ② friend가 선행사이므로 whom[that] 혹은 who라고 써야 한다. ③ where to go 혹은 where I should go라고 쓰는 것이 옳다. ⑤ 선행사가 a puppy이므로 are가 아닌 is이다.

15 목적격 관계대명사는 생략할 수 있다. ④번은 주격 관계대명사이다.

16 '무엇을 주문해야 할지'라고 하였으므로 의문사 what을 사용하여 문장을 만든다.

17 선행사가 사물이므로 첫 번째 빈칸에는 관계대명사 that 혹은 which가 들어가는 것이 옳으며 영화는 이미 만들어진 것이고 the film이 주어이므로 단수동사 was를 써야 한다.

18 '의문사+to부정사'는 '의문사+주어+should ~'와 같다. 따라서 ②번이 옳다.

19 사람과 사물을 모두 선행사로 받을 수 있는 것은 관계대명사 that이다.

20 선행사가 the man이므로 관계대명사 who나 that을 쓰고, '어디로 가야 할지'는 '의문사+to부정사'를 쓴다.

21 ①, ②, ⑤ 선행사를 사물로 하는 목적격 관계대명사 which 혹은 that, ④ 주격 관계대명사 who를 쓰는 것이 옳다.

22 where we should meet이라고 써도 무방하다.

23 I bought a book from the boy who(또는 that) was talking with my sister.에서 '주격 관계대명사+be동사'를 생략할 수 있으므로 ④, ⑤번이 옳다

24 '의문사+to부정사'는 '의문사+주어+should ~'와 같다.

서술형 시험대비   p.78~79

01 (1) who is visiting a place for pleasure and interest
(2) which were painted by your mom
(3) who want to be rich
(4) which is veryuseful for you
02 (1) where to find the bathroom
(2) what to do next
(3) which class to sign up for
03 what to do after graduation.
04 who(m)
05 How to say hello varies in different cultures.
06 There are children who are playing in the garden.

07 where to go

08 The apartment which was empty is no longer available.

The boy who cut his finger is now in the hospital.

Do you want to buy the pictures which are very expensive?

Bruno Mars is a singer who is very popular all over the world.

I must thank the people who congratulated me.

An artist is a person who draws or paints pictures as a job.

09 who[that], what to do

10 who[that] are doing / doing

11 who[that] read it how to think

12 who[that] helped me

13 Did you finish the book which[that] you were reading?

14 I don't know what to say.

I don't know what I should say.

01 (1) 선행사가 someone이므로 관계대명사 who 또는 that을 쓰는 것이 옳다. (2) 선행사가 사물이므로 which나 that을 써서 문장을 하나로 만든다. (3) 선행사가 사람이므로 관계대명사 who를 쓴다. (4) a tip이 사물이므로 관계대명사 which 혹은 that을 사용한다.

02 (1) 그녀는 내게 어디에서 화장실을 찾아야 할지 물어보았다. (2) 다음에 무엇을 할지는 네가 결정하기에 달려 있어. (3) 어느 수업에 등록할지 아직 결정하지 못했어.

03 '무엇을 해야 할지'이므로 what to do를 쓴다.

04 위 문장에는 '누구에게 말을 걸어야 할지'라는 의미로 who[whom]가 들어가고, 아래 문장에는 목적격 관계대명사 whom이 들어간다. whom 대신에 who를 쓸 수 있다.

05 '안녕이라고 말하는 방식'이므로 how to say hello라고 쓴다. vary: 다양하다

06 who 대신에 that을 써도 무방하다.

07 대화의 내용으로 미루어 보아, '어디로 가야 하는지 아느냐?'는 물음에 대한 답임을 알 수 있다.

08 available: 이용할 수 있는 cut one's finger: 손가락을 베다 congratulate: 축하하다

09 주격 관계대명사 who를 대신하여 that을 써도 무방하다.

10 '주격 관계대명사+be 동사'는 생략 가능하다.

11 '그것을 읽는 사람들'이므로 who read it이 people을 수식하게 만든다.

12 '나를 도와준 그 경찰관에게 감사하다고 했어'라는 의미이다.

13 finish: ~을 끝내다

14 '의문사+to부정사'는 '의문사+주어+should 동사원형'과 같다.

확인문제   p.80

1 T   2 F   3 T   4 F

확인문제   p.81

1 F   2 T   3 T   4 F   5 T

교과서 확인학습 A   p.82~83

Prepare

01 what to do, strikes   02 Take, how to be, during   03 to shake, quickly

04 Stay away   05 Use, to get out of

06 When, hold on to   07 How, on

08 survive an earthquake safely   09 Here are, which, helpful   10 them one by one, what to do

11 when things are shaking   12 Find, take cover

13 to protect yourself   14 stay away from

15 They, during   16 go outside, the shaking stops

17 To get out of 18 Take   19 much safer

20 Once, find an empty space, is, from

21 who want to hold on to, but   22 because it, fall on   23 Earthquakes, anytime

24 They, scary experiences

25 how to be safe   26 avoid injuries, protect yourself   27 Follow, be

교과서 확인학습 B   p.84~85

1 Do you know what to do when an earthquake strikes?

2 Take this quiz and think about how to be safe during this kind of natural disaster.

3 When things start to shake, run outside quickly.

4 Stay away from windows.

5 Use the stairs to get out of buildings.

6 When you are outside, hold on to a pole or a tree.

7 How did you do on the quiz?

8 Can you survive an earthquake safely?

9 Here are some safety tips which can be helpful in an earthquake.

10 Let's check them one by one and learn what to do.

11 Don't run outside when things are shaking.

12 Find a table or a desk and take cover under it.

13 You can hold on to the legs to protect yourself.

14 Also, stay away from windows.

15 They can break during an earthquake and hurt you.

16 You can go outside when the shaking stops.

17 To get out of buildings, don't use the elevator.

18 Take the stairs.

19 It's much safer.

20 Once you are outside, find an empty space that is far from buildings.

21 There may be people who want to hold on to a pole or a tree, but think again.

22 That's a bad idea because it can fall on you.

23 Earthquakes can strike anytime.

24 They can be scary experiences for everyone.

25 So learn how to be safe in an earthquake.

26 You can avoid injuries and protect yourself.

27 Follow these tips and be safe!

시험대비 실력평가   p.86~89

01 ⑤	02 what to do	03 ②	04 shake
05 ⑤	06 ③	07 are	08 ③, ④
09 ③	10 a quiz	11 ⑤	12 a table or a desk
13 ④		14 whose legs, under it	
15 ③	16 ⑤	17 ③, ④	18 ④

19 the shaking stopped   20 ③   21 empty

22 There are many situations which can be dangerous.   23 ③   24 safe

25 A wet floor and broken glass can be dangerous to people.   26 ②   27 ③   28 ②

29 ③   30 ⑤   31 how to get / take the stairs   32 We should look for an empty space(far from buildings).

01 안전 지침이 있다는 주어진 글에 이어 (D)에서 them이 주어진 글의 safety tips를 가리키므로 다음에 오고 (B)에서 설명을 시작하며 (A)에서 the legs가 (B)의 탁자나 책상의 다리를 말하므로 다음에 나오고 (C)의 They가 (A)의 windows를 가리키므로 다음에 나온다.

02 '의문사+주어+should+동사원형'은 '의문사+to부정사'와 같다.

03 '이러한 종류의 자연 재해가 발생하는 동안'이라는 의미가 가장 적절하다.

04 앞뒤 혹은 아래위로의 짧고 빠른 움직임은 '흔들림, 떨림'이다.

05 퀴즈는 지진이 발생했을 때 무엇을 해야 하는지를 확인하는 문제이다.

06 survive는 '살아남다, 생존하다'라는 의미이다.

07 some safety tips가 주어이므로 복수동사 are를 쓴다.

08 ⓒ에는 주격 관계대명사 which 혹은 that이 들어간다.

09 ⓓ에는 '하나씩'이라는 의미로 one by one을 완성하는 전치사 by가 들어간다. ① at: 시간 앞에 쓰이면서 '~에'라고 해석 ② be interested in: ~에 흥미가 있다 ③ by: 교통수단 앞에서 쓰이며 '~로'라고 해석 ④ be crowded with: ~으로 붐비다 ⑤ look forward to: ~를 고대하다

10 이 글 앞에, 우리가 풀어야 하는 퀴즈가 있었다.

11 빈칸에는 '하나씩'이라는 의미가 들어가는 것이 가장 적절하다. ① 사례별로 ② 나란히 ③ 조금씩, 서서히 ④ 하나씩

12 탁자나 책상을 가리키는 대명사이다.

13 ④번 뒤 문장의 주어인 They가 가리키는 것은 창문이다.

14 스스로를 보호하기 위해서, 당신은 다리를 붙잡을 수 있는 탁자나 책상을 찾아서 그 아래에 숨어야 한다.

15 ⓒ는 to부정사가 '~하기 위하여'라는 의미의 부사로 쓰이고 있다. ① 목적보어 ② 진주어 ③ 부사적 용법 중 목적(~하기 위하여) ④ 목적어 ⑤ something을 수식하는 형용사로 각각 쓰이고 있다.

16 창문으로부터 멀리 떨어져야 할 이유로 창문이 깨져 다칠 수 있기 때문이라고 하였다.

17 사람을 선행사로 받는 관계대명사 who가 들어가야 하며, who를 대신하여 that이 쓰일 수 있다.

18 (A) '건물에서 나가기 위해서'라는 목적을 나타내는 to부정사, (B) 비교급을 강조하는 much, (C) 부사절을 이끄는 접속사 because가 들어가는 것이 옳다.

19 흔들림이 멈추었을 때 밖으로 나가라고 하였다.

20 건물과 멀리 떨어진 공터를 찾아야 한다고 하였으므로 ③번 '건물 가까이에서 가만히 서 있어야 한다.'는 내용과 일치하지 않는다.

21 사람이 없거나 아무것도 담고 있지 않는 상태는 '비어 있는'이다.

22 which를 대신하여 that을 써도 좋다.

23 '의문사+to부정사'는 '의문사+주어+should 동사원형'으로 바꿔 쓸 수 있다.

24 위험한 상황에서 무엇을 해야 할지 배우고 안전하자는 의미이다. dangerous의 반의어인 safe를 쓰는 것이 옳다.

25 젖은 바닥과 깨진 유리가 위험할 수 있다고 하였다.

26 바닥이 젖어 있으면 닦아야 한다고 하였다.

27 hold on to: ~을 붙잡다 fall on: ~위로 떨어지다

28 빈칸 (C)에는 방법을 나타내는 how가 들어간다. ②번에는

How+형용사+명사+주어+동사!의 감탄문이 들어가며 나머지는 모두 What이 쓰인다.

29 기둥이나 나무가 넘어질 수 있으므로 그것들을 붙잡는 것은 나쁜 생각이라고 보는 것이 옳다. 따라서 bad라고 써야 한다.

30 ① outside ② empty ③ far from ④ safe의 반의어이다.

31 had better+동사원형: ~하는 편이 낫다

32 밖으로 나오면 (건물에서 떨어진) 공터를 찾으라고 하였다.

서술형 시험대비   p.90~91

01 how to be safe

02 an earthquake

03 to shake (또는 shaking)

04 strike

05 Here are some safety tips.
   They can be helpful in an earthquake.

06 some safety tips

07 what we should do

08 ⓐ are ⓑ learn ⓒ to protect

09 Also, stay away from windows which can break during an earthquake and hurt you.

10 Because tables and desks can protect us when things fall.

11 Find an empty space that(또는 which) is far from buildings.

12 When the shaking stops

13 Taking the stairs, using the elevator

14 it can fall on us

15 Don't use the elevator.
   Don't hold on to a pole or a tree.

16 how to be safe during an earthquake

17 learn how to be safe in an earthquake

---

01 '어떻게 해야 안전할 수 있는지'라는 의미이다. 의문사+to부정사 형태를 활용하여 답을 쓴다.

02 '이러한 종류의 자연 재해'는 지진을 가리킨다.

03 start는 to부정사와 동명사를 모두 목적어로 취하는 동사이다.

04 어떤 사람이나 사물에 손상이나 해를 끼치게 위해 갑자기 나쁜 방식으로 영향을 미치는 것은 strike이다.

05 선행사가 some safety tips이므로 대명사로 쓸 경우 They를 쓰는 것에 유의한다.

06 몇몇 안전 지침을 가리키는 대명사이다.

07 '의문사+to부정사'는 '의문사+주어+should+동사원형'과 같다.

08 ⓐ some safety tips가 주어이므로 are, ⓑ 무엇을 해야 할지 배워 보자는 것이 자연스러우므로 learn이며 check와 병렬 관

계이므로 learn을 그대로 쓴다. ⓒ '스스로를 보호하기 위해서'라고 해석해야 하므로 to부정사를 사용하여 빈칸을 채운다.

09 They가 가리키는 것이 windows이므로 사물을 가리키는 주격 관계대명사 which를 써서 문장을 만든다. that을 써도 무방하다.

10 질문: 탁자 아래에 숨는 것이 왜 도움이 되나요?

11 주격 관계대명사 which 혹은 that을 사용하여 하나의 문장으로 만든다.

12 흔들림이 멈추면 밖으로 나갈 수 있다고 하였다.

13 계단을 이용하는 것이 엘리베이터를 이용하는 것보다 훨씬 더 안전하다.

14 기둥이나 나무가 넘어질 수 있으므로 이것을 붙잡고 있는 것은 좋은 생각이 아니라고 하였다.

15 승강기를 이용하지 말고 기둥이나 나무도 붙잡지 말라고 하였다.

16 위 글은 지진이 발생하는 동안 지켜야 할 안전 수칙에 관하여 이야기하고 있다.

17 지진은 모두에게 무서운 경험이기 때문에 지진으로부터 안전을 지키는 법을 배워야만 한다.

영역별 핵심문제   p.93~97

01 ④   02 ①   03 ①   04 ⑤

05 (1) Keep in mind   (2) one by one   (3) ake a rest
(4) Why don't you

06 (1) You should hold on to your hat.
(2) I tried to stay away from crowded places.
(3) My younger brother took cover behind the car.

07 ①   08 ⑤   09 ⑤

10 Remember to be home by six o'clock.

11 ⑤   12 (A) interesting, (B) worried, (C) cover   13 They are worried about earthquakes these days.   14 I should take cover under a table. 15 ③   16 safety   17 ⑤

18 ③   19 what to say   20 ③

21 ⑤   22 ④   23 ②, ③

24 You should know how to use your money wisely.

25 ⑤   26 Where is the ketchup which(또는 that) was in the refrigerator?   27 ⑤

28 what to write about   29 ③   30 ③

31 safety tips which, can be helpful[useful]   32 ③

33 ④   34 ②   35 ④

---

01 홍수, 가뭄, 지진, 폭풍우를 포함할 수 있는 것은 disaster(재난)이다.

02 위험하거나 해롭지 않은 상태를 가리키는 말은 safety(안전)이다.

03 ① slippery: 미끄러운

04 cover: (비용을) 감당하다, 감싸다; 표지

05 keep in mind: ~을 기억하다, one by one: 하나씩, take a rest: 휴식을 취하다, Why don't you ~?: ~하는 게 어때?

06 hold on to: ~을 꼭 잡다, stay away from: ~에서 떨어져 있다, take cover: 숨다

07 주어진 문장은 무엇이 문제인지에 대한 질문의 답변으로 적절하므로 (A)가 적합하다.

08 대화에서 Yujin이 왜 의사에게 안 갔는지는 나와 있지 않다.

09 (A)에 들어갈 말로 ⑤번을 제외한 나머지는 모두 충고하는 표현이다.

10 'Don't forget ~'은 '~할 것을 잊지 마.'라는 의미로 'Remember ~'와 바꾸어 쓸 수 있다.

11 Jack은 방청소를 먼저 한 후 외출할 것이다.

12 (A) sound interesting: 흥미롭다 (B) be worried about ~: ~에 대해 걱정하다 (C) take cover: 숨다, 피난하다

13 Brian과 Jane은 요즘 지진에 대해 걱정한다.

14 프로그램에 따르면 지진 발생시, 탁자 아래로 숨어야 한다.

15 영화가 시작하기까지 20분이 남았으므로 뛰자는 Emily의 제안에 다칠 수 있다는 내용이 이어져야 하므로 (C)가 알맞다.

16 비록 Tom과 Emily는 영화관에 조금 늦었지만 그들은 안전(safety)보다 중요한 것은 없다고 동의하였다.

17 목적격 관계대명사 whom은 who나 that이 대신할 수 있으며 생략 가능하다. ⑤ 전치사 뒤의 관계대명사는 생략할 수 없다.

18 ③번은 who 대신 소유격 관계대명사 whose를 써야 한다.

19 '의문사+to부정사'는 '의문사+주어+should 동사원형'과 같다.

20 '책의 표지'라는 의미이므로 첫 번째 문장에는 소유격 관계대명사 whose가 들어가는 것이 옳으며, 두 번째 문장에는 bought의 목적어가 비어 있으므로 목적격 관계대명사 which나 that이 들어가는 것이 옳다.

21 where to wash 혹은 where I should wash라고 쓰는 것이 옳다.

22 목적격 관계대명사로 사용되면서 동시에 '어느 드레스'라는 의미로 쓰일 수 있는 which가 공통으로 들어간다.

23 주격 관계대명사가 쓰이는 자리이다. 사람을 선행사로 취하고 있으므로 who나 that을 쓰는 것이 옳다.

24 '돈을 현명하게 쓰는 법'이므로 how를 사용하여 문장을 만든다.

25 모두 관계대명사 who이지만, ⑤번은 의문대명사 who로 '누구'라고 해석된다. betray: 배신하다

26 냉장고 안에 있던 케첩이 어디 있는지를 묻는 문장으로 쓰면 된다.

27 what do you think about ~?: ~에 대해 어떻게 생각하니? what to do: 무엇을 해야 할지

28 '의문사+to부정사'를 이용하여 빈칸을 채운다. write about: ~에 대하여 쓰다

29 ⓐ는 '안전할 방법'이고 ⓑ는 '퀴즈가 어땠는지'를 묻는 말이다. 따라서 둘 다 how가 들어가야 한다.

30 글쓴이는 안전 지침에 관하여 이야기하기를 원한다.

31 which를 대신하여 that을 써도 무방하다.

32 지진 발생 시에 유의해야 할 점을 열거하고 있으므로 ⓐ에는 '더욱이, 또한'에 해당하는 moreover를 쓰는 것이 옳다. ① 그러나 ② 그러므로 ④ 마찬가지로 ⑤ 반면에

33 ④ 탁자 아래로 숨으라고 하였다.

34 ⓐ는 '~하기 위하여'라는 의미의 부사적 용법으로 쓰인 to부정사이다. 각 to부정사의 용법은 ① want의 목적어로 쓰인 명사적 용법 ② '~하기 위하여'라는 의미의 부사 ③ anything을 수식하는 형용사 ④ 진주어로 쓰인 명사적 용법 ⑤ 목적격보어로 쓰인 명사적 용법이다.

35 밖에 있을 때 공터를 찾으라고 하였으므로 ④번이 옳다.

단원별 예상문제
p.98~101

01 (B) → (C) → (D) → (A)
02 is a person who tells the actors what to do
03 I'm worried about my leg.
04 I hope you feel better soon.   05 ①
06 (A) earthquakes   (B) some helpful tips   (C) we need to take cover under a table
07 ⓑ to clean → cleaning   08 ③
09 You should keep that in mind.
10 ④   11 ③   12 ②   13 where to go   14 ②   15 ④   16 ②
17 The person who(또는 that 또는 whom) I talked with gave me good advice.   18 ④
19 ③   20 Find a table or a desk and take cover under it   21 ⑤   22 ①, ④
23 ③   24 how to protect   25 ⑤

01 (B) 걱정 표현 → (C) 고마움 표현 → (D) 충고하기 → (A) 대답

02 영화감독은 배우들에게 무엇을 할지 말해주는 사람이다.

03 be worried about: ~에 대해 걱정하다

05 useful: 유용한, handy: 편리한, friendly: 친근한, generous: 관대한, convenient: 편리한

06 오늘 나는 지진에 대한 프로그램을 보았다. 나는 요즘 지진에 대해 걱정하기 때문에 이는 매우 흥미로웠다. 내가 프로그램을 보고 있는 동안, 나는 Brian과 이야기를 나누었고 그에게 지진 안전에 대한 유용한 정보를 주었다. 프로그램은 우리 주변에 무언가가 흔들리기 시작할 때 우리는 탁자 아래로 숨을 필요가 있다고 하였다.

07 finish는 동명사를 목적어로 취하기 때문에 cleaning이 알맞

다.

08 ③ 대화를 통해 왜 Jack이 방청소를 나중에 하고 싶어 했는지 알 수 없다

10 주어진 문장은 안전 규칙에 관한 내용이므로 (D)에 위치해야 한다.

11 각각 지시부사, 관계대명사, 명사절 접속사로 쓰이는 that이 들어가야 한다.

12 ②번의 아래 문장은 'I know the man. I admire him.'을 하나로 만든 문장이다. 따라서 위 문장과 다르다.

13 '어디로 가야 할지'를 설명해주겠다는 의미로 볼 수 있다.

14 ⓐ which는 전치사 to의 목적어였던 the music을 받아주는 관계대명사이다. ⓑ 목적격 관계대명사가 생략되어 있으나 빠져도 무방하다. ⓒ 주격 관계대명사가 빠져 있다. people who don't have their own gardens로 쓰는 것이 옳다. ⓓ 목적격 관계대명사가 생략된 채로 두 문장이 이어지고 있으므로 대명사 it을 빼는 것이 옳다. ⓔ be into ~: ~에 관심이 많다

15 ④ how to protect yourself 혹은 how you should protect yourself라고 쓰는 것이 옳다.

16 사람과 사물을 모두 선행사로 받을 수 있는 것은 관계대명사 that이다.

17 give someone advice: ~에게 조언을 해주다

18 ④번은 '차의 핸들'이 고장 난 것이므로 소유격 관계대명사 whose가 쓰이며, 나머지는 모두 that이 들어갈 수 있다.

19 (A) some safety tips를 가리키므로 복수명사를 지칭하는 them, (B) 주어와 목적어가 같을 때 목적어로 재귀대명사 사용, (C) 명사가 잇따라 나오므로 전치사 during을 쓴다. while은 접속사로 부사절을 이끈다.

20 'A: 물건들이 흔들리기 시작해. 지진이 오려나봐. 어디에 숨어야 할지 모르겠어. B: 책상이나 탁자를 찾아서 그 밑에 숨어.'

21 주어진 문장의 They가 가리키는 것은 Earthquakes이다.

22 since와 as는 모두 '~ 때문에'라는 의미로 사용될 수 있는 접속사이다.

23 사람들이 무언가를 붙잡는 이유는 글에 나와 있지 않다.

24 답변에서 조언을 따라함으로써 스스로를 보호할 수 있다고 하였으므로 '내 스스로를 보호할 방법을 모르겠어.'라고 말했다고 볼 수 있다.

25 ⓐ 계단을 이용하는 것을 가리키는 대명사이다. ⓑ which로 대체 가능하다. ⓒ '~일지도 모른다'는 가능성을 의미하고 있다. ⓓ hold on to: ~을 꽉 붙잡다

서술형 실전문제 　　　　　　p.102~103

01 ⓑ worrying → worried

02 She is concerned about her leg.

03 She is going to go see a doctor.

04 I like the people whom I work with. / I like the people with whom I work.

05 what to do after graduation. / what I should do after graduation.

06 (1) I want to have the cheese cake.
　　It is sold only online.
　(2) Where is the cap?
　　It was in the closet.

07 (A) I'm worried about you.
　(B) You should watch your hands when you use a knife.

08 how to dance

09 There may be people.
　They want to hold on to a pole or a tree.

10 기둥이나 나무를 꼭 붙잡으려는 것

11 (C) strike (D) avoid (E) protect (F) Follow

12 We should use the stairs because it is much safer.

13 We can learn how to be safe in an earthquake.

14 It's because they can break and hurt us.

15 which[that], helpful[useful]

01 be worried about: ~에 대해 걱정하다

02 Yujin은 그녀의 다리를 걱정하고 있다.

03 Yujin은 방과 후에 의사에게 갈 것이다.

04 'I like the people. I work with them.'을 하나로 만든 문장이다.

05 graduation: 졸업

06 is sold: 판매되다 closet: 옷장

08 대화의 흐름을 보아 춤추는 방법을 알려줄 수 있는지를 묻는 말이 들어가는 것이 옳다.

09 They 대신 People을 써도 좋다.

10 Holding on to a pole or a tree를 의미하는 것이다.

11 strike: 발생하다

12 계단을 이용하는 것이 훨씬 더 안전하다고 하였다.

13 위 글에서 무엇을 배울 수 있는지 묻고 있다. 지진에서 안전할 수 있는 방법을 배울 수 있는 지문이다.

14 창문에서 떨어져 있어야 하는 이유는 창문이 깨져서 우리를 다치게 할 수 있기 때문이다.

15 글쓴이가 독자들에게 주는 조언은 유용하다.

창의사고력 서술형 문제 　　　　　　p.104

|모범답안|

01 (A) the people there
　(B) they all followed the safety rules
　(C) cover my nose and mouth with a wet towel

02 (1) Do you know how to prepare for natural disasters?

(2) I want to learn how to cook spaghetti.

(3) Tell me when to go to the theater.

(4) I don't know what to buy.

(5) Let's decide when to meet.

03 (1) A pilot is a person who flies a plane.

(2) A nurse is a person who takes care of patients.

(3) An architect is a person who designs buildings.

(4) A dentist is a person whose job is to examine and treat people's teeth.

(5) A farmer is a person who owns or manages a farm.

---

01 나는 어제 시립 도서관에 큰 불이 났다고 들었다. 나는 Brian과 그것에 대해 이야기를 나누었다. 나는 거기 있는 사람들에 대해 걱정했었다. Brian은 그들 모두 안전 규칙을 따랐기 때문에 안전하다고 이야기해 주었다. 솔직히, 나는 화재 시 무엇을 해야 하는지 알지 못했다. Brian은 젖은 수건으로 코와 입을 가리고 몸을 낮게 유지하여 탈출해야 한다고 이야기해 주었다. 나는 그것을 명심했다. 또한, 나는 안전 규칙에 대해 좀 더 알아볼 것을 다짐했다.

단원별 모의고사

01 ③   02 ①   03 ③

04 (C) → (A) → (D) → (E) → (B)

05 (1) How can we prepare for a natural disaster?

(2) When an earthquake strikes, buildings can shake and fall down.

(3) Don't run on the stairs. You might fall or get hurt.

06 earthquake   07 ②, ③

08 물건들이 흔들리기 시작하면 탁자 아래에 숨는 것

09 (A) play basketball with Minu

(B) clean his room

(C) be home by six o'clock

10 ⑤   11 ⓐ → accident   12 ②

13 ④   14 ②, ⑤   15 decide what to eat

16 is the day that comes before   17 ③

18 ④   19 Taking, how to be safe, strikes

20 ④   21 ③   22 ③   23 We can hold on to the legs of the table.

24 drinking   25 ⑤

---

01 앞뒤로 또는 위 아래로 짧고 빠른 움직임을 나타내는 말은 shake(흔들림)이다

02 주어진 문장에서 fall은 '떨어지다'를 뜻한다. 이와 같은 의미로 쓰인 것은 ①번이다. ②, ③, ④번은 '가을', ⑤번은 '폭포'를 의미한다.

03 take a break: 휴식을 취하다, break: 부서지다, (기록을) 깨다

04 (C) 영화가 몇 시에 시작하는지 질문 → (A) 대답 → (D) 반응 및 뛰자고 제안 → (E) 거절 및 충고하기 → (B) 동의

05 prepare for: ~을 준비하다, ~을 대비하다, natural disaster: 자연 재해, strike: 발생하다, stairs: 계단, get hurt: 다치다

06 종종 큰 피해를 야기하는 지구 표면의 한 부분이 흔들리는 것을 가리키는 말은 earthquake(지진)이다.

07 tip은 '조언, 정보'를 뜻하며 이와 바꾸어 쓸 수 있는 것은 information(정보), guidance(지침)이다.

09 Jack은 Minu와 농구하기로 되어 있었다. 아빠는 그에게 외출하기 전에 방청소를 먼저 할 것을 충고했지만 Jack은 이를 미루고 싶어 했다. 하지만 아빠는 이를 먼저 할 것을 요구했고, 그래서 Jack은 그의 방을 청소하기로 결정했다. 농구하러 나가면서 Jack은 6시까지 귀가할 것을 약속했다.

10 수진은 친구에게 전화를 해서 다른 날에 소풍을 가려고 한다.

11 accidental: 우연한, accident: 사고

12 바닥이 미끄럽다는 상대방의 말에 너의 침실 실내화가 마음에 든다는 대답은 어색하다.

13 주어진 문장의 빈칸에는 주격 관계대명사 who 또는 that이 들어간다. 관계대명사 that은 who, whom, which를 대신하여 쓰일 수 있다. ④번에는 소유격 관계대명사 whose가 들어간다.

14 눈이 크다는 표현은 'She has big eyes.' 혹은 'Her eyes are big.'이다.

15 '무엇을 먹을지'이므로 what to eat이라고 쓰는 것이 옳다.

16 월요일은 화요일 앞에 오는 날이다.

17 위 문장에는 주격 관계대명사, 아래 문장에는 소유격 관계대명사가 들어가야 한다. 소유격 관계대명사 뒤에는 관사가 없는 명사가 온다.

18 (A) '빠르게'라는 의미가 옳으므로 부사 quickly, (B) stay away from: ~에서 떨어져 있다, (C) '건물 밖으로 나오기 위해서'이므로 부사로 쓰인 to부정사를 쓰는 것이 옳다.

19 이 퀴즈를 푸는 것은 지진이 발생할 때 우리가 어떻게 해야 안전할 수 있는지를 생각하도록 돕는다.

20 퀴즈는 자연 재해가 발생하는 동안 해야 하는 일을 제대로 알고 있는지를 확인하는 것이다.

21 지진 발생 시 주의해야 하는 사항을 첨가하여 이야기하고 있으므로 '게다가'라는 의미의 연결어가 들어가는 것이 옳다.

22 ⓑ, ⓒ, ⓔ가 글의 내용과 일치한다

23 스스로를 보호하기 위하여 탁자나 책상의 다리를 잡을 수 있다고 하였다.

24 전치사의 목적어 역할을 하도록 동명사를 쓰는 것이 옳다.

25 Darlene이 지진 발생 후 15일 후에 발견되었다고 나와 있을 뿐 지진이 며칠 동안 지속되었는지는 언급되지 않았다.

19

Lesson 3

Happy Others, Happier Me

06 어떤 것에 관한 정보를 제공하는 글귀나 사진들이 위에 있는 종이나 나무 등을 가리키는 말은 sign(표지판)이다.

교과서 Conversation

핵심 Check   p.114~115

1 me help you   2 Do you need any help
3 deep / Don't worry, help you
4 glad you like it   5 My pleasure
6 for saying so

교과서 대화문 익히기

Check(√) True or False   p.116

(1) T   (2) F   (3) T   (4) F

교과서 확인학습   p.118~119

Listen & Speak 1 A

give out / Let me help you then / volunteer club activity / mean / It means that, each other, better place

Listen & Speak 1 B

my mentee / Do you teach her every weekend / You are a good mentor

Listen & Speak 2 A

this is for you / How did you know that / the other day / How nice / I'm glad you like it

Listen & Talk 2 B

I read a story about a special boy in India / Why is he special / had to work / I'm glad you like it

Real Life Communication

Are you feeling better / on my own / Let me help you, join my study group / we can learn better when we teach each other / Thanks for helping me

Let's Check 1

looks heavy. Let me help you / Where is the bus stop around here / No problem

---

시험대비 실력평가   p.112

01 ②   02 ③   03 ①   04 danger
05 ①   06 (1) confusing   (2) decide   (3) soap
(4) secret

01 국가, 마을, 강 등을 보여주는 지구의 표면 또는 그것의 일부의 그림이나 도면을 나타내는 것은 map(지도)이다.
02 say: (글이) 쓰이다, 말하다
03 sign: 표지판
04 주어진 단어의 관계는 반의어 관계이다. danger: 위험, safety: 안전
05 주어진 문장에서 'free'는 '무료의'를 의미한다. 이와 같이 쓰인 문장은 ①번이다. 나머지는 '자유로운'을 의미한다.
06 confusing: 혼란스러운, secret: 비결, soap: 비누, decide: 결정하다, 결심하다

서술형 시험대비   p.113

01 impossible
02 (A)good   (B)help   (C)try   (D)tip   (E)glad
03 (1) He put up a 'For Sale' sign in front of his house.
    (2) I finished this work earlier thanks to his help.
    (3) We have to do our homework on our own.
04 (1) Thanks to   (2) the other day   (3) give out
05 (1) give out   (2) come up with   (3) put up   (4) One day
06 sign

01 주어진 단어의 관계는 반의어 관계이다. possible: 가능한, impossible: 불가능한
03 (1) put up: ~을 세우다 in front of: ~ 앞에 (2) thanks to: ~ 덕택에 (3) on one's own: 자기 스스로
04 thanks to: ~ 덕분에, the other day: 며칠 전에, give out: ~을 나누어 주다
05 give out: 나누어 주다, come up with: 제시하다, put up: 세우다, 설치하다, one day: 어느 날

01 ②   02 ④   03 ⓒ which → that

04 ④

01 'Let me help you.'는 '내가 도와줄게.'라고 도움을 제안하는 표현이다.

02 Henry는 Sujin과 같이 버스 정류장으로 가고 있다.

03 명사절을 이끄는 접속사 that이 적절하다.

01 ②   02 Let me help you.   03 ④

04 smile   05 ③   06 ⑤   07 (A) her mentee (B) her old books (C) she felt happy (D) she was a good mentor   08 She suggested joining her study group to him.

09 Because she thought that they can learn better when they teach each other.

10 (B) → (D) → (A) → (C)   11 a massage

12 He gave Aram a massage.

03 ④번은 유감을 나타낸다.

04 스티커는 웃음의 중요성을 강조한다.

05 주어진 문장의 앞에서 그가 많은 학생들을 집에서 가르치는 이유를 설명하고 있으므로 (C)번이 알맞다.

06 Yujin이 인도에 있는 많은 학생들을 돕기 위해 무엇을 했는지는 알 수 없다.

07 오늘 나는 지민이 인상 깊었다. 그녀는 매주 아동 센터에서 그녀의 멘티를 가르친다. 게다가 그녀는 그녀의 멘티에게 그녀가 보던 책을 주려고 하였다. 그녀는 멘티를 가르칠 때 행복을 느낀다고 말했다. 나는 그녀가 좋은 멘토라고 생각했다. 상자가 무거워 보여서 나는 그녀를 도와주었다. 나는 타인을 돕는 것이 세상을 더 나은 곳으로 만들어 준다고 생각한다.

08 Emily는 Brian에게 그녀의 공부 모임에 함께 할 것을 제안했다.

09 Emily가 공부 모임을 시작한 것은 서로 가르칠 때 더 잘 학습할 수 있다고 생각했기 때문이다.

10 (B) 고민 이야기 및 조언 구함 → (D) 도움 및 방법 제안 → (A) 시도할 계획 나타내기 및 고마움 표현 → (C) 칭찬에 대해 응답하기

12 Jack은 Aram의 기분이 나아지도록 마사지를 해 주었다.

01 I feel happy when I teach her.

02 (m)entor

03 many children in his town

04 (A) a special boy in India

(B) he was special

(C) couldn't go to school and had to work

05 She is going to give out free stickers.

06 **서로에게 미소 지을 때 세상은 더 좋은 곳이 될 것이다.**

02 경험이 별로 없거나 종종 어린 사람에게 도움이나 조언을 주거나 가르치는 사람을 가리키는 말은 mentor(멘토)이다.

04 오늘 Yujin은 나에게 인도의 어느 특별한 소년에 관한 이야기를 해주었다. 나는 왜 그녀가 그가 특별하다고 하는지 궁금했다. Yujin은 그 소년이 그의 마을에서 학교에 갈 수 없고 일을 해야 하는 많은 아이들을 자기 집에서 매일 가르친다고 이야기했다. 그것은 정말 좋은 이야기였다.

05 Sora는 Tom을 돕기 위해 무료 스티커를 나누어 줄 것이다.

Grammar

1 (1) which(또는 that)   (2) who(m)(또는 that)

2 (1) persuaded, to shake   (2) expect, to eat   (3) told, not to be

01 (1) who → which 또는 that   (2) were → was

(3) continue → to continue   (4) to passing → to pass

02 (1) lives   (2) which   (3) to stay   (4) to start

03 (1) This is the table that[which] they needed.

(2) She came to a meeting that[which] I ran.

(3) We can't force them to work hard.

(4) What made you think so?

01 (1) 사물이 선행사이므로 which 또는 that, (2) The building이 주어이므로 단수동사 was, (3), (4) enable과 allow는 to 부정사(to+동사원형)를 목적격보어로 취하는 동사이다.

02 (1) 주어가 The man이므로 단수동사 lives를 쓴다. (2) 사물을 선행사로 취하는 목적격 관계대명사 which를 쓰면 된다.

(3), (4) tell과 encourage는 5형식으로 쓰일 때 to부정사를 목적격보어로 사용한다.

03 (1) 'They needed the table.'을 관계절로 만든다. (2) 'I ran a meeting.'을 관계사절로 만든다. (3) force는 to부정사를 목적보어로 취하는 동사이다. (4) '네가 생각하게 만들다'이므로 make를 사역동사로 사용한다.

시험대비 실력평가 p.127~129

01 ③, ④ 02 ④ 03 ④ 04 He didn't allow me to use all the money that I have.
05 ⑤ 06 ③ 07 ⑤ 08 which you should do, to boil 09 ③ 10 ②
11 ⑤ 12 Do you remember those people who(m) you met on holiday? 13 ⑤
14 ④ 15 ③ 16 to help me with math
17 ⑤ 18 which I did yesterday
19 we will force you to
20 The only thing that you should not do is to cut in while others are talking. 21 ⑤ 22 ④
23 taught us to love

01 사물을 선행사로 받아주면서, 이끄는 문장에 동사의 목적어가 비어 있으므로 목적격 관계대명사 which가 들어간다. which를 대신하여 that을 쓸 수 있다.

02 'My mom bought the shoes for me."를 관계절로 만든 것이다. 따라서 ④번이 옳다.

03 사역동사 make는 원형부정사를 목적격보어로 취한다.

04 '내가 가진 모든 돈'이므로 I have가 all the money를 수식하도록 문장을 만든다. 관계대명사 which를 써도 좋다.

05 목적격 관계대명사를 생략할 수 있다. ⑤번은 명사절을 이끄는 접속사로 생각할 수 없다. go bad: 상하다

06 '작은 가게들'이 주어이므로 복수동사 are를 쓴다. be crowded with: ~으로 붐비다

07 allow, encourage는 to부정사를 목적격보어로 취하는 동사이며, decide와 refuse는 to부정사를 목적어로 취하는 동사이다. ⑤번은 전치사 in의 목적어로 동명사가 들어간다.

08 목적격 관계대명사 which를 대신하여 that을 써도 무방하다.

09 cause는 to부정사를 목적격보어로 취하는 동사이다. 따라서 to stop이 옳다.

10 ⓐ The toys가 주어이므로 동사는 are를 쓴다. ⓑ, ⓔ want, require는 to부정사를 목적격보어로 취하는 동사이므로 각각 to do the job, to hand in the reports라고 쓰는 것이 옳다. ⓒ look for~ : ~을 찾다

11 빈칸에는 to부정사를 목적격보어로 취하는 동사가 들어가야 한

12 who(m)을 대신하여 that을 써도 무방하며 목적격 관계대명사이므로 생략해도 좋다.

13 <보기>의 that은 관계대명사로 동사의 목적어가 빠져 있는 불완전한 문장을 이끈다. 따라서 ⑤번이 관계대명사이다. 나머지는 모두 명사절을 이끄는 접속사 that으로 완전한 문장을 이끈다.

14 선행사가 사람이 아니므로 관계대명사 which를 쓰고, persuade는 to부정사를 목적격보어로 취하는 동사이므로 to tell, '내가 돈을 지불하게 만들었다'는 사역동사로 쓰인 make이므로 원형부정사 pay를 쓰는 것이 적절하다.

15 불완전한 문장을 이끄는 관계대명사와 완전한 문장을 이끄는 명사절 접속사로 모두 쓰일 수 있는 것은 that이다.

16 수학을 도와줄 멘토가 필요하다고 하였으므로 help me with math를 어법에 맞게 to help me with math로 쓰면 된다.

17 모두 목적격 관계대명사가 들어가지만 ⑤번에는 주격 관계대명사가 들어간다.

18 목적격 관계대명사 which 대신 that을 써도 좋다.

19 force는 to부정사를 목적격보어로 취하여 '목적어가 V하게 강요하다'라는 의미로 쓰인다.

20 'The only thing is to cut in while others are talking. You should not do it.'을 목적격 관계대명사를 이용하여 하나로 합친 문장이다.

21 need는 5형식으로 쓰일 때 to부정사를 목적격보어로 취한다. 따라서 to do라고 쓰는 것이 옳다.

22 would like는 5형식으로 쓰일 때 to부정사를 목적격보어로 취한다. to부정사는 'to+동사원형' 형태이다.

23 '우리가 삶을 사랑하도록'이므로 teach를 5형식으로 사용하며, 목적격보어로 to부정사를 쓴다. 시제에 유의한다.

서술형 시험대비 p.130~131

01 are, know, to believe, to clean, to focus
02 Hannah's cousin taught her how to play the piano.
03 What do you want me to do
04 the girl to turn down the music.
05 (1) Kyle has the money.
　　 He found it on the street.
　 (2) Is this the book?
　　 You are looking for it.
06 James advises Olivia to see a doctor.
07 I want to get the job that I applied for.
08 allows him to go shopping with Ann on Monday.
09 to play the guitar for her.
10 The technology that they have developed

22 정답 및 해설

enables us to drive a car safely.

11 I like the cat that John found at the park.

12 cause people to have headaches.

13 (1) Osaka is the city which my sister visited last week.

(2) Robert is an actor whom we like very much.

(3) My dad gave me the wallet which I really wanted to have.

14 that I can do is to be quiet

15 told me to have

01 관계사절의 수의 일치는 선행사에 달려 있다. people이 선행사이므로 be동사는 are를 쓴다. let은 목적격보어로 원형부정사를 취하는 사역동사이며, expect, get, order는 to부정사를 목적격보어로 취하는 5형식 동사이다.

02 teach+목적어+how 'to부정사'의 형을 취한다.

03 want는 to부정사를 목적격보어로 취하는 동사이다.

04 ask는 to부정사를 목적격보어로 취하는 동사이다.

05 동사와 전치사의 목적어를 목적격 관계대명사로 만들었으므로 the money, the book을 동사와 전치사의 목적어로 하여 문장을 둘로 나눈다.

06 James는 Olivia에게 병원으로 가서 진찰 받을 것을 권하고 있다.

07 apply for: ~에 지원하다

08 allow는 to부정사를 목적격보어로 취하는 동사이다.

09 Emma가 자신을 위해 기타를 연주해 줄 수 있는지 내게 묻고 있다. to부정사를 목적격보어로 취하는 동사 ask를 이용하여 빈칸을 채운다.

10 enable은 to부정사를 목적격보어로 취하는 동사이며, the technology가 주어이므로 enable을 단수동사로 만드는 것에 유의한다.

11 'John이 공원에서 발견했던 고양이'이므로 목적격 관계대명사가 이끄는 문장 'John found at the park'가 the cat을 수식하도록 문장을 만드는 것이 옳다.

12 cause는 목적격보어로 to부정사를 취하는 동사이다. '사람들에게 두통을 일으키는 것'이므로 목적어로 people, 목적격보어로 to have를 사용하여 문장을 만든다.

13 (1), (3) which를 대신하여 that을 쓸 수 있다. (2) whom을 대신하여 who, that을 쓸 수 있으며, 모두 목적격 관계대명사이므로 생략이 가능하다.

14 The only thing이 주어이므로 단수 동사를 쓰는 것에 유의한다.

15 tell은 5형식으로 쓰일 때 to부정사를 목적격보어로 취한다.

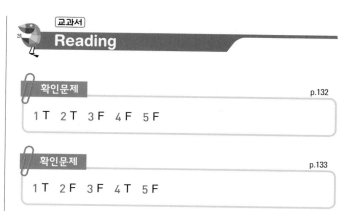

확인문제   p.132

1 T 2 T 3 F 4 F 5 F

확인문제   p.133

1 T 2 F 3 F 4 T 5 F

교과서 확인학습 A   p.134~135

01 are, which   02 to hear, them   03 You Love
04 had   05 However, nobody
06 came up with   07 stuck, to   08 put up, that
   said   09 were using   10 When, whom
   they loved, smiling   11 a big success
12 During, disappeared   13 because,
   happiness to   14 Arrow Man   15 A few years
   ago, were, confusing   16 enough
   information   17 ask others to explain
18 Where, on, go to   19 often took,
   wasted   20 decided to solve
21 lots of red arrow stickers   22 rode, around,
   stuck, on   23 asked him to do
24 wanted to help
25 Thanks to, easily, save time

교과서 확인학습 B   p.136~137

1 Here are two stories which I read yesterday.

2 Do you want to hear about them?

3 Call Someone You Love

4 New York had many pay phones on its streets.

5 However, nobody really used them.

6 One day, a man came up with an idea.

7 He stuck coins to one of the phones.

8 He also put up a sign that said, "Call Someone You Love."

9 Soon, many people were using the phone.

10 When they were talking to someone whom they loved, they didn't stop smiling.

11 His idea became a big success.

12 During the day, all the coins disappeared.

13 The man was very happy because his small idea

gave happiness to many people.

14 The Red Arrow Man

15 A few years ago, the maps at bus stops in Seoul were very confusing.

16 They didn't have enough information.

17 People had to ask others to explain the maps.

18 "Where is this bus stop on the map? Does this bus go to Gwanghwamun?"

19 Many people often took the wrong bus and wasted their time.

20 One day, a young man decided to solve this problem.

21 He bought lots of red arrow stickers.

22 Every day he rode his bicycle around the city and stuck the stickers on the bus maps.

23 Nobody asked him to do this.

24 He just wanted to help others.

25 Thanks to his effort, people could understand the maps easily and save time.

시험대비 실력평가
p.138~141

01 two stories which I read yesterday

02 ⑤   03 who, whom, that   04 ②

05 ③   06 ④   07 ③

08 It said, "Call Someone You Love."   09 ②

10 wasted

11 **화살표 모양의 스티커를 사서 서울 시내를 돌아다니며 버스 지도에 스티커를 붙이는 것**

12 ③   13 ③   14 Because there wasn't enough information on the maps.   15 ④

16 ⓐ to hear ⓒ talking   17 ⑤

18 disappear 19 ④   20 ②   21 which, stuck coins to   22 ③

23 (B)—(A)—(C) 24 ②   25 explain → to explain

26 ③   27 ⑤   28 They didn't have enough information.   29 ③   30 Seoul, right, save their time

01 어제 내가 읽은 두 개의 이야기를 가리키는 대명사이다.

02 길거리에 공중전화가 많이 있었지만 아무도 사용하지 않았다는 의미이므로 However를 쓰는 것이 옳다.

03 사람을 선행사로 받아주는 목적격 관계대명사 whom이 들어가야 한다. whom을 대신하여 who 혹은 that을 써도 좋다.

04 4형식 동사를 3형식으로 전환할 때 동사 give는 간접목적어 앞에 전치사 to를 붙인다.

05 한 남자가 표지판을 설치하자 곧 많은 사람들이 전화기를 사용하기 시작했다고 이어지는 것이 옳으며, ③번 뒤 문장의 they가 가리키는 것은 주어진 문장의 many people이다.

06 (A) hear about: ~에 관하여 듣다, hear from: ~로부터 소식을 듣다 (B) pay phones를 가리키고 있으므로 복수명사를 지칭하는 them (C) 명사를 이끌고 있으므로 전치사 During, While은 접속사로 부사절을 이끈다.

07 어떤 남자가 공중전화 하나에 동전들을 붙였다고 하였다.

08 표지판에는 '당신이 사랑하는 사람에게 전화 하세요'라고 쓰여 있었다.

09 빈칸 ⓐ에는 좁은 장소 앞에 쓰이는 전치사 at이 들어간다. ① turn off: ~을 끄다 turn on: ~을 켜다 ② be surprised at: ~에 놀라다 ③ pick somebody up: ~을 (차에) 태우러 가다 ④ take care of: ~을 돌보다 ⑤ wait for: ~을 기다리다

10 시간을 낭비했다는 의미이다.

11 간단하게 '버스 지도에 스티커를 붙이는 것'이라고 써도 좋다.

12 청년의 노력 덕분에 사람들이 지도를 쉽게 이해할 수 있게 되었다는 의미이다. Depending on: ~에 따라

13 (A) 셀 수 있는 명사를 수식하는 것은 a few, (B) 지도가 혼란을 유발하는 것이므로 confusing, (C) 사람들의 시간을 가리키는 것이므로 복수 명사를 지칭하는 their를 쓰는 것이 옳다.

14 사람들이 서울에서 버스를 잘못 탔던 이유는 지도에 충분한 정보가 없었기 때문이었다.

15 아무도 이 청년에게 이 일을 하라고 요청하지 않았다고 하였다.

16 ⓐ want는 to부정사를 목적어로 취한다. ⓑ '누군가에게 전화하고 있을 때'라는 의미이므로 진행형을 만들어 주는 것이 옳다.

17 ⓑ 길거리 위에 공중전화가 있다는 의미이므로 전치사 on을 쓴다. ① be interested in: ~에 흥미가 있다 ② be satisfied with: ~에 만족하다 ③ pay attention to: ~에 주목하다 ④ take care of: ~을 돌보다 ⑤ depend on: ~에 의지하다

18 '보여지는 것을 멈추다'는 '사라지다'이다.

19 (A)는 관계대명사 that이다. ④번은 명사절을 이끄는 접속사 that이다.

20 Soon은 '곧'이란 의미로 before long과 같다. For a long time: 오랫동안 Hardly: 거의 ~하지 않는 Still: 그럼에도 불구하고 Lately: 최근에

21 which를 대신하여 that을 써도 무방하다.

22 'nobody really used them'은 아무도 실제로 그것을 사용하지 않았다는 의미로 'not everyone used the pay phone'과는 의미가 다르다. 후자는 모두가 공중전화를 사용한 것은 아니었다는 의미로 누군가는 사용했다는 뜻이다.

23 공중전화(pay phones)가 있지만 → (B) 누구도 그것들(them)을 사용하지 않아 한 남자가 좋은 아이디어를 떠올리고 동전을 붙여 둠 → (A) 또한(also) 표지판을 설치하자 곧 많은 사람들이 전화기를 사용함 → (C) 그들이(they) 통화할 때 계속 미소를

지음

24 지도에 정보가 부족하다고 하였고, 사람들이 다른 사람들에게 지도를 설명해 달라고 요청해야 하므로 '혼란스러운 (confusing)'이 들어가는 것이 옳다.

25 ask가 5형식으로 쓰일 때는 to부정사를 목적격보어로 취한다.

26 지도상에서 정류장을 확인하고 지도 위에 스티커를 붙이는 것이다. 전치사 on은 '~(위)에'라는 의미로 어떤 것의 표면에 닿거나 그 표면을 형성하는 것을 나타낼 때 쓰인다.

27 내용상 청년은 다른 사람을 돕기 위해 스티커를 붙였다고 볼 수 있으며, 또한 청년의 노력 덕분에 사람들이 지도를 쉽게 이해할 수 있게 되었다고 하였으므로 bother는 help를 쓰는 것이 옳다.

28 서울의 버스 지도가 가진 문제는 충분한 정보가 없다는 것이다.

29 광화문으로 가는 버스 번호는 위 글에 나와 있지 않다.

30 버스를 잘못 타서 시간을 낭비했다고 했으므로, 청년의 노력 덕분에 서울 사람들은 버스를 제대로 타서 시간을 절약할 수 있었다고 말할 수 있다.

서술형 시험대비 p.142~143

01 (A) happy (B) happiness
02 Here are two stories. / I read them yesterday.
03 Call Someone Who(m) You Love
04 pay phones (on its streets)
05 they kept smiling
06 coins, which(또는 that) nobody really used
07 who, coins
08 A: stick, B: stuck coins, to use, someone whom
09 put up a sign
10 The maps at bus stops in Seoul
11 who asked him to do this
12 they(또는 the maps) didn't have enough information.
13 He stuck red arrow stickers on them.
14 His effort enabled people to understand the maps easily.
15 which, was red
16 confusing, them, waste
17 wanted the maps at bus stops to have enough information.
18 It's because he just wanted to help others.

01 (A) be동사의 보어가 들어가야 하므로 형용사 happy (B) 목적어가 들어가야 하므로 happiness로 쓰는 것이 옳다.

02 목적격 관계대명사를 이용하여 하나로 만들어진 문장이다. two stories가 선행사이므로 복수명사 them을 이용하여 문장을 둘로 나눈다.

03 목적격 관계대명사 whom이 생략되어 있다. whom을 대신하여 who 혹은 that을 써도 좋다.

04 길거리에 있는 공중전화를 가리키는 대명사이다.

05 didn't stop Ving는 'V하는 것을 멈추지 않았다'는 의미이므로 keep Ving를 써서 '계속 V하다'로 쓸 수 있다.

06 누구도 사용하지 않았던 공중전화기 중 하나에 동전들을 붙여 놓은 것을 의미한다.

07 who를 대신하여 that을 써도 좋다.

08 whom을 대신하여 who 또는 that을 써도 무방하다.

09 B as well as A: A 뿐만 아니라 B도

10 서울의 버스 정류장에 있는 지도들을 가리키는 말이다.

11 who를 대신하여 that을 써도 좋다.

12 사람들이 다른 사람들에게 지도를 설명해 달라고 요청해야 했던 이유는 지도에 충분한 정보가 없었기 때문이었다.

13 청년은 버스 지도에 스티커를 붙였다.

14 enable은 목적격보어로 to부정사를 취하는 동사이다.

15 청년이 산 스티커의 색깔은 빨간색이었다. 관계대명사 which를 대신하여 that을 써도 무방하다.

16 don't have to V: V할 필요가 없다

17 want는 to부정사를 목적격보어로 취하는 동사이다. '정류장의 지도가 정보를 갖는 것'이므로 목적어로 the maps at bus stops를 쓰고 목적격보어로 to have ~를 쓴다.

18 남자가 매일 스티커를 지도에 붙인 이유는 다른 사람들을 돕고 싶어서였다.

영역별 핵심문제 p.145~149

01 ② 02 ② 03 (1) waste your time (2) on your own (3) stopped playing
04 mentee 05 (1) come up with (2) The other day (3) on your own 06 ⑤ 07 ②
08 volunteer 09 ⑤ 10 ① 11 ④, ⑤
12 ⑤ 13 ② 14 He made a basket with plastic bags for his mom.
15 She talked about it when they were having dinner the other day.
16 (D) → (C) → (E) → (B) → (A)
17 ④ 18 ⓐ which 또는 that ⓑ to save
19 ③ 20 ① 21 ④ 22 ask her to copy 23 ⑤ 24 ⑤ 25 ⑤
26 whom(또는 that) they loved 27 ②
28 ④번 used → using 29 ⑤
30 (A) to explain (B) to solve (C) to do 31 ①
32 ④ 33 ③ 34 People often took the wrong bus and wasted their time.

25

01 사물들을 차갑게 유지하기 위해 사용되는 장치나 공간을 가리키는 말은 refrigerator(냉장고)이다.

02 ② effort: 노력

03 waste one's time: ~자신의 시간을 낭비하다, on one's own: 자기 스스로, stop ~ing: ~하기를 멈추다

04 주어진 단어의 관계는 상대어 관계이다. mentor: 멘토, mentee: 멘티

05 come up with: ~을 생각해 내다, the other day: 며칠 전에, 지난번, come across: ~을 우연히 만나다 on one's own: 자기 스스로

06 주어진 문장을 포함한 나머지는 모두 '휴식'을 의미하지만 ⑤번은 '나머지'를 의미한다.

07 ②번은 '그러면 내가 도와줄게.'라는 의미로 도움을 제안할 때 쓴다. 나머지는 도와달라는 의미로 쓴다.

08 보수를 받지 않고 무언가를 해주는 사람을 가리키는 말은 volunteer(자원봉사자)이다.

10 주어진 문장은 상자에 든 것이 무엇인지 묻는 질문에 대한 대답이므로 (A)가 알맞다.

11 amazing: 놀라운 discouraged: 낙심한

12 Mike는 지역 아동 센터에서 책을 읽을 것이라는 설명은 대화 내용과 일치하지 않는다.

13 이어지는 대답으로 어떻게 새 바구니를 필요로 하는지 알게 된 것을 설명하는 내용이 이어져야 하므로 ⓑ가 적절하다.

14 Alex는 엄마를 위해 비닐봉지로 바구니를 만들었다.

15 Alex와 엄마는 며칠 전 저녁을 먹으며 새 바구니에 대해 이야기했었다.

16 (D) 이야기 주제 언급 → (C) 주인공이 특별한 이유 질문 → (E) 이야기 내용 설명 → (B) 반응 → (A) 칭찬에 답하기

17 warn은 '~하지 말라고 경고하다'라는 의미로 쓰일 때 to부정사를 목적격보어로 취한다. leak: (물 따위가) 새다

18 ⓐ에는 두 개의 문장을 이어주는 주격 관계대명사를 써야 하며, ⓑ에는 내용상 '물을 절약하도록 조언한다'는 내용이 들어가는 것이 옳다. advise는 to부정사를 목적격보어로 취하므로 to save를 쓴다.

19 want는 to부정사를 목적격보어로 취하는 동사이며, 두 번째 빈칸에는 목적격 관계대명사 which 혹은 that이 들어가는 것이 옳다.

20 목적격 관계대명사로 쓰이면서 동시에 '어느, 어떤'이라고 해석되는 의문사는 which이다.

21 ④ would like는 5형식으로 쓰일 때 to부정사를 목적격보어로 취한다. 따라서 to accept라고 쓰는 것이 옳다.

22 ask가 5형식으로 쓰일 때는 목적격보어로 to부정사를 취한다. '그녀가 복사하는 것'이므로 목적어로 her, 목적격보어로 to copy를 쓴다.

23 주어가 The bananas이므로 복수 동사를 쓰는 것이 옳다.

24 주격 관계대명사는 생략할 수 없다.

25 say는 to부정사를 목적격보어로 취할 수 없다.

26 글의 내용상 그들이 사랑하는 사람에게 전화하고 있다고 보는 것이 옳다.

27 (A) 공중전화기가 많지만 아무도 쓰지 않는다는 것이 옳으므로 nobody, (B) come up with: (생각을) 떠올리다, come down with: (병으로) 앓아눕다 (C) 낮 동안에 모든 동전이 사라졌다는 것이 내용상 적절하다.

28 사람들이 그 전화기를 사용했다는 것이므로 현재분사를 써서 수동태가 아닌 진행형으로 표현하는 것이 옳다.

29 사람들이 몇 통의 전화를 했는지는 글을 읽고 알 수 없다.

30 ask는 5형식으로 쓰일 때 to부정사를 목적격보어로 취한다. decide는 to부정사를 목적어로 취하는 동사이다.

31 ①번에 이어지는 문장에서 the stickers는 청년이 산 lots of red arrow stickers를 의미한다.

32 ⓐ는 (교통수단 등을) 타다[이용하다]는 의미로 쓰였다. ① 넣다, ② 선택하다, 사다, ③ 가지고 가다, ④ 타다, ⑤ 잡다

33 사람들이 버스를 잘못 타는 일이 종종 있었다고 했을 뿐 사람들이 항상 버스를 잘못 탔다는 것은 글의 내용과 맞지 않는다.

34 버스 정류장 지도로 인해서 사람들은 종종 버스를 잘못 타서 시간을 낭비하였다.

단원별 예상문제 p.150~153

01 ① 02 ⑤ 03 ⑤
04 ①, ⑤ 05 I'm glad (that) you like it. 06 ⑤
07 (A)many children in his town (B)couldn't go to school and had to work
08 How about joining my study group?
09 ⓓ disagree → agree 10 ⑤ 11 ④
12 ② 13 ③ 14 The car that I want to buy is minivan.
15 (1) He gave some candies to the little kids who(m) he saw.
(2) There was a festival which many people took part in.
(3) The dish which you broke was not that expensive.
16 to close the window 17 ③
18 that, which 19 ② 20 ④
21 the man was very happy 22 (D)–(A)–(C)–(B)
23 빨간 화살표 스티커를 버스 지도에 붙이다. 24 ⑤
25 People could understand the maps easily and save time.

01 주어진 문장은 도움을 제공하고자 하는 표현으로 Tom의 고민에 대한 대답으로 적절하므로 (A)번이 적절하다.

02 ⓐ는 '무료의'라는 의미로 이와 같은 의미로 쓰인 것은 ⑤번이다.

03 왜 Hojun이 봉사활동을 하러 나오지 않았는지는 알 수 없다.

04 (A)는 '정말 멋있구나!'라는 표현으로 ①, ⑤번과 바꾸어 쓸 수 있다.

07 인도의 소년이 특별한 이유는 그의 마을에서 학교에 갈 수 없고 일을 해야 하는 많은 아이들을 매일 그의 집에서 가르쳤기 때문이다.

08 'Why don't you ~?'는 '~하는 게 어때?'라고 제안하는 표현으로 'how about ~?'으로 바꾸어 쓸 수 있다.

09 이어지는 대화에서 좋은 구성원이 되기 위해 열심히 노력한다고 하였으므로 상대방의 의견에 동의하는 'I agree.'가 적절하다.

10 ⑤ Brian은 혼자서 병원에서 공부하려고 노력했었다.

11 ask는 to부정사를 목적격보어로 취하는 동사이다. 목적격 관계대명사 which 혹은 that과 to부정사가 짝지어지는 것이 옳다.

12 '내가 답변하는 것'이므로 목적어로 me, 목적격보어로 to answer를 써서 문장을 만든 ②번이 가장 적절하다.

13 주어가 복수 명사 men이므로 수의 일치는 복수 동사로 하는 것이 옳으므로 are를 쓴다.

14 'The car is minivan. I want to buy it.'을 하나로 합친 문장이다. 목적격 관계대명사를 이용하여 문장을 쓴다.

15 관계대명사 who(m), which를 대신하여 that을 쓸 수 있으며 목적격 관계대명사이므로 생략해도 좋다.

16 창문이 열려 있어 추웠다고 하였다. 창문 옆에 앉아 있던 Jimmy에게 창문을 닫아 달라고 요청하는 말을 쓰는 것이 옳다.

17 <보기>의 that은 동격의 명사절을 이끄는 접속사이다.

18 사물을 선행사로 받아주는 주격 관계대명사가 쓰인다.

19 ⓐ와 ⓓ가 글의 내용과 일치한다.

20 두 가지 이야기를 읽었다고 하였으므로 다른 한 가지 이야기가 이어질 것이라고 보는 것이 옳다.

21 그 남자가 행복한 이유는 많은 사람들에게 행복을 주었기 때문이라고 하였다. so는 결과를 이끄는 접속사이다.

22 (D)에서 They는 주어진 문장의 the maps를 가리키고, (A)는 사람들이 지도에 대한 설명을 요구하는 글이며, (C)는 이에 대한 해결책을 한 남자가 떠올려 스티커를 사서 (B) 그 스티커를 붙이고 다녔다는 순서가 가장 적절하다.

23 do this=stick the stickers on the bus maps

24 매일 스티커를 붙였다고 하였다. 따라서 주말마다 붙였다는 것은 글의 내용과 일치하지 않는다.

25 남자의 노력이 있은 후 사람들은 지도를 쉽게 이해하고 시간을 절약할 수 있었다.

01 She is going to give her old books to her.

02 Jimin feels happy when she teaches her mentee.

03 He is going to carry the box.

04 to open

05 Do you have the book which we checked out from the library?

06 My mom allowed me to stay out late.

07 asks Jimmy to get in line

08 Is the book which you are reading interesting?

09 you were talking to[with]

10 ④번 to smile → smiling

11 sticking coins / to call, they love

12 his small idea gave happiness to many people

13 that he bought to solve the problem

14 They had to ask others to explain the maps.

01 지민은 오늘 멘티에게 그녀가 보던 책을 줄 것이다.

02 지민은 멘티를 가르칠 때 행복을 느낀다.

03 Mike는 지민을 도와주기 위해 상자를 날라 줄 것이다.

04 입을 벌리라고 했지만 너무 무서워서 벌릴 수 없었다는 의미가 되므로 tell의 목적격보어로 to부정사를 사용하여 답을 쓴다.

05 check out: (도서관에서 책을) 대출하다

06 3인칭 단수 주어에 let을 썼으므로 과거 시제임을 알 수 있다. 따라서 allowed를 쓴다. let+목적어+V: 목적어가 V하게 허락하다

07 Paul은 Jimmy에게 줄을 서라고 요청하였다. ask는 to부정사를 목적격보어로 취하는 동사이다.

08 which를 대신하여 that을 써도 무방하다.

09 목적격 관계대명사를 생략해야 빈칸에 맞게 답을 쓸 수 있다. talk to[with]: ~와 이야기하다

10 stop to V: ~하기 위해 멈추다, stop Ving: ~하던 것을 멈추다

11 뉴욕 사람들 누구도 공중전화를 사용하지 않는 것에 대하여 좋은 생각을 떠올린 한 남자와의 대화이다. enable은 목적격보어로 to부정사를 취한다.

12 그의 생각이 많은 사람들에게 행복을 주었기 때문에 남자는 행복했다.

13 that을 대신하여 which를 써도 무방하다.

14 사람들은 올바른 버스를 타기 위해서 다른 사람들에게 지도를 설명해 달라고 요청해야 했다

|모범답안|

01 (A)on my own   (B)joining her study group.
   (C)we can learn better when we teach each
   other   (D)be a good member

02 (1) A painter is an artist who paints pictures.
   (2) A purse is a small bag which people keep their
     money in.
   (3) A baker is a person whose job is to bake and
     sell bread.
    (4) A chair is a piece of furniture which people
      sit on.

03 (1) She asked me to go there with her.
   (2) The teacher encourages me to try again.
   (3) They forced him to tell the truth.
   (4) Computers enables us to live convenient lives.
   (5) I allowed my friend to use my pen. / We told
     them to stay calm.

01 나는 학교에 다시 돌아오게 되어 행복했다. Emily는 나를 매우 따뜻하게 반겨주었다. 우리는 공부를 포함한 많은 것들에 대해 이야기했다. 내가 병원에 있는 동안 나는 혼자 공부하려고 노력했지만 어려웠다. 내가 이것에 관해 Emily에게 이야기했을 때 그녀는 나를 도와주었다. 그녀는 내게 그녀의 스터디 모임에 가입할 것을 제안했다. 그녀는 우리가 서로 가르칠 때 더욱 잘 배울 수 있다고 생각했기 때문에 스터디 모임을 시작했다. 나는 그녀의 생각에 동의했다. 나는 좋은 구성원이 되기로 결심했다. 나는 정말로 그녀에게 고마웠다.

단원별 모의고사   p.157~160

01 outside   **02** ①

03 (1) Bats mostly sleep during the day.
   (2) I used a pay phone to call my mom.
   (3) He came up with a great idea at the meeting.

04 ②   **05** ②   **06** ⑤

07 (A)on (B)that (C)like   **08** ⑤   **09** ⑤

10 She was looking for the bus stop.

11 He helped Sujin by carrying her bag to the bus
stop.

12 ⑤   **13** ①   **14** to eat   **15** ⑤

16 I want to make a movie which many people will
love.

17 The teacher told us to be on time.   **18** ④

19 ③, ⑤   **20** ②   **21** Thanks to a man's
idea, many people in New York became happy when
they called someone they loved.   **22** ⑤

23 ②   **24** ③   **25** people to understand

01 주어진 단어의 관계는 반의어 관계이다. inside: 안쪽에, outside: 바깥에

02 더 경험이 있는 사람에 의해 조언을 받거나 도움을 받는 사람을 가리키는 말은 mentee(멘티)이다.

04 'How+형용사(+주어+동사)!'의 감탄문이다.

05 엄마는 Alex의 선물을 받고 기뻐하였으므로 happy(행복한)가 적절하다.

06 대화를 통해 Alex가 어디에서 바구니 만드는 법을 배웠는지는 알 수 없다.

07 (A) on own's own: 혼자서, (B) 명사절을 이끄는 접속사 that이 알맞다. (C) 명사절의 주어 you 다음이므로 동사 like가 알맞다.

08 나머지는 모두 감사함에 대한 대답을 나타내며 ⑤번은 비난을 거부하는 표현이다.

09 Emily와 Brian이 공부 모임에서 무엇을 배웠는지는 알 수 없다.

10 Sujin은 버스 정류장을 찾고 있었다.

11 Henry는 버스 정류장까지 Sujin의 가방을 들어주며 그녀를 도왔다.

12 ⑤ 그 말을 들으니 기쁘다는 대답이 자연스럽다.

13 사람과 사물을 모두 선행사로 받아줄 수 있는 관계대명사는 that 이다.

14 엄마는 내가 야채를 먹기를 원한다는 말이 들어가는 것이 적절하다. want는 to부정사를 목적격보어로 취한다.

15 make는 목적격보어로 원형부정사를 취하는 사역동사이다.

16 which를 대신하여 that을 써도 좋다.

17 tell은 to부정사를 목적격보어로 취하는 동사이다.

18 (A)는 동명사이다. 모두 동명사이지만 ④번은 현재진행형을 만드는 현재분사이다.

19 이유를 나타내는 접속사가 들어가는 것이 적절하다.

20 한 남자가 뉴욕에서 사용되지 않는 공중전화기에 동전을 붙여두었다고 하였다.

21 한 남자의 아이디어 덕분에, 뉴욕에 있는 많은 사람들이 그들이 사랑하는 사람들에게 전화했을 때 행복해졌다.

22 much는 셀 수 없는 명사를 수식하는 수량형용사이다.

23 (A) 주어가 the maps이므로 복수 동사 were, (B) 빈도부사는 일반동사 앞에 위치하므로 often took, (C) 스티커들을 지도들에 붙였다는 의미이므로 them이 옳다.

24 ⓐ 서울 버스 정류장의 지도에 정보가 부족한 것이 문제였고, ⓓ 청년은 문제를 해결하기 위하여 화살표 스티커를 붙이고 다녔으며, ⓔ 사람들이 종종 버스를 잘못 탔던 이유는 지도에 정보가 부족했기 때문이었다.

25 help는 원형부정사나 to부정사를 모두 목적격보어로 취할 수 있다. 따라서 other people understand를 답으로 써도 좋다.

교과서 파헤치기

Lesson 1

1 beef, 소고기   2 during, ~ 동안
3 homeroom teacher, 담임 선생님   4 decide, 결정하다
5 email, 이메일을 보내다   6 bite, 물다   7 nail, 손톱
8 wish, 소망   9 handle, 손잡이   10 personal, 개인적인
11 planet, 행성   12 hobby, 취미   13 try, 시도하다
14 art, 미술   15 traffic, 교통   16 print, 인쇄하다

단어 TEST Step 1   p.02

01 행성	02 물다; 물린 자국	03 사실, 진실
04 곧	05 청소하다, 깨끗하게 하다	
06 친애하는	07 깨뜨리다, 부수다	08 ~ 동안
09 소고기	10 이메일을 보내다	11 장난감
12 손잡이	13 달리기	14 거짓말을 하다
15 손톱	16 틀린, 거짓의	17 소망
18 확실한, 확신하고 있는		19 시도하다
20 방학	21 담임 선생님	22 화난, 속상한
23 건강한, 튼튼한	24 결정하다	25 똑똑한, 명석한
26 개인적인	27 취미	28 인쇄하다
29 교통	30 조언, 정보	31 가을
32 우주	33 더 이상 ~하지 않다	
34 ~할 생각이다	35 그건 그렇고, 그런데	
36 요즈음에	37 ~로 변하다	38 실현되다
39 ~에 열중하다	40 최선을 다하다	41 서로
42 집에 오는 길에	43 ~에 흥미가 있다	

단어 TEST Step 2   p.03

01 soon	02 traffic	03 tip
04 false	05 smart	06 spring
07 print	08 art	09 healthy
10 fall	11 space	12 decide
13 kind	14 cupcake	15 personal
16 hold	17 care	18 hobby
19 upset	20 funny	21 vegetable
22 lie	23 planet	24 break
25 bite	26 truth	27 vacation
28 beef	29 false	30 handle
31 nail	32 toy	33 each other
34 on one's way home		35 be into
36 make changes	37 come true	38 by the way
39 not ~ anymore	40 do one's best	41 those days
42 change into	43 be interested in	

대화문 TEST Step 1   p.05~06

Listen & Speak 1 A

how, winter vacation / You know what, during the vacation / you were interested in / really fun / want to try

Listen & Speak 1 B

know what, homeroom teacher / His sciene class, a lot of fun / this year / new teacher / What does she teach / teaches art

Listen & Speak 2 A

are thinking of starting / What kind of club / learn about stars, planets, thinking, starting / Sounds, How often, going / once a week / will, meet / want to join our club / I'm interested in, too

Listen & Speak 2 B

made, I'm thinking, of cooking, for dinner / sounds great / at home / What about beef / vegetables, don't have, I'll buy some for you on my way home

Real Life Communication A

know what, I'm thinking of taking, painting class / decide to take / I want to go to an art high school / Are, thinking of becoming / interested in painting / comes true / do my best

Real Life Communication B

going to move / didn't tell me about / learned about, upset / I can understand her feelings, going to miss / keep in touch with

대화문 TEST Step 2   p.07~08

Listen & Speak 1 A

Brian: Julia, how was your winter vacation?
Julia: It was great. You konw what? I took muay thai lessons during the vacation.
Brian: That's amazing. I didn't know that you were interested in muay thai.
Julia: Yes. It was really fun.

Brian: Really? I want to try it.

Jimin: You know what, Tim?

Mr. Smith is my homeroom teacher this year.

Tim: That's great, Jimin. His science class last year was a lot of fun.

Jimin: Who's your homeroom teacher this year?

Tim: It's Ms. Kim. She's a new teacher.

Jimin: What does she teach?

Tim: She teaches art.

Jane: Minsu, Sujin and I are thinking of starting a club.

Minsu: Really? What kind of club?

Jane: We want to learn about stars and planets. So, we're thinking of starting a space science club.

Minsu: Sounds good. How often are you going to meet?

Jane: Maybe once a week.

Minsu: I see. Where will you meet?

Jane: In Room 101. Minsu, do you want to join our club?

Minsu: Yes, I'm interested in space, too.

Alex: Mom, I made bulgogi at school today. I'm thinking of cooking bulgogi for dinner.

Mom: That sounds great, Alex.

Alex: Do we have any vegetables at home, Mom? What about beef?

Mom: We have some vegetables, but we don't have beef. I'll buy some for you on my way home

Alex: Great.

Emily: You know what, Junsu? I'm thinking of taking a painting class.

Junsu: Really? Why did you decide to take a painting class, Emily?

Emily: Because I want to go to an art high school.

Junsu: Are you thinking of becoming an artist in the future?

Emily: I hope so. I'm interested in painting pictures.

Junsu: That's great. I hope your wish comes true.

Emily: Thanks. I'll do my best.

Sue: You know what? Jenny's family is going to move to Japan.

Jack: Is that right? Jenny didn't tell me about it.

Sue: She learned about it just last week and she's very upset now.

Jack: I can understand her feelings. I am going to miss her so much.

Sue: Me, too. She said she would keep in touch with us.

---

01 made, changes during
02 emailed, other, about   03 Dear Eric
04 It, spring in   05 last, vacation, time for
06 made, personal, during
07 One, my, hobby
08 making cupcakes   09 Making, own, is
10 other change, breaking, habits   11 past, bit, nails
12 don't anymore
13 feel, about, made   14 If, try, fell, like
15 hope, hear from   16 Your friend
17 Dear Junho   18 In, it, fall
19 talked about, changes
20 time to talk about
21 These days, into
22 printed, things with   23 One, of, dream
24 traffic, heavy, change into
25 other, special, for
26 hold, because, sick
27 handles, so, to hold   28 My, happy
29 By, to try, some   30 Take care
31 Best wishes

---

01 made some interesting changes during the vacation
02 emailed each other, talked about our changes
03 Dear   04 It, beautiful spring in
05 The last winter vacation, time
06 made, personal changes during
07 One, new hobby
08 making cupcakes
09 Making, own, is, lot
10 The other change, breaking, habits
11 past, often bit my nails   12 don't anymore
13 feel great about, changes, made
14 If, try to make, sure, will feel, like
15 hope to hear from   16 Your friend
17 Dear   18 In, it, in March
19 talked about, changes

20 time to talk about

21 These days, into 3D printing

22 printed two things with

23 One, model of, dream car

24 If, is heavy, will change into a flying car

25 The other, special cup for

26 can't hold, well because, sick

27 three handles, easy to hold   28 My, happy

29 By the way, to try, some day   30 Take care

31 Best wishes

1 My friend Eric and I made some interesting changes during the vacation.

2 We emailed each other and talked about our changes.

3 Dear Eric

4 It's a beautiful spring in Seoul.

5 The last winter vacation was a great time for me.

6 I made two personal changes during the vacation.

7 One is my new hobby.

8 It's making cupcakes.

9 Making my own cupcakes is a lot of fun.

10 The other change is breaking one of my bad habits.

11 In the past, I often bit my nails.

12 Now I don't anymore.

13 I feel great about the changes I made.

14 If you try to make some changes, I'm sure you'll feel great like me.

15 I hope to hear from you soon.

16 Your friend, Junho.

17 Dear Junho,

18 In Sydney, it's fall in March.

19 You talked about your changes in your email.

20 Now, it's time to talk about my new changes.

21 These days, I'm into 3D printing.

22 I printed two things with a 3D printer.

23 One is a model of my dream car.

24 If the traffic is heavy, it will change into a flying car.

25 The other is a special cup for my grandfather.

26 He can't hold his cup well because he's sick.

27 My special cup has three handles, so it is easy to hold.

28 My grandfather is very happy.

29 By the way, I want to try your cupcakes some day, Junho.

30 Take care.

31 Best wishes, Eric.

1 내 친구 Eric과 나는 방학 동안 흥미로운 변화가 있었다.

2 우리는 서로에게 이메일을 보냈고 우리의 변화에 관해 이야기했다.

3 안녕 Eric,

4 서울은 아름다운 봄이야.

5 지난 겨울 방학은 나에게 멋진 시간이었어.

6 나는 방학 동안 두 가지 개인적인 변화가 있었어.

7 하나는 나의 새로운 취미야.

8 그것은 컵케이크를 만드는 거야.

9 나만의 컵케이크를 만드는 것은 정말 재미있어.

10 나머지 다른 변화는 나의 나쁜 습관 중 하나를 없애는 거야.

11 예전에 나는 종종 손톱을 물어뜯곤 했어.

12 이제 나는 더 이상 그러지 않아.

13 나는 내가 만든 변화가 정말 기분 좋아.

14 만약 네가 변화하려고 노력한다면, 너도 나처럼 기분이 좋을 거라고 확신해.

15 곧 소식 전해 줘.

16 너의 친구 준호가.

17 안녕 준호,

18 시드니에서는 3월이 가을이야.

19 너는 이메일에서 너에게 일어난 변화들을 말해 주었지.

20 이제 나의 새로운 변화를 말해 줄 차례야.

21 요즈음, 나는 3D 프린팅에 빠져 있어.

22 나는 3D 프린팅 2가지를 인쇄했어.

23 하나는 나의 꿈의 자동차의 모형이야.

24 교통이 혼잡할 때, 그것은 날 수 있는 차로 바뀌어.

25 나머지 다른 하나는 우리 할아버지를 위한 특수 컵이야.

26 할아버지는 편찮으셔서 컵을 잘 들지 못하셔.

27 나의 특수 컵은 손잡이가 3개 있어서 들기 쉬워.

28 할아버지는 아주 행복해 하셔.

29 그건 그렇고, 너의 컵케이크를 언젠가 먹어 보고 싶다, 준호야.

30 잘 지내.

31 행운을 빌어, Eric.

Real Life Communication - Step 2

1. what, thinking of keeping

2. Why, decide to do

3. because, be good at

4. great

구석구석지문 TEST Step 2   p.20

Real Life Communication - Step 2

1. A: You know what? I'm thinking of keeping a diary in English.
2. B: Why did you decide to do that?
3. A: It's because I want to be good at English writing.
4. B: That's great.

My Writing Portfolio

1. Dear me,
2. You are very smart and funny.
3. However, you still want to make two changes, don't you?
4. One is to have more good friends. The other is to become healthier.
5. Here are my tips for your wishes.
6. If you are nicer to others and eat more vegetables, you'll make these changes.
7. Love, Me

Culture Link

1. Bobo is my pet dog.
2. She has two brothers.
3. One is black. The other is white.
4. She has two toys.
5. One is a ball. The other is a plastic duck.
6. She has two habits.
7. One is watching TV. The other is sleeping on my chair.

단어 TEST Step 1   p.21

01 흔들림, 떨림; 흔들다		02 해결하다
03 비어 있는, 빈	04 넘어지다	05 따르다, 따라가다
06 이상한, 낯선	07 공간	
08 다치게 하다, 아프게 하다		09 바닥, 마루
10 상처, 부상	11 기둥, 장대	12 칼
13 낮은	14 약	15 안전
16 놀라운	17 깨다, 부수다, 부서지다	
18 두려운, 무서운	19 결정하다, 결심하다	
20 미끄러지다	21 발생하다	22 젖은
23 보호하다	24 탈출하다	25 심각한
26 걱정, 근심; 걱정하다		27 방지하다, 막다, 피하다
28 아픈	29 위험한	30 미끄러운
31 지진	32 잊어버리다	33 재난, 재해
34 살아남다, 생존하다		
35 (~에서) 나가다, 떠나다		36 숨다
37 약간, 좀	38 ~에서 떨어져 있다	
39 ~에 대해 걱정하다		40 ~을 꼭 잡다
41 ~을 기억하다	42 (기분이) 나아지다	43 휴식을 취하다

단어 TEST Step 2   p.22

01 cover	02 wipe	03 escape
04 serious	05 disaster	06 forget
07 floor	08 sore	09 avoid
10 stair	11 by	12 worry
13 survive	14 prepare	15 elevator
16 slippery	17 dangerous	18 protect
19 situation	20 earthquake	21 throat
22 program	23 safety	24 empty
25 slip	26 break	27 injury
28 solve	29 wet	30 strange
31 rule	32 space	33 shake
34 medicine	35 take a rest	36 be worried about
37 feel better	38 hold on to	39 stay away from
40 keep ~ in mind		41 one by one
42 Why don't you ~?		43 get out of

단어 TEST Step 3   p.23

1 solve, 해결하다   2 protect, 보호하다

3 forget, 잊어버리다   4 safety, 안전   5 wipe, 닦다

6 empty, 비어 있는, 빈　　7 fall, 넘어지다

8 shake, 흔들림, 떨림　　9 pole, 기둥, 막대

10 earthquake, 지진　　11 follow, 따르다, 따라가다

12 avoid, 방지하다, 막다, 피하다　　13 hurt, 다치게 하다

14 injury, 상처, 부상　　15 disaster, 재난, 재해

16 break, 깨다, 부수다

대화문 TEST Step 1　　　　　p.24~25

Listen & Speak 1 A

wrong / I'm worried about, hurts a lot / Why don't you go see / going to go / you feel better / hope so, too

Listen & Speak 1 B

are, watching / program about earthquakes / Sounds interesting, I'm worried about earthquakes / Me, too / helpful tips / does, say / start to shake, take cover / didn't know

Listen & Speak 2 A

going out to play / finish cleaning your room / not yet, later / You should clean your room first / clean, play basketball / Don't forget, by six o'clock

Listen & Speak 2 B

What time / left . Let's run / You might fall and hurt yourself, should walk on the stairs / right, a little late / Better safe than sorry

Real Life Communication

a big fire, city library / heard about, I was worried about the people there / Don't worry, followed, safety rules / What / cover, with a wet towel, stay low, escape / didn't know / keep that in mind, helpful some day

Let's Check

raining, worried about our picnic / until late afternoon, You should go another day / call, choose, another day

대화문 TEST Step 2　　　　　p.26~27

Listen & Speak 1 A

Tom: Yujin, what's wrong?

Yujin: I'm worried about my leg. It hurts a lot.

Tom: Why don't you go see a doctor?

Yujin: I'm going to go after school today.

Tom: I hope you feel better soon.

Yujin: I hope so, too.

Listen & Speak 1 B

Brian: What are you watching?

Jane: It's a program about earthquakes.

Brian: Sounds interesting. I'm worried about earthquakes these days.

Jane: Me, too. This program has some helpful tips.

Brian: Really? What does it say?

Jane: When things start to shake, you need to take cover under a table.

Brian: Oh, I didn't know that.

Listen & Speak 2 A

Jack: Dad, I'm going out to play basketball with Minu.

Dad: Did you finish cleaning your room?

Jack: No, not yet. Can I do it later?

Dad: No. You should clean your room first.

Jack: Okay. I'll clean my room and then play basketball.

Dad: Good. Don't forget to be home by six o'clock.

Jack: Okay.

Listen & Speak 2 B

Emily: What time is the movie?

Tom: It starts at 4:30.

Emily: Oh, no. We only have 20 minutes left. Let's run!

Tom: No! You might fall and hurt yourself. You should walk on the stairs.

Emily: You're right. We can be a little late.

Tom: Yes. Better safe than sorry.

Real Life Communication

Brian: There was a big fire at the city library yesterday.

Mina: Yes, I heard about it. I was worried about the people there.

Brian: Don't worry. Everybody was okay. They all followed the safety rules.

Mina: Really? What are the rules?

Brian: You need to cover your nose and mouth with a wet towel. Then stay low and escape.

Mina: Oh, I didn't know that.

Brian: You should keep that in mind. It might be helpful some day.

Let's Check

Sujin: It's raining. I'm worried about our picnic in the afternoon.

Mom: It is going to rain until late afternoon today. You should go another day.

Sujin: You're right, Mom. I'll call my friend and choose another day.

01 what to, when, strikes
02 Take, how, during, disaster
03 things, shake, outside   04 Stay away
05 Use, out of   06 outside, hold, pole
07 How, on   08 survive, safely
09 Here, safety, which, helpful
10 check, by, what
11 run, when, shaking
12 Find, take cover
13 hold on, to protect
14 stay away from
15 break, earthquake, hurt
16 go outside, shaking stops
17 get out, don't use   18 Take, stairs
19 much safer   20 Once, find, empty, far
21 may, hold, pole, but
22 because, fall on
23 can strike anytime
24 scary experiences, everyone
25 how, safe, earthquake
26 avoid injuries, protect
27 Follow, tip, safe

01 what to do, earthquake strikes
02 Take, how to be, during, natural disaster
03 to shake, quickly   04 Stay away from
05 Use, to get out of
06 When, outside, hold on to
07 How, on the quiz
08 survive, an earthquake safely
09 Here are, which, helpful in an earthquake
10 Let's, them one by one, what to do
11 Don't, when things are shaking
12 Find, take cover under
13 hold, to protect yourself
14 stay away from windows
15 They, break, during
16 go outside, the shaking stops
17 To get out of, don't use   18 Take, stairs
19 much safer
20 Once, find an empty space, is far from
21 who want to hold on to, but think
22 because it, fall on
23 Earthquakes, strike anytime

24 scary experiences for everyone
25 how to be safe
26 can avoid injuries, protect yourself
27 Follow these tip, be

1 지진이 발생할 때 해야 할 일을 알고 있습니까?
2 이 퀴즈를 풀며 이러한 종류의 자연 재해가 발생하는 동안 어떻게 해야 안전할 수 있는지를 생각해 보세요.
3 물건들이 흔들리기 시작하면, 빨리 밖으로 뛰어나가세요.
4 창문으로부터 멀리 떨어지세요.
5 건물에서 나갈 때는 계단을 이용하세요.
6 밖에 나가서는 기둥이나 나무를 붙들고 있으세요.
7 퀴즈가 어떠셨나요?
8 당신은 지진에서 안전하게 살아남을 수 있나요?
9 여기에 지진 발생 시 도움이 될 수 있는 안전 지침이 있습니다.
10 하나하나 확인하면서 무엇을 해야 하는지를 배워 봅시다.
11 물건이 흔들리기 시작할 때 밖으로 뛰어나가지 마세요.
12 탁자나 책상을 찾아서 그 밑에 숨으세요.
13 자신을 보호하기 위해 탁자나 책상 다리를 붙들고 있으세요.
14 또한, 창문으로부터 멀리 떨어지세요.
15 지진이 일어나는 동안 창문들이 깨져 다칠 수 있으니까요.
16 흔들림이 멈추었을 때 밖으로 나가도 됩니다.
17 건물에서 나가기 위해 엘리베이터를 이용하지 마세요.
18 계단을 이용하세요.
19 그것이 훨씬 더 안전합니다.
20 일단 밖으로 나가면, 건물로부터 멀리 떨어진 공터를 찾으세요.
21 기둥이나 나무를 꼭 잡고 있으려는 사람들이 있을 수 있지만, 다시 생각해 보세요.
22 그것이 당신 위로 넘어질 수 있으므로 그것은 좋지 않은 생각입니다.
23 지진은 언제든지 발생할 수 있습니다.
24 지진은 모두에게 무서운 경험일 것입니다.
25 따라서 지진이 날 때 안전을 지키는 법을 배우세요.
26 부상을 방지하고 자신을 보호할 수 있습니다.
27 이 지침을 따르고 안전을 지키세요!

1 Do you know what to do when an earthquake strikes?
2 Take this quiz and think about how to be safe during this kind of natural disaster.
3 When things start to shake, run outside quickly.

4 Stay away from windows.

5 Use the stairs to get out of buildings.

6 When you are outside, hold on to a pole or a tree.

7 How did you do on the quiz?

8 Can you survive an earthquake safely?

9 Here are some safety tips which can be helpful in an earthquake.

10 Let's check them one by one and learn what to do.

11 Don't run outside when things are shaking.

12 Find a table or a desk and take cover under it.

13 You can hold on to the legs to protect yourself.

14 Also, stay away from windows.

15 They can break during an earthquake and hurt you.

16 You can go outside when the shaking stops.

17 To get out of buildings, don't use the elevator.

18 Take the stairs.

19 It's much safer.

20 Once you are outside, find an empty space that is far from buildings.

21 There may be people who want to hold on to a pole or a tree, but think again.

22 That's a bad idea because it can fall on you.

23 Earthquakes can strike anytime.

24 They can be scary experiences for everyone.

25 So learn how to be safe in an earthquake.

26 You can avoid injuries and protect yourself.

27 Follow these tips and be safe!

Real Life Communication B

1. heard about, was worried about

2. hurt, not serious

3. should watch, when, close

4. right, will

Culture & Life

1. When, struck, thanks to

2. found, after the earthquake struck

Culture & Life Project

1. Here are, our survival bag

2. packed some food

3. need, to survive

4. packed, matches, in disasters

5. put, in, too

6. need, injuries

Real Life Communication B

1. A: I heard about your accident. I was worried about you.

2. B: Thanks. I hurt my hand, but it's not serious. I'll be okay.

3. A: Good. You should watch your hands when you close the door.

4. B: You're right. I will.

Culture & Life

1. When an earthquake struck in Italy in 2016, people found Georgia thanks to Leo, a dog.

2. Leo found the eight-year-old girl 16 hours after the earthquake struck.

Culture & Life Project

1. Here are the items for our survival bag.

2. We packed some food and water.

3. We need them to survive.

4. We also packed some matches that might be helpful in disasters.

5. We put medicine in the bag, too.

6. We might need it for injuries.

10 refrigerator, 냉장고　　11 arrow, 화살표
12 mentee, 멘티　　13 sign, 표지판
14 rest, 쉬다, 휴식하다　　15 map, 지도　　16 mentor, 멘토

단어 TEST Step 1　　p.40

01 쉬다, 휴식하다　02 피하다　03 공중전화
04 활동　05 화살, 화살표　06 위험
07 (글 · 글씨 등이) 쓰이다　08 노력
09 성공　10 가능한　11 자원 봉사 동아리
12 ~하려고 계획하다　13 해결책
14 멘티　15 훌륭한, 굉장한　16 거리
17 설명하다　18 혼란스러운　19 냉장고
20 필요로 하다　21 잊어버리다　22 쓰레기
23 비밀, 비결; 비밀의　24 사라지다
25 다른　26 틀, 테　27 바깥의, 외부의
28 아동 센터　29 동전　30 해결하다
31 지도　32 무료의　33 비닐봉지
34 표지판　35 (생각) 찾아내다, 제시하다
36 낮 동안　37 자기 스스로
38 시도하다, 한번 해 보다　39 설치하다, 세우다
40 ~하는 것을 멈추다　41 ~ 덕분에
42 ~해야 한다　43 (과거의) 어느 날

단어 TEST Step 2　　p.41

01 sticker　02 basket　03 coin
04 sign　05 confusing　06 secret
07 solve　08 few　09 bus stop
10 children's center　11 disappear
12 frame　13 free　14 soap
15 glad　16 hear　17 map
18 different　19 mentor　20 outside
21 plastic bag　22 trash　23 refrigerator
24 explain　25 effort　26 decide
27 avoid　28 trash　29 danger
30 rest　31 success　32 pay phone
33 solution　34 forget　35 the other day
36 give out　37 come up with　38 during the day
39 stop -ing　40 on one's own　41 put up
42 thanks to　43 give it a try

단어 TEST Step 3　　p.42

1 few, 몇몇의　2 confusing, 혼란스러운　3 start, 시작하다
4 disappear, 사라지다　5 free, 무료의　6 secret, 비밀의
7 activity, 활동　8 hear, 듣다　9 success, 성공

대화문 TEST Step 1　　p.43~44

Listen & Speak 1 A

planned to give out / think, forgot / Let me help you then, going, give out / part, volunteer club activity / mean / It means that, smile at each other, become a better place / wonderful idea

Listen & Speak 1 B

in the box / my mentee, going to give / Do you teach her every weekend / feel happy, teach / You are a good mentor, looks heavy, Let, help

Listen & Speak 2 A

this is for you, made, with / How did you know that, needed / talked about, the other day / How nice, many different colors / I'm glad you like it

Listen & Speak 2 B

I read a story about a special boy in India, hear about / Why is he special / couldn't go, had to work, taught, every day / great story / I'm glad you like it

Real Life Communication

Are you feeling better / tried to, on my own, but / Let me help you, join my study group / study group / we can learn better when we teach each other / try hard, Thanks for helping me / welcome, glad, like

Let's Check 1

looks heavy, Let me help you / Where is the bus stop around here / over there, carry / very kind / No problem, going, too

대화문 TEST Step 2　　p.45~46

Listen & Speak 1 A

Tom: Hojun and I planned to give out free stickers today, but I think he forgot.
Sora: Really? Let me help you then. Why are you going to give out stickers?
Tom: It's part of our volunteer club activity.
Sora: I see. What does this sticker mean?
Tom: It means that when we smile at each other, the world will become a better place.
Sora: That's a wonderful idea.

Mike: Jimin, what are all these things in the box?

Jimin: They're for my mentee at the children's center. I'm going to give her my old books today.

Mike: Do you teach her every weekend?

Jimin: Yes. I feel happy when I teach her.

Mike: You are a good mentor. Oh, the box looks heavy. Let me help you.

Jimin: Thanks.

Alex: Mom, this is for you. I made it with plastic bags

Mom: That's very cute, Alex. How did you know that I needed a new basket?

Alex: You talked about it when we were having dinner the other day.

Mom: How nice! I really like this basket. It has many different colors.

Alex: I'm glad you like it.

Yujin: I read a story about a special boy in India. Do you want to hear about it?

Jack: Sure. Why is he special, Yujin?

Yujin: Many children in his town couldn't go to school and had to work . So he taught them in his house every day.

Jack: That's a great story

Yujin: I'm glad you like it.

Emily: Welcome back, Brian. Are you feeling better?

Brian: Yes, thanks. I tried to study on my own in the hospital, but it was hard.

Emily: Let me help you. Why don't you join my study group?

Brian: Did you start a study group? That's wonderful.

Emily: Thanks. I think that we can learn better when we teach each other.

Brian: I agree. I'll try hard to be a good member. Thanks for helping me.

Emily: You're welcome. I'm glad you like my idea.

Henry: Your bag looks heavy. Let me help you.

Sujin: Thanks. Where is the bus stop around here?

Henry: It's over there. I'll carry your bag to the bus stop for you.

Sujin: You're very kind.

Henry: No problem. I am going that way, too.

01 are, which, read

02 want, hear about   03 Call, You Love

04 had, pay, on, streets

05 However, nobody, used   06 One, up with

07 stuck, to, of   08 put up, that

09 many, were using

10 When, talking, whom, smiling

11 His, became, success

12 During, all, disappeared

13 because, gave happiness   14 Arrow Man

15 few, ago, were, confusing

16 didn't, enough information

17 had, others, explain

18 Where, on, go to

19 often took, wasted

20 One, decided to solve

21 bought lots, arrow

22 rode, around, stuck, on   23 asked, to do

24 just, help others

25 Thanks, could, easily, save

01 are, which, read

02 to hear about 03 Call, You Love

03 Call, You Love

04 had, pay, phones

05 However, nobody, used   06 came up with

07 stuck coins to 08 put up, that said, Call, Love

09 many, were using

10 When, were talking, whom they loved, didn't stop smiling   11 became a big success

12 During the day, disappeared

13 because, gave happiness to

14 Red Arrow Man

15 A few years ago, were, confusing

16 didn't have enough information

17 ask others to explain

18 Where, on the map, go to

19 often took the wrong bus, wasted

20 decided to solve

21 lots of red arrow stickers

22 Every day, rode, around, stuck, on

23 asked him to do   24 wanted to help

25 Thanks to his effort, could understand, easily, save time

37

1 여기 내가 어제 읽은 이야기가 두 개 있어.

2 들어볼래?

3 당신이 사랑하는 누군가에게 전화하세요.

4 뉴욕에는 길거리에 공중전화가 많이 있었다.

5 그러나 아무도 그것들을 실제로 사용하지는 않았다.

6 어느 날, 한 남자에게 좋은 아이디어가 떠올랐다.

7 그는 공중전화 하나에 동전들을 붙였다.

8 그는 또한 "당신이 사랑하는 사람에게 전화하세요."라고 쓰인 표지판을 설치했다.

9 곧, 많은 사람들이 그 전화기를 사용하고 있었다.

10 그들이 사랑하는 누군가에게 전화하고 있을 때, 그들은 미소 짓기를 멈추지 않았다.

11 그의 아이디어는 커다란 성공이었다.

12 낮 동안, 모든 동전이 사라졌다.

13 그 남자는 자신의 작은 아이디어가 많은 사람에게 행복을 가져다 주었기 때문에 매우 행복했다.

14 빨간 화살표 청년

15 몇 년 전, 서울의 버스 정류장의 지도는 매우 혼란스러웠다.

16 지도에는 충분한 정보가 없었다.

17 사람들은 다른 사람들에게 지도를 설명해 달라고 요청해야 했다.

18 "이 버스 정류장은 지도의 어디에 있는 건가요? 이 버스가 광화문으로 가나요?"

19 많은 사람이 종종 버스를 잘못 타서 시간을 낭비하곤 했다.

20 어느 날, 한 젊은 청년이 이 문제를 해결해 보기로 했다.

21 그는 빨간 화살표 스티커를 많이 샀다.

22 매일 그는 자전거를 타고 서울 시내를 돌아다니며 버스 지도에 스티커를 붙였다.

23 아무도 그 청년에게 이 일을 하라고 요청하지 않았다.

24 그는 단지 다른 사람들을 돕고 싶었다.

25 그의 노력 덕분에, 사람들은 지도를 쉽게 이해하고 시간을 절약할 수 있었다.

1 Here are two stories which I read yesterday.

2 Do you want to hear about them?

3 Call Someone You Love

4 New York had many pay phones on its streets.

5 However, nobody really used them.

6 One day, a man came up with an idea.

7 He stuck coins to one of the phones.

8 He also put up a sign that said, "Call Someone You Love."

9 Soon, many people were using the phone.

10 When they were talking to someone whom they loved, they didn't stop smiling.

11 His idea became a big success.

12 During the day, all the coins disappeared.

13 The man was very happy because his small idea gave happiness to many people.

14 The Red Arrow Man

15 A few years ago, the maps at bus stops in Seoul were very confusing.

16 They didn't have enough information.

17 People had to ask others to explain the maps.

18 "Where is this bus stop on the map? Does this bus go to Gwanghwamun?"

19 Many people often took the wrong bus and wasted their time.

20 One day, a young man decided to solve this problem.

21 He bought lots of red arrow stickers.

22 Every day he rode his bicycle around the city and stuck the stickers on the bus maps.

23 Nobody asked him to do this.

24 He just wanted to help others.

25 Thanks to his effort, people could understand the maps easily and save time.

Real Life Communication B

1. not good at, What

2. Let me help, Why don't

3. give it a try

4. problem, glad

Let's Write

1. Be

2. in the second grade

3. want to help, with

4. can meet, after school

5. ask, to be

6. think, can be

7. whom my mentee can trust

Culture & Life

1. see, inside

2. wash their hands, to get

3. Washing, can prevent

4. Thanks to, fewer, getting sick

Real Life Communication B

1. A: I'm not good at science. What can I do?

2. B: Let me help you. Why don't you start with easier books?

3. A: Okay, I'll give it a try. Thanks for the tip.

4. B: No problem. I'm glad you like it.

Let's Write

1. Be a Mentor!

2. My name is Semi and I'm in the second grade.

3. I want to help my mentee with her homework.

4. I can meet my mentee after school.

5. I'll ask my mentee to be on time.

6. I think a good mentor can be a good friend.

7. So I want to become a good friend whom my mentee can trust.

Culture & Life

1. Do you see toys inside the bars of soap?

2. Children in South Africa wash their hands more often to get the toys.

3. Washing your hands can prevent many health problems.

4. Thanks to this idea, fewer children are getting sick.

MEMO

적중100

영어 기출 문제집

정답 및 해설

지학 | 민찬규